6/96

SCREENWRITERS ON SCREENWRITING

ALSO BY JOEL ENGEL

Rod Serling: The Dreams and Nightmares
of Life in The Twilight Zone

Gene Roddenberry:
The Myth and the Man Behind Star Trek

Addicted: Kids Talking about
Drugs in Their Own Words

SCREEN WRITERS ON SCREEN WRITING

THE BEST IN THE BUSINESS DISCUSS THEIR CRAFT

JOEL ENGEL

HYPERION

NEW YORK

Library of Congress Cataloging-in-Publication Data

Engel, Joel.
Screenwriters on screenwriting : the best in the business discuss
their craft / Joel Engel.—1st ed.
p.   cm.
ISBN 0-7868-8057-0
1. Motion picture authorship. 2. Screenwriters—United States—
Interviews. I. Title.
PN1995.E67 1995
808.2′3—dc20   94–36394
CIP

First Edition

BOOK DESIGN BY BRIAN MULLIGAN

10   9   8   7   6   5   4   3   2   1

To my cousin Irene,
who taught me the worth of a good story.

Contents

Foreword

Borden Chase was a Hollywood screenwriter. When he turned his western novella *Guns Along the Chisolm Trail* into *Red River* sometime in the late forties, the term "screenwriter" was somewhere between a condescending pejorative and calling a writer a pandering slut. In those far-off times the added qualifier "Hollywood" was not much more than gilding the hooking lady's lily.

Fifty years later I think it's fair to say the epithet is no longer so disreputable. Since *Cahiers du Cinema* and *The Village Voice* first helped turn movies into "film" I don't think it's unfair to say that there's a certain cachet associated with the term. Screenwriters are now the architects (or draughtsmen depending on what end of the artist-artisan scale the film critic decides to place us) of what is increasingly referred to as "the dominant art form of the twentieth century." Indeed a "serious" young writer-director can easily find himself and his first film referred to and discussed with increasingly risible gravity, a creative force whose very voice and self threaten to change the world of art and life as we know it, and all on a budget of less than twenty million.

Only when the contemporary film critic or *ET* host adds the "Hollywood" to "screenwriter" do we get any echo of the automatically low regard in which the screenwriter was once routinely held and routinely held himself. Such third-rate parttime scribblers for the screen as Fitzgerald, Faulkner, Dorothy Parker, Nathanael West, Clifford Odets, or those shabby more-or-less full-timers like Ben Hecht, Charles Brackett, Billy Wilder, Casey Robinson, Sidney Buchman, Morrie Riskind, Anita Loos, James Agee, Herman Mankiewiecz, Preston Sturges, dined out on anecdotes designed to point out how much they were paid and how little they were regarded.

I can't recall the studio or the studio head, it may have been Columbia and Harry Cohn (it sure *sounds* like Harry) but there's this paradigmatic story of the mogul in question and his writers under contract. Passing by the writers' bungalows at lunchtime, as was his custom, he cocked his ear and waited to hear typewriter keys slamming into foolscap, a sound he expected to be as continuous as the waves breaking on State Beach. There was dead silence. Indignation rising, the mogul peered into a bungalow window: the typewriters were unattended and his two writers were stretched out on a couch and studio divan, dead to the world. Before he could fire the lazy louts, one of them managed to catch the outline of their boss lurking ominously in the bungalow window. Waiting only a split-second, the writer smacked his hand to his forehead and leapt to his feet, yelling excitedly, "I've got it! I've got it! I've solved the third act!"

History, apocryphal or otherwise, does not record the mogul's reaction to this burst of inspired self-preservation but presumably he moved on satisfied that his scribes, vertical or horizontal, were ever and always on the case. Any lunch hour of these writers' building–commissary war stories had more entertainment value than can be found in most of our screenplays today. Movies were movies, men were men, screenwriters scribes, and their work sparkled with wit, joy, and subversive significance. The point being—if anyone were in doubt—that taking screenwriters more seriously today does not seem, on the whole, to have made us better screenwriters. Or made for better movies.

Over a number of years, I went to the bandy-legged Borden

Chase's house for a ritual Christmas dinner. Borden looked like a tougher, more glamorous version of James Gleason, Robert Montgomery's prizefight manager in *Here Comes Mr. Jordan.* Borden had been a sandhog and worked on the Holland Tunnel. He'd been a roughneck and a roustabout, a tough little bantam rooster with an eye for the ladies and a wonderful way with scenes involving confrontations between men (Clift and Wayne in *Red River;* Burt Lancaster and Gary Cooper in *Vera Cruz;* Jimmy Stewart and Dan Duryea in *Winchester 73*).

There's an especially memorable Mexican standoff between John Ireland as Cherry Valance and Montgomery Clift as Matthew Garth, two young bucks who it appears will inevitably shoot it out, in *Red River.* The scene is not one of tough-guy, in-your-face posturing. On the contrary, it is playful and polite. They engage in target practice on the open plains, taking a break from the business of driving John Wayne's cattle herd to market. Ireland shoots and knocks the shit out of some bottles and rocks. Clift admires the display. Then Clift shoots the shit out of some bottles and rocks on the ground *and* in the air. Ireland is hugely admiring of the display. *"Now* I know who you'd be," he says with a wide grin, fairly licking his lips at the prospect of facing a gunfighter of Clift's skills and reputation, "you'd be Matthew Garth! You're as good as they say you are." Clift returns compliment for compliment. They exchange weapons to see what the other fellow's got for equipment in a shamelessly Freudian I'll-show-you-my-gun-if-you'll-show-me-your-gun display. They admire the hell out of each other's long barrels, stroking them, purring over them, before they return them, Ireland wistfully adding, "There's nothing like a good gun or a Swiss watch—or a woman from anywhere. Ever had a . . . good Swiss watch?"

There was one particular part of the Chases' Christmas dinner that sometimes involved a bit of writing. Everyone at the table was obliged to come up with a toast. They were sometimes inventive, amusing, elaborate, but there was always one that brought the table to a respectful silence—"To absent friends."

I'm old enough to have glimpsed those writers and their times but too young to have lived and worked with them. I have no regrets about having missed that semifabled epoch when men were men, women women, and writers rogues, but I increasingly feel—I suspect we all do—that the history of life on earth is not one of evolution so much as devolution. With each succeeding generation we get weaker and smaller; the Titans are always in the past. They're the original, we're the Xeroxed copies, each generation growing progressively more blurred and degenerate.

This is a romantic fancy of course, but having succumbed to it I should add that the writers interviewed here have talents that would serve them well in any age.

Still, I can't help but look back from the vantage of relative respectability and say, "To absent friends."

Robert Towne
January 19, 1995

Introduction

When approached to star in a proposed movie, Julia Roberts and Mel Gibson (and Michelle Pfeiffer and Jack Nicholson and Denzel Washington, et al.) naturally inquire about the director, the costars, and the producer. Only after reading the script, however, do they make their decisions.

How important is the script to moviemaking? Good scripts can be made into bad movies, but good movies can't be made from bad scripts. Bad movies may not share anything in common; good movies certainly do. While the script may not be everything, everything else is worthless without it.

If that seems overstated, think again. Hollywood's tendency is to "package" movies. Executives and producers bundle all the elements that they believe audiences want—stars, exotic locales, pyrotechnics, etc.—and often pay little mind to the script. It's no surprise that so many films end up like the emperor parading without his clothes.

It wasn't always so. The business and artistic message of a terrific film like *North by Northwest,* for example, is that those elements worked because they slipped perfectly into Ernest Lehman's extraordinary screenplay.

Case in point: Before *Rocky,* conventional wisdom held that boxing movies were box-office poison. After *Rocky,* so-called boxing movies were hot—which led to several bad boxing movies (including the *Rocky* sequels). Mistaking the trees for the forest, too many people missed that *Rocky* was no more a boxing movie than *Silence of the Lambs* was about cannibalism. *Rocky,* above all, was a good story that just happened to take place against a boxing backdrop.

In any event, this isn't a primer on dealmaking, nor is it intended for studio executives. This is a book for screenwriters—aspiring and maybe even established—and for those who love movies, want to learn more about their genesis, and understand the value of inventive writing. Each of the screenwriters included in this compilation of interviews contributes something substantial to these goals.

How I came to ask these thirteen men and women to submit to a long interview doesn't have much of a backstory. While I feel varying degrees of passion and awe for their work, I remain appreciative of their accomplishments. They've all written at least one movie that either held me in thrall or inspired deep admiration.

I asked them questions, ranging from pragmatic to aesthetic, that I believed reflected the uncertainty and ignorance that beginning screenwriters feel (and frequently, as I learned, accomplished ones as well). I wanted to know how they got started, what kept them going when they weren't yet successful, and how they access their muses. The interviews lasted anywhere from seventy-five minutes to nearly four hours. I edited the transcripts for clarity, length, and appropriateness to the subject of movies and writing them.

My sense of these interviews is that they are like the chapters of a good novel. By itself, a chapter satisfies, but, more importantly, it contributes to a whole that is greater than the sum of its parts.

As someone who's profoundly interested in screenwriting, I can point to an illuminating message in each interview—something that would prove helpful were I ever to attempt a screenplay of my own. Collectively, the interviews confer a new perspective on screenwriting, one that has pleasantly altered my relationship to the big screen in the darkened theater. After listening to some of the best in the business talk about how they do what they do, I watch movies from a different angle and with a more educated eye.

I think you will, too, whether your goal is emulation, inspiration, or appreciation. Remember, it wasn't Humphrey Bogart who said, "It doesn't take much to see that the problems of three little people don't amount to a hill of beans in this crazy world." It was Julius Epstein, Philip Epstein, and Howard Koch.

Joel Engel
Topanga, California
July 1994

SCREENWRITERS ON
SCREENWRITING

BRUCE JOEL RUBIN

Bruce Joel Rubin was an aspiring writer until well into his forties, when he finally began to meet with "overnight" success and became the oldest rookie in Hollywood. His story of perseverance, at least as far as concerns his career, reached its zenith in 1991, when he won an original screenplay Oscar for Ghost.

Meeting Rubin, it's hard not to think that those years of struggling served him well. He seems extraordinarily calm, a trait he attributes to his spiritual pursuits, which also inform every aspect of his writing.

We talked in his office behind his San Fernando Valley home, which is located close to ground-zero of the monstrous 6.8 earthquake that destroyed much of Los Angeles in January of 1994. At the time, two weeks after the event, aftershocks were still palpable nearly every hour.

JOEL ENGEL: How do you find a story? Do you start with a character, a plot idea, or something else?

BRUCE JOEL RUBIN: I go to theme first. That's what works for me most.

JE: Well, the four you've made do seem similar thematically.

BJR: Pretty much. That's my theme. I may make movies about that theme until I die. My problem is not stories. I have so many of them—drawers full of ideas for stories. You read a newspaper, there's this whole thing that blows up in front of you.

JE: Fully hatched?

BJR: Not really. In fact, just the opposite. Just a great idea for a movie. What I find in a movie is that a single idea is not enough. What really seems to work for me is when I see ideas for, say, three different films start to move into one film. That really intrigues me. A film gets richer and richer. What started *Ghost* going was just *Hamlet*—watching *Hamlet,* the ghost of the father on the parapet telling his son to avenge his death. I thought that was a great idea to put in contemporary terms. It seemed so simple, and I'd never seen it. That started to be the story for the movie. Then I heard a woman on television tell how her husband had left home. It was the one day he hadn't said "I love you" to his wife. Well, that day he died. She said, "This man said he loved me every day of his life when he left the house. This one day he didn't." She's suffered continually since then because he didn't say it.

I began thinking about not only how it was for her, missing that, but also for this guy, who hadn't done the one thing he normally did and should have done. That was the love story element combined with the murder element—I decided he got killed, not just that he died. Now I had two layers to the story. Then I was telling some friends of mine about a fake psychic, Oda Mae. They began laughing hysterically. But the story wasn't funny yet. They thought it should also be a comedy. It had never dawned on me before that it could be funny, too. That's when Oda Mae emerged as a comic character. Now I had something to lighten and leaven the movie; I knew it needed that. All of these pieces started coming together. So when I wrote the film, I had this rich stew—all these things I could start to put in there. It was fun to write.

JE: Do you block out a story first?

BJR: I write treatments a lot. Not always scene by scene, but the basic story points. Usually three to ten pages. I just get the basic idea. Most of my treatments have been too elaborate, much more novelistic than cinematic. When I finished the treatment for *Ghost,* I remember showing it to my wife. I said it was too thin, not enough there. She said, "No, this is perfect. This is what it should be. Not these other things that go on for thirty episodes. This is clean." It was wonderful for her to say that to me. It finally taught me how simple a movie really is. A lot of people write novels from movies. They're not novels; they're very simple things. The more I write now, the more I think about movies, the simpler it seems to get.

Movies to me are only about wanting something, a character wanting something that you as the audience desperately want him to have. You, the writer, keep him from getting it for as long as possible, and then, through whatever effort he makes, he gets it. The power of the rooting interest to me is the essence of moviedom. It's everything. So simple. A film works when you, the audience, want something for a character as much as he wants it for himself.

JE: Are there tricks to creating out of nothing a character whom we root for?

BJR: You create someone who is sympathetic, who has a need. D. W. Griffith, in *Birth of a Nation,* just had the hero holding a cat. By his petting the cat, you liked him. That's a trick. Show him being nice to people. Show a person who is in some ways a person you like. I had an interesting dilemma while rewriting *Sleeping with the Enemy*. I had to create the character in the middle whom Julia Roberts falls in love with. Since this guy emerges in the middle of the film, I didn't have time to build him as a character. You have to like him right off. So I had this idea that she would spy him outside the window, watering the grass, singing a song from *West Side Story*. He'll be holding the hose and doing a dance. Then he'll look up at the window, see her, and be totally embarrassed. In that moment, you like him. Instantaneously. It's just a gimmick. But you do whatever you can to create for people a likability quotient if they're your hero. I don't want to limit it to that, though. Sometimes you should not let your character be so likable.

Michael Keaton in *My Life* was an interesting problem. At the beginning you're not supposed to like him, and by the end you are. So you have to see redeemable quality, and you have to see something in that character that you invest in. So I opened with his character wishing on a star. You invest in whatever that is; you give over to it. By the end, when the payoff hits, you've been wanting him to get it. Now, I don't know if I was all that successful with *My Life*. Where that's really successful is in *Ghost*. This guy wants to come back and tell his wife he loves her. That's what he wants to do. He's got to say "I love you" to this woman. How do you do that? That's a great dilemma, because he's dead. He's on the other side, yet he's still there and can see everything that's going on. He can walk around, do a lot of stuff, but he cannot communicate the one thing he wants to communicate to this woman. Luckily, he discovers the psychic, who's not a real psychic, who doesn't believe in it, which is a great twist. She has to go through a conversion, which takes the whole audience through a conversion, because they don't believe in this stuff, either. So as she goes through this conversion and the hero finally gets to talk to his wife, whom he has to save, there's this extraordinary rooting for him to say those words. They're saved for the end. Inside, you're aching for that. You want it to happen. So when it finally does happen, it's orgasm. That's what you want.

But how do you do it? If everyone could follow the recipe like that we'd have a million great movies out there. I don't know exactly how to do it, either. The rules are not rules. They're just something you feel. You intuit your way into the process of writing. You tell the story from inside the character. That's probably the most important thing in writing, and the thing that least happens in Hollywood.

JE: From inside *each* character?

BJR: Yeah, you become that person. You know who's great? John Patrick Shanley. I love his writing. *Moonstruck.* There aren't two characters in that film who have the same voice. They each have totally distinct real lives and real voices that are separate from and different from everyone else. Wonderful. That's great writing. Most films in Hollywood, however, have one voice—the writer's. Sure, actors play it a little differently, but you don't get the sense of their dimensionality. Good writing, you get into that character. It's very hard to do. You lose you to them. And you have to trust that you can write a black woman, or a Latino man, or a gangster, or a hero; every aspect of humanity.

You're as good a writer as you are able to get out of the way. This has always fascinated me. You have to become and sensitize yourself to other human beings. And what you discover in writing, which is why it's such a powerful growth tool—at least for me—is where you're limited, where you're blocked, where you cannot access another human being, where you cannot empathize with someone's inner life. Writing by trying to become those characters shows you that.

JE: Give me an example of a character you had a hard time getting to.

BJR: Jerry Zucker always used to say that we were going to have to bring in someone else to write the bad guys. "Bruce," he said, "you can't write bad guys. Everyone you write is good, is nice." I said, "No, I can write bad guys." And I think I did. There was Willie, the guy who committed the murder. And Carl, the best friend whose character takes this twist. I had fun writing him. A fascinating thing I found in the screenings is that the audience hated him more for trying to seduce Molly than for killing Sam. That was amazing to me. Audiences are so connected to those things. Killing we can deal with, but seducing someone else's wife or girlfriend is unacceptable.

In *Ghost,* we had people talking to the screen all time. I love that. I love going to the theater and watching people yelling at Molly, "Don't let him do it. He's a bad guy." They're totally caught up. Writing to create that effect is wonderful.

JE: That was a magical movie, I think, in that everything worked.

BJR: It was rare. It really came together. A wonderful experience from conception to the Oscar.

JE: In *Jacob's Ladder,* you wanted what he wanted, even though you didn't know what he wanted.

BJR: Mostly, you wanted to know what was happening to him—

JE: Because *he* wanted to know what was happening.

BJR: Right. That's very compelling. Often the solution to a problem is enough to carry you through a movie. Scratching the itch to know what really happened. A lot of movies get made with that. Or *The Fugitive,* which is nothing about justice. It's just letting this guy escape, survive, and prevail. Really, the ultimate film story is nothing more than good over evil.

JE: What do you think of films in which evil triumphs over evil; films in which there's no retribution or heroism for the greater good?

BJR: My feeling is, it's okay to take people there if "there" illuminates something else—if the absence of light reveals light or makes you reflect on light. But if the absence of light leads only to dark, then I don't think it's worthwhile. I'm certainly not opposed to violence in films, so long as it's violence in the service of the greater good. If it's only to wallow in the dark side, that doesn't appeal to me.

JE: The components today of what's hip are cynicism and nihilism.

BJR: Nihilism fits the tenor of the times. As a writer, I'm trying to promote some alternatives to nihilism. Art, I think, has a larger purpose than just diversion. Art is a transcendent view of the mundane. So much of what we look at has no transcendence in it. The brackets are in the wrong place. It doesn't leave us complete. It doesn't leave us with a vision that allows us to see life from another angle. Sometimes, if the experience is powerful enough, the transcendence takes place a week later, and you can say that maybe it was worth looking at; the reverberations of it have honestly found their way into my system, enough to cause a transformation of self. So maybe it was an artful experience, even though it wasn't necessarily in the watching.

The Wild Bunch, for me, was a very difficult and powerful experience. When it was over I didn't walk away from it thinking that it had been a particularly great work of art. On the other hand, as days and weeks went by, it lingered in a powerful way. I kept thinking, finally, that what I had responded to was the dance of Shiva; that the film was so much about destruction that it had transcended destruction; so much about death and bloodshed that, in the end, as much as my ego responded to it in a kind of uncomfortable way, something in me rose beyond that and saw the dance of life and death in the movie.

JE: Your films seem to feature protagonists who take a sort of classical journey, like Jonah, from light to darkness and back to light again.

BJR: I really think one has to go from darkness to light; I don't think one just goes from light to light. That's the journey of a human being. I don't think anyone goes on a different journey than that. And truly, all of one's positivity has to be measured against that journey. When one starts to take that journey seriously is when one's real character begins to show itself. I don't consider the way we pass time in the world is particularly significant. What's significant is how you deal with the reality of your mortality. That affects one's life very dramatically. Most people I know don't deal with it at all.

JE: The reality of the mortality meaning the knowledge that you're going to die?

BJR: The knowledge that your life is finite. Really looking into that has a major impact on how that life is lived. Not to be morbid, or to be caught up in some endless psychological or philosophical involvement with death, but to recognize that there is a total package here. At some point we leave this world. How you are prepared to deal with that—in an existential mode or a philosophical or religious mode—has an enormous amount to do with who you are as a human being and how you live your life. For many people, living in denial of that finality allows them to live a carefree, happy, sweet existence. But at some moment you have to pass through this portal. Some people believe that you pass through that portal and cease to exist. Some people believe that you pass through that portal and continue on in some fashion. Obviously, I embrace that. How you live your life is what you believe happens at that juncture. If you can just say "I don't know—I'll find out when I get there," you probably believe in the ashes to ashes, dust to dust end of existence at death. Or you can see it as a launching pad for something bigger or—and this is perhaps the least Western idea—as a launching pad for a journey that transcends what you've been through. Or you can see it in Judeo-Christian terms as either punishment or reward for how you've lived your life.

JE: Judging by *Ghost,* I would say you believe in the punishment-reward scenario.

BJR: I don't, actually. *Ghost* was for me an attempt to tell a story that could reach a particular audience. My real sensibilities are more transcendental, more Eastern than Western, not so much reward/punishment.

JE: That was implied in *Ghost.*

BJR: Yes, it shows that there are consequences for behavior. If you were a bad guy and killed people, there are black shadows taking you off to the nether world. If you were a good guy, you float off into some heavenly realm. That's enormously simplistic, and I knew it was simplistic when I wrote it. But that wasn't a movie that tried to raise people's consciousness, whereas *Jacob's Ladder* was a bit more about what's known in the Tibetan Book of the Dead as the Bardo Cycle, the passage of the soul after death, which is a journey from darkness into light. *Jacob's Ladder* was very much a depiction of that journey in much more Eastern terms than Western terms.

I'm fascinated by all this stuff. It compels me as a writer more than just about anything. My vision of life is that life is hardly what it appears to be; we live in a universe that is vastly different from what our senses present to us. Even the idea of death is a false idea. We see death as a biological event, where, in a deeper sense, it has more to do with the ego. The world is less a material construct than we imagine. It has great physicality and great sensuality, but we experience it on a limited frequency. There's a huge spectrum of reality that our brain is incapable of witnessing or tuning in to.

JE: Incapable or not tuned in to?

BJR: Let's say not tuned in to—that supposed ninety percent of the brain that we don't even use. There is a transcendent mode to life that is not part of Western experience, not something we're taught to pursue here. Whereas, in the Eastern world, for centuries people were taught to pursue the life of the spirit or soul, that the journey inward was as important as the journey outward.

So, as a writer, my objective is to show people another direction, to try to turn them inward rather than have them simply live in this outer framework.

JE: Let's use my friend Allen as an example. Seeing *Jacob's Ladder* incited in him a sort of midlife crisis. He went back to teaching after several years as a businessman. I'm not sure if he holds the universe in a different context now, though he certainly, as you talked about before, became acutely aware that his days are not infinite.

BJR: I'm not necessarily trying to change people's inner land-scape. I'm simply trying to awaken them to the opportunity to think in a different way, or to look in a different way, or to sense life in a different way. As a writer, you see that so many stories have been told, so many of the journeys people have have been expressed, at least in the literature—less, perhaps, in film, because it's such an action-oriented medium. I really feel that in our West-ern culture, so many film journeys deal with the resolution of outer conflict. I just want to take people on a little bit of a differ-ent ride—to tell a little bit different story.

JE: It's not easy to film a Henry James novel successfully.

BJR: Exactly. But I would like to shift the arena a little bit from the world of action into the world of spirit. Not that you can't have action. It's a journey where great drama does take place. I'd like people to perceive some of that. *Jacob's Ladder* is a journey into a man's mind in the hours of his death—what his mind goes through. For some people that was fairly clear; some didn't have a clue as to what was going on.

We actually toyed with the idea of telling people up front that this was a journey through the mind of a man who's dying, so that the mystery of it was no longer the issue, that it was all about watching the journey, watching him resolve these issues.

JE: But the wonder of it, the mystery, was interesting; the reve-lation was to be a surprise.

BJR: For some people, the question of what was going on was the compelling issue. For other people, it was the pure intensity of what was happening to this guy, this pure sort of inner devastation that was occurring in which everything that he held on to with some kind of reality was being pulled out from underneath him. The one thing that could not survive this journey was his hold on anything. Finally, he had to let go of it all in order to find the light.

As the character Louis so clearly says in the movie, holding Jacob, that if you're afraid of dying—I forget the words exactly—you see creatures pulling you from your life. But if you're open to this transition, these same creatures become angels freeing you, freeing your spirit. Really, that's the key idea of that movie: Here's a man fighting that process who learns to surrender to it, learns to give into it. The lesson is not just for dying but for living: How have you lived your life? Stop fighting it so much and surrender to a larger process. But where it really does have an impact is in this dying process. In the end, you really do have to let go of everything; you take nothing from this world.

JE: So the question then is, apropos of writing: How do you take your world view and turn it into something dramatic that is accessible to people who don't already know that they should take that journey or remain open to its possibilities?

BJR: Let's talk about writing as opposed to philosophy.

JE: Don't they intersect all along the way?

BJR: That all depends on what motivates your writing. When I first started writing, a long, long time ago, all I cared about was telling a story that had a beginning, middle, and end. I was so thrilled to find a script that tied together the pieces in the last reel that I'd established at the beginning, it didn't matter what it was about. It just mattered to me that it was a whole piece of cloth. That, to me, was very exciting as a writer.

JE: Can you give a specific example?

BJR: Well, nothing, thank God, that was ever produced. These weren't significant works—just me learning how to tell a story. They were exercises for me, and not intended to be turned into movies. Twice in my life when I was really desperate to create film and had very little time to do that, I locked myself in a hotel room. Once for eight days, the other for ten or eleven days. I told myself, "You're not coming out of this room until you have a script. Period."

In both instances, I walked into the room without even an idea of what I was going to write. But I had to force the issue, had to force myself.

JE: How early in your career was this?

BJR: Before I even had a career. This is way back. I didn't have huge periods of time to sit and write on a daily basis. My objective was to just get something on paper that I could look at that was a script. In both instances I wrote full movies. Neither of them is a particularly great work, though both are full of interesting ideas and have some wonderful scenes, and both are 120 pages of real material that I put down on paper. When I look at what I did there, I realize that I was involved in a very important process in writing. You need to get what I call "the lump of clay" on the table. You can't mold it until it's there. So if you get ten pages down and then start being judgmental and critical of your work, you'll never get that lump of clay on the table. What happens to a lot of writers is they obstruct the process early on by saying, "Oh, this isn't going where I want it to go. It's not how I want it to be." The point is, just let it be; just let it happen. I really learned to just write a script, just put it out there and get it down. Then, once it's on the table, you go back to it and you can bring all of your critical faculties into play. You can say, "Okay, this intent was right; this played out poorly; this character ain't gonna work; this scene at the end of the movie shows me how the beginning should have worked."

There's all this stuff that starts to come out when you see the whole thing that you cannot understand until that moment. My advice to writers, and often to myself, is, just get it out there. Get a draft done, even if it's wrong, even if it's got lots of holes, even if characters don't sound the way you want them to sound yet. It's okay, because when you go back, at least when I go back, I discover that the intent somehow had true inspiration there; that there was something in the original effort that was right. Often it's filled with a lot of wrong elements, but within the initial presentation is the key or the seed to something that will make the scene work. And that's always extraordinary. You discover, hey, this part was good or, that idea was wonderful.

I did that twice, and both of those scripts remain unshot. Neither of them, even with all that clay on the table, is a film I believe has been molded into anything worth producing. They both tell stories. They're both even compelling stories, on a certain level. The question comes down to something that Jerry Zucker [director of *Ghost*] said to me when we first met on *Ghost*. He said, "What's this movie about?" I said, "It's about a guy who dies and comes back to save his wife." He said, "No, no. What is it *about?*" I had no idea what he was getting at. Then it slowly dawned on me, being thick and slow to understand anything, that movies have to have a theme—something that they're trying to say to the world, a reason for being. Not just to tell a story; it needs to have purpose. *Ghost* and *Jacob's Ladder*, *Brainstorm* and *My Life* are four films for me that have purpose, a thematic drive; films, I think, that make them worthy of being made—and of me putting a year or two of life into getting them made. Whereas these other stories have no purpose other than to divert. Not that that isn't okay;

many of our most enjoyable films are pure diversions. But I realized that, for myself, diversion wasn't enough. Just to divert was too big an effort to have that consequence, that people only get two hours of distraction.

JE: How did you finally answer Jerry Zucker?

BJR: In the end the film was about spirit, about the fact that our lives are embued with spirit. It's really about trying to affirm that spirit in man—though in a very quiet way. I said something about that when I accepted my Oscar, and I could hear everybody laughing in the auditorium, like, *Oh, come on, this is just entertainment.* But it wasn't just about entertainment. I think one of the reasons the film enjoyed such acceptance was because it addressed this issue that somehow there is a higher aspect to man. Also, there was that wonderful idea that love goes with you, that love has some sort of transcendent purpose, that love is the one thing you take with you, that having love in your life is worthy. I think these themes and ideas sort of seep into people, and I think it's something they want when they go to the movies. Some of the really great movies—*Star Wars, Raiders of the Lost Ark*—have that. *Star Wars* talks about the Force—not that people come out of the movie saying that the Force was the particular thing they loved most of all. But it's an extraordinary concept.

JE: It's not an accident that the "Force" has become part of the cultural language. It has a life of its own outside the movie.

BJR: Exactly. I love that. I feel that a movie that has thematic purpose is something that I can spend my time on, whereas a movie that doesn't, I won't. As a writer, you have two hours to talk to the world; what do you want to tell them? This is an extraordinarily privileged opportunity. Again, I don't want to require that every filmmaker have some deep, powerful message to convey to the world. But is there something that you personally want to communicate to another human being? If there is, this is a great opportunity to do it. And, sometimes, making movies is where to discover what you do care about, what you do want to say.

I personally have a problem with films that have no purpose. I don't mind films that just entertain, I guess. Like *Fatal Attraction* had an extraordinary power behind it because there was a great moral dilemma that came along with it. So as much as it entertained and put you through all sorts of twists and turns inside yourself—and every man I know who saw it was just writhing with the discomfort—I prefer that film to films that have no reason for being other than to slash people up and to create a lot of mayhem. To what end? What was its purpose?

JE: *Fatal Attraction* and *Indecent Proposal* both created major stirs, and both relied on ethical and moral dilemmas thematically. Regardless of their artistic worth, maybe the films that have the power to compel—whether it's action or discussion or whatever—require a plot that revolves around some sort of moral complexity.

BJR: Movies that are about something, when you come out of the theater and the experience isn't finished; there's still something that you're digesting and taking away with you. I often liken films to meals. One likes to go to a film and get a three-course meal or a five-course meal. What's so frustrating is, you go to so many meals and get the hors d'oeuvres tray and you're lucky to pick up one or two little morsels, and you walk out of the theater feeling hungry and thirsty; it took away rather than gave you. And I think a film should give. The great films give and they keep giving. *The Wizard of Oz* and *Citizen Kane* and *2001*. On and on.

Every time you sit down, you get the taste of that meal all over again, and really love it and digest it. How often does that happen to people going to movies these days? So I would like to feed people, to have them walk out of the theater and say, "Wasn't that good?" And then start talking about it.

JE: Not to be overly glib, but how do you do it? What do you begin with?

BJR: You have to find what it is you have a passion for. What do you want to say?

JE: When you went into that hotel room to write a script—

BJR: I had no passion; I had only the desire to write a script. That was the big distinction. All I wanted was to write a script that would sell and that would tell a whole story and that would get me onto the road to moviedom. Of course, neither script did because they were empty pieces of storytelling; much ado about nothing.

JE: A lot of movies like that get made.

BJR: That's a whole other issue. Both of those movies, based on where I am in my career today, I could get made if I wanted. In fact, I have a number of unproduced screenplays, all of which I know I could get made, but I don't want to. I wouldn't waste people's time to watch them. That's not what it's about for me anymore, just getting movies made. It's about making movies that mean something to me. Otherwise, why bother? There are scripts that I do have, dating way back, that have something to them that I may one day refashion, based on what I've learned in the last few years of filmmaking and storytelling. I think I'm a better writer today than I was when I wrote them, and I think they'd benefit.

My second script was what became *Brainstorm*. The thing that was wonderful about that was I was very passionate about the idea, and the only way I could possibly have written it was through an arrangement I made with my wife. At the time I had a nine-to-five job as a film curator at the Whitney Museum in New York. I did that for four years. I didn't start out as the curator; I became that after my friend the curator died. I didn't want to be curator. I didn't want to show other people's movies; I wanted to be making my own. What I loved about the films I showed at the Whitney—which were equivalent to the types of films now shown in Park City [at the annual Sundance film festival]—is that they were independent films that were based on people's passions. They weren't even all just storytelling; a lot of them were non-narrative and wonderfully experimental and poetic. I thought of them as poetic cinema more than anything because they were so personal. I wanted to make them, too, but I wanted to make them for a mass audience. I was very hungry to make films, not just to program them and show them. So what I did was strike a bargain with my wife: She said she would do the dishes, and after dinner every night for three months I would write one scene of this movie. I couldn't go to bed until I finished the scene. Sometimes I would write a scene in half an hour. Sometimes it took me four or five hours. But I always finished; and after three months I had a screenplay. And it was a screenplay that got made. Sure, it got changed quite a bit, but it did get made [*Brainstorm*]. Everyone who tells me they don't have time to write, I just say "One scene a night for three months, and you'll have a movie—you can even use the weekends." It's possible to be a writer if you want to be a writer, even without all the time in the world. Even without a wife who'll support you by doing the dishes. After doing the dishes, instead of turning on the television or reading a book or going to the movies, write one scene. Whatever you do, write a scene.

JE: It does help to have a wonderful, supportive spouse.

BJR: If you want, I can talk for two hours about my wife. She's been extraordinary. She's responsible for me having a career at all. Sometimes she supported me while I would write, and sometimes I supported her while she did her art. We kind of leap-frogged careers: I supported her when she went back to school. What finally happened is, we came out to Los Angeles for the opening of *Brainstorm* and had lunch with Brian De Palma, who'd been a classmate [at NYU film school]. He said, "You know, if you really want a career in Hollywood, you have to move out here." I had always known that and never wanted to accept it. We were living in De Kalb, Illinois. My wife was a professor at Northern Illinois University, and I was thinking that I could be a writer and send my scripts to Hollywood. They'd send me back huge checks, and I would have this very perfect life without actually having to live here. But they didn't send me back anything.

Anyway, we returned to De Kalb. My wife quit her job, put our house on the market, and said, "We're moving to Los Angeles." The most astounding vote of confidence I've ever had from anybody. She just said, "Let's do it." We did. We had two kids at the time, eleven and three. We arrived here ten years ago with four thousand dollars in our pocket.

JE: What do you think your wife saw in you that inspired her to do that?

BJR: She saw someone who had a real need to have this happen.

JE: Do you have a need to write novels?

BJR: Never.

JE: Plays?

BJR: No.

JE: Just movies. You just love movies.

BJR: I've loved movies since I saw my first movie, which was when I was four. My parents took me to a nightclub in Detroit, when they still had nightclubs, at the Statler-Hilton. My parents said that I could watch the floor show or go see a movie. I chose the movie. The maître d' tried to convince me to stay and watch the show—"Beautiful girls and dancing," he said. I said I wanted the movie. My parents said okay, so we went over to the theater and saw *The Al Jolson Story*. When it was over my parents said, "Wasn't that wonderful. Now let's go." I said, "No. I want to see it again." I would not leave the theater. I refused to leave. I held on to the seat. They had no choice but to watch the movie a second time. It was that early, four years old, when I knew that whatever this was, I loved it; I just loved it. I have never stopped loving it. Although, for a while during my teenage years and a little earlier, I thought that movies were just entertainment and diversion, and that what really mattered was theater. I spent all my time as a teenager really involved in theater. I used to usher at all the theaters in Detroit and watch all these plays and shows over and over again. Saw some really remarkable works—O'Neill's *Long Day's Journey into Night;* Lunt and Fontaine in *The Visit*.

Then, when I was sixteen, I went to see *Wild Strawberries*. Art films, to that point, were just films with a little bit of flesh. Suddenly there was this movie. It changed my life. I realized that film could be something else, that it wasn't necessarily just Westerns and thrillers and comedies; there was content, substance. I loved what Bergman was doing. That opened me up to the most exciting time of my life in terms of creative input and what was happening in film. I discovered Antonioni, Truffaut, Goddard; all these guys. I couldn't breathe. I was just so thrilled by the reality of what was happening in movies and what movies could be. I loved the whole arena of foreign films—storytelling and art and grand visions. It was so wonderful to me.

Then I went to school with Marty Scorsese. He and I were very friendly in college. He used to talk to me about John Ford and Howard Hawks. Those names didn't compute in my mind. I thought, *These aren't artists. The Europeans are artists. These guys just tell stories.* Marty tried to show me that Ford was an auteur, that there was a body of work. At that point, Truffaut hadn't really established the auteur theory, so it was just Scorsese saying these things to me. I started to see the Americans differently. I really think I became this person who wanted to combine the American sensibility of mass entertainment with European content-filled stories. That's how it all emerged. Then it took a long time for me to learn to be a writer.

JE: Was there a single epiphanic moment?

BJR: No, not other than a friend of mine after high school telling me that there were a few colleges—UCLA, NYU, USC—where you could study filmmaking. *You mean, there's a way to learn to make movies?* I wouldn't exactly call it an epiphany, but that moment was important because I learned that there was access, that there was a way to become a filmmaker. The hardest thing about becoming a filmmaker in Hollywood is that there is no road to it; no avenue; no plotted way to get here.

JE: It works as a weeding-out process: Only those willing to give blood and guts need apply.

BJR: In a sense it does. But unfortunately it weeds out a lot of very creative people and leaves standing a lot of people who have power and that ego-drive to get through, but who, once they're through, don't have anything to say. They have their career in mind, but nothing to bring along with it.

JE: *My Life* has something to say. But very few people, evidently, went to hear it.

BJR: If you want to make a movie about serious subjects of that nature [death, dying, love, legacy, and the examined life], and you want to point arrows at the subject, don't expect a mass audience to go to it, because mass audiences don't want to be deluged with seriousness. They want entertainment.

JE: But you knew that anyway.

BJR: I thought that if I gave it to them in an entertaining way, and I made the film with real emotional access, that they would go see it; they would tell their friends, "This really moved me. Go see it." I was wrong. The comments from the preview audience were much better than even *Ghost,* and that was pretty great. We ended up with ninety-six percent "excellent to very good," and an eighty percent "definite recommend." I thought that it was going to be huge, which I was excited about because I've had the experience of huge, and that was a nice experience. Then, it wasn't huge. It's considered respectable, and because of the modest investment was, I've been told, the second most profitable film the studio [Columbia] had [in 1993], next to *Groundhog Day.*

JE: I sat next to someone who sobbed through much of it, then said to his friend when the lights came up that he didn't like it.

BJR: There are people who have that experience, and I don't know what to say. Maybe they found it overly sentimental. I don't want to be a defender of the film just because I wrote it. The thing that bothers me about a lot of recent films is that they refuse to go for the emotion, to touch sentiment. Revered films tend to restrain themselves, but I find that frustrating. I want films that deliver something.

JE: All right, you've made your directorial debut. Question is, what do you learn about writing from directing?

BJR: It's a good question. I don't think it should change your writing. What happens to a lot of writers after they direct, they write much tighter; they don't write the scenes they know won't make it into the movie, all of the fat they know is going to get cut out later. Well, try to sell a Pritikin meal to someone over a good steak dinner. Studios buy the juice, the steak, the thing that's really rich and tasty and delicious. That's what they want. On the page, if you don't have that, your film is going to look dry and empty. What ends up on the screen is a cinematic translation of a verbal literary work. The first job of a writer is to create a literary work, not the blueprint purely for what's going to be on the screen. Because what comes on the screen benefits from performance, locale, decor, camera, lighting—all of these things that are not on the page add to the cinematic moment. It's much richer on a certain level than that literary moment in the sense that you're playing with multiple realities. On a page it's all suggestion, all images that your mind conjures for yourself—but it's not realized, just suggested. If as a writer you limit yourself to such a severe regime that all you give the reader is what's finally going to be on the screen, no one's going to like reading your work, and no one's going to buy your work. Not unless you are such a good storyteller that you can create *The Fugitive*—boom, boom, boom, one quick moment after another after another—which is less about character than about plotting and movement and action. When you do that, yes, you can bombard the page with quick stuff and staccato editing and structure.

JE: I have a copy of Scott Frank's script for *Dead Again*. What Kenneth Branagh shot is exactly that script.

BJR: That can happen. With the kind of plotting in *Dead Again,* you almost can't lose a thread. You lose one and you're in trouble. That's the problem you run into with most thrillers. With *The Firm* they were going crazy because they were running into two and a half hours.

Often when you're writing you put in scenes you know aren't going to make it into the movie. There was a scene in the script for *My Life* with the Michael Keaton character getting angry at the videotape he'd been making and throwing the camera on the floor. After breaking the camera, he goes back to Circuit City; and in the process of him trying to connive this salesman into giving him a free camera, you start to establish a character. He does wonderful things. He sees the salesman watching the Dodger game in the background and lets him know that he represents Tommy Lasorda [the Dodger manager]. He says he can get him a Tommy Lasorda autograph; does this whole number. When he leaves the store, you find out he doesn't know Lasorda at all. He just does this thing to get the guy in. He tells his secretary to find out who represents Lasorda and send one to this guy. So he's a good guy, but conniving. The voice of that was very important to me, even though I knew when I wrote it that I couldn't play a scene in Circuit City; I didn't have time. When I finally cut it, I knew it was going to go. I had a lot of scenes that got me through writing. Some even survived the draft that got to the studio.

That brings up another point. You should always leave a number of scenes in your script for the studio that you know will never make it into the final script, because the studio is going to see those scenes and ask you to cut them. That's how the game is played; they're going to force you to cut something. So give them something to cut that doesn't cost anything.

JE: How do you know whether what you put down on the page is worthy of your having confidence? How do you know if it's any good? Hemingway talked about the shit detector.

BJR: The shit detector is something I think you do need. But it has to be turned off for the first draft. That's easier to do on a typewriter, which is what I used to use, than it is on a word processor. Rewriting on a typewriter means retyping the whole page. That's a big deal. On a computer, I rewrite all the time. In fact, my process on a computer is different than what it was on a typewriter.

When a scene works, there's something in you that knows it's working.

JE: Yeah, but you know that because you have obvious talent that's been validated. How do know if you have any talent, and whether you should trust that something in you?

BJR: I can't answer whether or not someone has talent. But you can answer whether or not you're a commercial screenwriter very simply: Does anyone want to buy your script? Let me tell you about an experience I had with *Ghost*. I had a lunch meeting at Paramount. As I was walking back with the executives, they said, "This is the best script we've ever read." I was wowed. I was flying high. Mr. Talent. Cut to a week later. I'm walking out of the studio, and the executives are in front of me talking to another writer. One of them says, "You know, this is the best script we've ever read." I said to myself, "Oh, *that's* how it works. *Now* I get it." They're *all* the best script they've ever read, and it's always going to be like that. And, in a certain sense, it's easy to tell people that—but you know when they mean it when they pay you; when the check goes to the bank, they've put their money where their mouth is. That's when you know whether you have whatever it takes. When they say, "Here's twenty million dollars to make a movie"—your script generated that.

JE: But for years and years you went on without ever hearing that or seeing that. What enabled you to continue without that external validation?

BJR: You just have to trust in yourself. I knew *Jacob's Ladder* was a good script. I knew it was. I could tell when I read it over that it was good, that it was better than other things I'd written. For years it had the dubious distinction of being on that list as one of the ten best unproduced screenplays in Hollywood. That meant something to me, because at least it was a distinction, dubious or not; an acknowledgment. I so liked the script that I turned down director after director after director, all of whom wanted to make it in ways that I thought would be wrong for the material. I knew what it was, what would work.

One of the things that happens after you finish a script is, you show it to people you love. Usually the people you love tell you it's wonderful. My wife always loves my work and thinks it's wonderful. Thank God for that, because she's the first person who sees it, and it would be devastating if she didn't love it. She seems to authentically love it. Then there are people like your parents or siblings. They also love it. Now, there's a problem here: Because everyone you've showed the script to has loved it, it's good. What are people going to say when they see the material, that it's worthless? Most people get off the hook as fast as they can: "It's fantastic. I loved it." So you walk away with this puffed-up feeling and think that you're a great writer. The only way I've ever found to get true feedback is the studio. You can tell if they're telling the truth by whether they pay for it. So how do you know if what you're writing is good and there's no studio executive to tell you? You have to ask yourself continually: "Is this good enough for someone to hand out twenty or thirty or forty or fifty million dollars?" Ask yourself if your script is the kind of thing that somebody will want to put that kind of money into in order to make.

The reality is, Hollywood is such an unpredictable place. Nobody knows.

JE: To answer yes to those rhetorical questions, isn't there a dangerous temptation to try to copy a successful formula, like *Lethal Weapon*? By page twenty-five this has to happen; page fifty, this; ninety-five, that.

BJR: Then it's about your aura as a film writer. Let's say I wrote a *Lethal Weapon* type of script today that was not as good as Shane Black wrote, but it had my name on it. It would probably sell, solely because my name now has the patina of success. If we put someone else's name on it who didn't have that patina, it probably wouldn't sell. That's another thing that happens in Hollywood all the time. Many people absolutely know that their scripts are better than what gets made. It's about that thing which starts to shine and makes you luminous enough to catch someone's attention. I tend toward optimism, the belief that if something is really, really good that, like cream, it'll rise to the top—attention will be paid somewhere along the way. It may take a while, but I think it'll probably happen. Enough people out there are looking for good stuff. It doesn't mean it'll get made, or get made easily.

I pitched the story of *Ghost* for three years; same story. It wasn't until near the end of those three years that it started to gather some interest from the right people. I think it's because my career was starting to become a little more visible that they paid attention. I was starting to be a bit more of a presence in the business. Finally they became interested in the story.

JE: Can you name your three favorite films?

BJR: Probably the ones I mentioned before: *Wizard of Oz, Citizen Kane,* and *2001: A Space Odyssey.*

JE: If you could somehow put those three together, merge them thematically, you'd end up with a pretty good summation of what your work is about.

BJR: What my work aspires to be—to see that much creativity in one work. If I could create on those levels, I would be very thrilled. I'm very clear about my talent. I've read Shakespeare and Chekhov; I read what I write. We're not talking great literature here. My hope is to be a good popular entertainer.

It's tricky, though. The success of *Ghost* was very debilitating to me. It took me a year to get over just the fear of sitting down again to write. There were so many expectations. People would say, "We know the next thing you write is going to be great." I kept saying, "Who are you talking to? How do you know that? What are you privy to? I haven't got a clue what my next project is going to be, and I know how capricious it is, and I know how hard it is." To think that it's going to be great just because something you did was successful commercially is an absurdity. In some ways, the fact that *My Life* was not a huge success is liberating, because now I can go back to being a normal writer. I don't have to live up to *Ghost.*

ERNEST LEHMAN

One of my first questions to Ernest Lehman elicited the most startling answer of our entire conversation. Anticipating a chance to get a close look, I asked how many screenwriting Oscars he'd won. After all, he'd written the adaptations of West Side Story *and* The Sound of Music, *which together earned four Academy Awards just for producer-director Robert Wise. His other film credits read like a list of all-time movie greats.*

"None," he said.

It's a disturbing thought to contemplate the fact that Pillow Talk *beat* North by Northwest *for best screenplay. So much for awards.*

Mr. Lehman, who was seventy-eight years old when we met, began his writing career in the 1930s as a journalist. Before going to Hollywood in the 1950s, he was also a press agent and a short-fiction writer. For all his considerable talent at creating character, dialogue, and plot, it seems that Mr. Lehman has spent little time analyzing the source of his creativity or wondering how the hell he does what he does so well. He just accepts that it happens. Nonetheless, it's as instructive as it is entertaining to hear his stories about bringing to the screen such disparate works as West Side Story, Who's Afraid of Virginia Woolf? *and* North by Northwest."

We met in the large, freestanding poolroom of the home he and his wife have lived in for nearly four decades.

ERNEST LEHMAN: Hitch[cock] once said to me, "If a director can get eighty-five percent of the writer's intention on the screen, the writer should consider himself fortunate."

JOEL ENGEL: Most writers now take it for granted that their scripts are merely "blueprints."

EL: Blueprint, my God. In the old days they used the word "scenarist," as though the writer was only creating scenarios. It wasn't the play that was going to be put on the screen, just a scenario.

JE: Do you have a favorite of all the films you've written?

EL: I can't say that I do. Years ago a group of writers traveled to what was then the Soviet Union to show some films. Each of us brought one film. I took *Somebody Up There Likes Me.* They'd already seen *West Side Story* and *The Sound of Music.* They used to see everything. But I loved that picture, though I can't say it's my favorite. When I see *Sound of Music,* I feel every frame is a thing of beauty, which I attribute to Bob Wise.

JE: Wasn't somebody besides Paul Newman supposed to get the role of Rocky Graziano in *Somebody Up There?*

EL: James Dean. He was killed in an auto crash before we started filming. I was at the Writers Guild when my wife called to say that he'd been killed. I said, "Oh my God." That night, on television, there was a drama based on an Ernest Hemingway short story called "The Battlers." The role of the punch-drunk fighter was played by a relatively unknown actor named Paul Newman. Charles Schnee, the producer, and I both watched the show independently of each other. He called me, and we both instantly agreed that this guy Newman was Rocky Graziano.

JE: Dean was probably too frail for the role anyway. And he'd have played it like Hamlet.

EL: I don't know what the thinking was when they cast him. I met Dean once, when he walked into John Houseman's office; I guess John was considering him for a picture. I don't know how he would have done it. He was very slight.

JE: Newman was terrific in the role.

EL: I think it started his whole career. Anyway, you asked about my favorite movies of mine. *The Sound of Music. North by Northwest. Somebody Up There Likes Me. The King and I. Who's Afraid of Virginia Woolf?*

JE: You're naming them all.

EL: Well, it's impossible. It's ridiculous.

JE: Tell me about adapting *Virginia Woolf.*

EL: I never wrote so many different drafts for a film before, and then to arrive at a picture that was very true to the play. I went in many different ways, even had a real son who committed suicide at age sixteen, by hanging himself in the closet. That's what Martha couldn't face.

JE: As opposed to the son whom we find out George and Martha invented?

EL: Yes.

JE: Why did you experiment with that?

EL: We're talking about the mid 1960s. At the time, when I saw the play, I was not the only one bothered a bit by the fantasy of the imagined child. I wondered if I could make it work.

JE: Because it didn't ring true?

EL: There's a whole history of how this play script had been sent to me by Abe Lastfogel of the William Morris Agency, because no one else would touch it. I was a writer, not a producer. At the time I was working on *The Sound of Music*. After reading the play, I resolved never to see it on the stage, because it disturbed me. The nakedness, the openness of the way George and Martha talked *to* each other and *at* each other. It disturbed me. I felt that I didn't need that in my life—in my married life. Every time I went to New York, people said, "You've gotta see *Virginia Woolf*." I said, "You gotta, I don't gotta. I don't want to see it." And I didn't—until it came out to California. Friends of ours had two extra tickets for opening night. I was recovering from the flu and in a sort of weakened condition. In a weak moment, I said yes. I went to the theater. And for the first twenty or twenty-five minutes I wondered what I was afraid of; I laughed. It was fun. Then, "You're a flop. You're a big, fat flop." Crash. Suddenly, the whole thing turned, and there I was, trapped, surrounded by people I knew. I couldn't control my emotions. I was absolutely torn to pieces by that play. I barely got out of the theater alive. I was devastated by the experience. Never, not for a moment, did I consider that for a movie.

One day, when Abe Lastfogel called me, I said, "By the way, I finally saw that play. And it knocked the crap out of me. It killed me." He said, "That's very interesting. There's another man in this town on whom it had the same effect. Jack Warner. He was devastated by that play." And that was that. End of discussion. A week later he called back: "Ernie, is there any chance you'd be

interested?" "Absolutely not, Abe, I'm busy working on a picture." "But you told me the play devastated you." "Why are you
telling me this?" I said. "Because," he said, "I happen to know
that Fred Zinnemann is interested in directing it. I'm going to try
to sell it, because nobody else will buy it. I'm going to get a clear-
ance [from playwright Edward Albee]." "That's your business," I
said. "Don't bother me." But he never stopped. One day he
called me and said he was about to sell it to Jack Warner. "Should
I mention you?" I said, "No. What you do with Jack Warner is
your business, not mine." That was that. Back to *The Sound of
Music.*

Then came another phone call, maybe a week later. "Ernie,"
he said, "this is official. Jack Warner has bought *Who's Afraid of
Virginia Woolf?* and wants you to write and produce it." I said,
"Oh my God. You mean I'm going to have to say yes or no?" He
said, "You've got the weekend to think about it. It's official." So
I called my friend [producer] Larry Turman. I'd been through this
on *The Graduate* with him, when he couldn't figure out whether
he should buy the [Charles Webb] novel. I told him, "If you love
it, get it." So he came over and we sat beside my pool, and I told
him, "I don't know how to do it. It can't be done. But you know
what? How can I not? If I can create, in a movie theater, the
emotional effect that that play has on an audience, that would be
something."

I called Abe Lastfogel and told him I wanted to meet with Jack
Warner and all his executives. We met in Warner Brothers' tro-
phy room. I told them that the picture was impossible. "We all
know that," I said. "I'll get out on a limb and try to do it, but it's
so risky that I have to be in control of who does what to whom
and who's in it. Everything." Warner agreed—provided that he
had the right to approve my decisions.

I sat alone in the back half of the bungalow that George Cukor
had used when he directed *My Fair Lady,* because I was only

writing then and therefore couldn't have the front half of the bungalow, too, according to Warner. I sat and thought, got phone calls from people who had ideas—actors who wanted to be in it, directors who wanted to direct. I couldn't figure it out, how to do it, how to turn this play into a movie. It was all in one room. How do you do that? This went on for a long, long time. I even went to England to see the original cast, Uta Hagen and Arthur Hill. On the way, I went to New York to meet with Edward Albee. He didn't show up for the meeting. So I called his agent, who said he'd get in touch with him. I waited the next day, and he didn't show up again. I called his agent and said, "Give me his phone number." I called him and said, "Edward, I don't think you really want to meet with me." He said, "I'll be right over." I didn't blame him. If I'd been him I wouldn't have wanted to sit in a room with me knowing that I, Edward Albee, had nothing to say about this movie; I'd hope that this character from California doesn't destroy my work.

JE: Well, he had sold the rights, and he was getting Ernest Lehman, not Joe Blow.

EL: You didn't know Edward Albee in those days. Anybody who could write *The Zoo Story* and *The American Dream*—he was very cautious. And I was very defensive. I didn't want to have to account to him for whatever I was going to do with the play. We literally never talked again after that.

Not to go into too much detail, but I discussed the show with so many people. Finally, after at least half a year of my being alone in the picture, the late agent Hugh French called me and said, "Ernie, did you ever think of Elizabeth Taylor and Richard Burton to play George and Martha?" I said, "No, I didn't. But thanks." The idea almost went in one ear and out the other. It was as preposterous an idea as Edward Albee's: He wanted Bette Davis and James Mason. I guess he'd seen the late-late shows and thought they were still photographable.

Well, a month or two went by. I was standing on line waiting to get into *The Night of the Iguana*. Richard Burton was in that. Looking around at the audience, I was thinking about Elizabeth Taylor—thirty-two years old and beautiful; what a ridiculous idea to cast her. But I'd seen a photo of her chewing out [her late husband] Mike Todd at an airport. It was exactly like Martha. I sort of made the decision to cast Elizabeth Taylor. I thought that George and Martha's marriage could be twelve years old instead of twenty. She can be in her forties instead of her fifties. We can make her look older. I suddenly thought, "I've got a secret." It was a sensational secret. I'd always thought of her as a marvelous movie actress.

I called Jack Warner to tell him that we needed to meet because I'd decided on my Martha. "You gotta be kidding," he said when I told him. "We'll make her look the right age," I said. "But she gets a million dollars a picture, and this is a low-budget picture." he said. "It'll be worth it," I said. "But Ernie," he said, "she's a beautiful child, for God's sake. How are you going to do it?" "Wigs," I said, "and she'll add weight." I did the whole pitch. Finally he said, "What do you want me to say?" I said, "I want you to say yes." "Okay," he said, "yes." Of course, I had no idea whether Elizabeth Taylor was even interested, or whether she'd seen the play. She and Burton were off in Europe filming *The Sandpiper*. It was being shot in Paris, with locations in Santa Barbara for tax purposes.

So began a long odyssey. I called Hugh French, her agent. Turns out they were coming into town on the way to Santa Barbara and were going to stay at the Beverly Hills Hotel. I went to meet her. She was at the dentist when I got there. I was alone with Richard Burton. I was embarrassed. I hadn't said I wanted him for the movie. I hadn't even thought about it. We spent about an hour together. He was wonderful, telling all the reasons why she had to take the part. "She comes through that box like nobody else," he said.

Finally, she walked into the room. I'll tell you, when Elizabeth comes in, it's like electricity. Richard Burton started in on her with all the reasons why she should do the part. "Shut up, love," she said. "I don't want to hear it from you. I want to hear it from Ernie." She took me into the bedroom. "Why in the world would you want me for this?" she said. "Forgive me," I said, "but you're Martha." We talked and talked and talked. It was an incredible meeting for me; I'd never produced a picture before. And here I am dealing with internationally headlining stars at the height of their fame. She said she'd think about it.

Word came down from Santa Barbara that she said yes. Negotiations started, and we signed her. When it was announced in the papers, I read some unpleasant comments from Edward Albee about the casting. I had to defend myself.

Now came the next order of business: George. Well, they planned to stop at the Beverly Hills Hotel on the way back to Europe. I took my list of actors over there to get her thoughts and approval. Richard Burton's name was not on the list. He was, in my opinion, too strong, too powerful. Elizabeth approved of some of the names on the list. Then she said, "Well, what about schmuck here?" He's sitting right there in the room. I said, "Richard, you've got to understand. I think you're the greatest actor in the world. I just think you're too strong. I'm embarrassed to be talking in front of you." He said, "I understand, Ernie. Just remember that if you don't get who you want, I'll be in the bullpen."

Elizabeth and I agreed on a couple of names. But before I left I said, "Do me a favor, Richard. When you get back to Paris, think about whether you really feel you could play this weak man. And I'll do the same." He said he would. So every day I realized more and more what an asshole I had been, how stupid I'd been. What happened was, Jack Lemmon said he would do it, then he went off to do *The Great Race*. I think that between Tony Curtis and Blake Edwards and his own wife and God knows who else, he probably decided he'd be chewed alive working as George with Elizabeth Taylor's Martha. It's dangerous for a man to be seen in that role. I began wondering what the production would be like with no one watching over Elizabeth Taylor.

Burton had played Hamlet, for God's sake. The fact that he had a slight accent didn't mean a thing; George was a college professor. Suddenly it became clear to me that Elizabeth Taylor and Richard Burton in *Who's Afraid of Virginia Woolf?* was perfect casting.

I wrote a long memo to Jack Warner, who was in New York, explaining my decision. I said that I thought Burton's presence on the set, working with his wife, would be very important to the dignity and prestige of this production; that he was a great actor, etc., etc., etc. Warner's response was, "We can't afford Richard Burton. Wait until I come home." When he got back we discussed it. I said that it wouldn't be a Liz and Dick picture; no one, no press, allowed on the set. So we got Richard Burton. A lot of money.

Now I had the problem of who was going to direct the picture. Elizabeth and Burton had director approval. I had to fly to Paris, where they were still shooting *The Sandpiper*. We had a lot of knockdown, drag-out meetings. Richard said that I should direct it. I said I wouldn't do it. Elizabeth said she wanted Fred Zinnemann. He said, "We don't want Zimmerman." She said, "It's Zinnemann." I said, "I happen to know that Fred Zinnemann doesn't want to direct this picture." There was a director, whom I won't name, that I was trying to sell them on. I screened his latest film for them. When the movie ended, Burton got up and said, "He doesn't know how to tell a story." That was that.

Before I got to Paris, Larry Turman had called me. He said, "Ernie, I want you to know that a friend of mine is standing here beside me and wants you to know that he would be interested in directing *Virginia Woolf*. It's Mike Nichols." When Burton was doing *Hamlet* on Broadway, Mike Nichols and Elaine May had performed in the theater right next door. He used to visit them when he finished every night. They'd all gotten friendly. I said, "Larry, whose friend are you, Mike's or mine?" That was my first impulse. You know, you make the dumb decisions first. You don't arrive at decisions smartly. So there I was in Paris, it hits me. Nichols was the darling of Broadway because he'd directed three hit comedies, *Luv, Barefoot in the Park, The Knack*. He was considered a genius. I was looking for the picture to be prestigious and respectable, not Hollywoodish.

Well, we had several kind of drunken scenes, battling names back and forth. When Nichols's name came up, I got the sense that they might have been a little afraid of him. They were in awe of him; didn't quite understand him. I got the idea that they wouldn't be able to eat him alive. Of all the directors that came up, only he inspired that kind of feeling from them.

Elizabeth made me call Fred Zinnemann's agent to make me confirm that he wasn't interested; we got that out of the way. Then I called Mike Nichols in Jamaica. I asked him if he'd consider. He said, "Send me a script and we'll talk." I was in Paris. How was I going to get him a script in Jamaica? So I flew to New York, and at the airport I found a young married couple on their way to Jamaica. They delivered it to him. Mike called me, said, "I'm interested. I've got a lot of things I want to talk about." He came to New York and we met. Now I had to call Jack Warner in Burbank. "Mike Nichols?! What are you talking about? You'd better come here immediately."

I flew to California, armed with a couple of magazine pieces on Nichols. I said a lot of good things. I must have been pretty persuasive. He said yes. The deal was, we had to wait for Mike Nichols to go out of town with a new play called *The Odd Couple*. I was in awe of Mike, in a way. He's a very scary sort of witty guy—not easy to deal with because he's so clever. He can kill you with a joke. Believe me, I've been through working with Billy Wilder, with Alfred Hitchcock. Mike scared me to death. He didn't know the front end of a camera from the rear. Meanwhile, I'd wanted Sandy Dennis for the supporting role, and had tested her for the role. When Mike came to Warner Brothers, Jack Warner and I ran the test, in which she was very, very good. Mike said no, he didn't want her. Jack said, "Okay, you shoot a test of someone." In twenty minutes, Mike said, "Sandy Dennis is fine."

For the other role, I wanted Robert Redford; turned out Mike did, too.

JE: He knew him from *Barefoot*.

EL: Sure. He said, "No problem, I'll get him." He picked up the phone. Redford said, "Absolutely not." Nobody wanted to be emasculated on the screen by Elizabeth Taylor. George Segal turned out to be a good choice. He had done *The Young Doctors* before for Larry Turman.

JE: This was a good time for Nichols, making *The Graduate* the year following both *Barefoot in the Park* and *Who's Afraid of Virginia Woolf?*

EL: Listen, Nichols had signed to do *The Graduate* before Larry called me with him.

JE: Great story, a slice of Hollywood in the 1960s. You'd already been writing for three decades by then.

EL: When I got out of college, I decided to write articles for the national magazines. [Producer] David Brown and I scratched around. Then I became a Broadway press agent and started writing fiction, a lot of it about Broadway, including *The Sweet Smell of Success* and *The Comedian*. That brought me to the attention of Paramount Pictures, which hauled me out to California. It was 1952 or '53. I soon became famous for turning down assignments. If I felt I didn't know how to write something, I didn't want to get mixed up in it.

JE: What particular gift did you bring to scriptwriting—imagination, taste, sense of character or structure?

EL: I wonder. I think whatever it is happens on many different levels, without my consciously being aware of it. I'd written many short stories, and, believe me, it's very difficult to come off in the restrictive length of a short story or novella. Apparently, I have a sense of how to develop conflict. This sounds bullshitty, because it's all happening on an unconscious level; you don't know what skills you bring. I try to maintain an awareness of whether the audience understands what the character is thinking and intending; whether the dialogue is more than mundane; whether something is being communicated and if it's entertaining. Are you developing a sense of conflict? Are characters in opposition to each other? I'm interested in how to be brief and how not to stay in a situation too long. I'm always aware of the audience: Do they still want to know what comes next?

JE: You have to rely on some sort of interior shit detector to know that. There aren't test screenings for drafts of a screenplay.

EL: It's not a conscious thought. It works on an unconscious level. Are characters in character? Would they do what they're doing? I've seen a lot of movies that have scenes in which characters act out of character, I guess for the convenience of the plot. Things have to be justifiable and communicable. Audiences should never say, "Wait a second, I don't understand that." What happens then is that the picture keeps going by, and they're playing catch-up.

JE: But you don't want them to get ahead of you, either.

EL: That's worse.

JE: Do you include in that list of things happening on an unconscious level that the camera should take the place of dialogue whenever possible?

EL: Absolutely. I've irritated many directors by putting the shot in the script, though I never felt that it had to be done that way necessarily. Bob Wise used to startle me. *My God. Just because I wrote it on paper—he's doing it?*

JE: You did that with Hitchcock, too?

EL: With Hitch, it's like the picture is all finished before it's filmed. It is all on paper. We sat together and figured out every shot.

JE: When you were writing *North by Northwest,* you were stuck for an ending; you didn't know what was going to happen once they got to Mount Rushmore. Then, suddenly, you got it. What do you think happens to enable that?

EL: I think humans are problem-solving organisms. Woe onto him who has no problems; he goes to hell. We create problems usually. If you're in a highly challenging craft like writing, everything's a problem. I remember pacing up and down Riverside Drive, wondering how to write *The Comedian*. *If I don't come up with a solution, I'll never write it, I'll never sell it, I'll be broke,* etc., etc. I was living from typewriter to mouth as a free-lance writer.

JE: Writing for publication, or even the theater, is a different animal than writing for the screen.

EL: They don't put it up on the stage and ask the writer, "What do you think? Listen to it." You see it when it's done. It's amazing that films turn out at all, because the writer's not there. He's someplace else, or he's not wanted, or the actors or the director want to change it, or he didn't know as he was sitting in his study writing it that the scene is too long. Playwrights sit in the theater during rehearsals: "Wait a minute, let me change that. It's too long; it's not playing." You don't get that chance with movies. When you see a really fine picture, wow, what a miracle. Writing for publication, you're everything. Writing for films, it's you plus the actors, plus the director, plus the producer, plus the art director, plus the composer, plus the editor, plus the studio executives.

JE: I watched *The Sound of Music* with my daughter the other night. They don't make 'em like that anymore.

EL: I'd change only one scene: When Maria is sitting with the children, thanking them for being nice to her and welcoming her. They all start crying. I don't believe it. I decided to put that scene in there, and I don't believe it now. It was nice, and it was fun that it irritated Von Trapp that, her first night on the job, she's already causing trouble for him: "Are we going to have this every night?" That sort of thing.

Christopher Plummer [Baron Von Trapp] was helpful to me.

Thank God he insisted that I make his character as good as it was, because it was not that good in the play. It was musical-comedy time. He'd walked off the picture, so they got me back to rewrite. For days we sat together working. One of the reasons he's so good in the picture is that he forced me to write his scenes well.

JE: I have an unanswerable question for you. Christopher Plummer sat with you as you wrote his scenes. What is it you can do that he can't? Why can't Chris Plummer, or 99.4 percent of us, do what you do?

EL: I'll tell you what I imagine it is. From my earliest days in high school, I think I had a particular facility or innate ability to deal with words. I could make them come out a certain way, in order to say what I wanted them to say. I know how to manipulate words. That's a mechanical way to put it. To me, that's not the essence of art. I admire something that's artistic and feel that I never could have done that.

JE: You don't think of what you do as art?

EL: Honestly, I don't think of it as art. When it works it's skill and craft and some unconscious ability.

JE: What is art?

EL: Art creates an effect, but is less obvious in what it's doing.

JE: How did you get the reputation as the big movie writer—the writer big producers, directors, and studio heads wanted for their lavish musicals and adaptations?

EL: Me saying no to this, no to that.

JE: I never saw *West Side Story* on the stage. What did you change for the screenplay?

EL: I think I improved the play a bit. For one thing, I completely rearranged the musical numbers. It's hard to believe that in the stage show, the song "Cool" wasn't done after the rumble between the Jets and the Sharks. "Cool" was done in the candy store, before they meet. "Officer Krupke," which I put before the meeting, where "Cool" was in the play, was originally done in the last act of the show. It didn't seem right to have a very funny number after the rumble. In the play, immediately after the rumble, when two bodies are lying there and the bell is tolling, Maria sang "I Feel Pretty"—a gay, happy, charming number. I took that and put it up front, in the afternoon at the dress shop, when she knows she's going to meet Tony. It wasn't there in the play. I thought, "My God, these are great people: [playwright] Arthur Laurents, [lyricist] Stephen Sondheim, [director and choreographer] Jerome Robbins." I got to play Monday morning quarterback—to see that, for instance, "Cool" is terrific, it really works, when they're coming apart emotionally after Riff has been killed. It works much better to stage it in a garage rather than on the street. And "Officer Krupke," you can afford to be funny putting it early; nothing's happened yet. But to put it where it was originally, after such grim undertakings, wasn't as good as allowing unrelenting drama. The movie built toward where it was going.

I think I have an innate sense of drama. I mean it. I see drama in my own life, in every little thing. Life is filled with it. I think everything can be made into a story. I used to write short stories based on things I observed happening—little things, anything— around me.

JE: Does your imagination, stimulated by these happenings, conceive of the drama, the story, in its entirely, or do you build the story one step at a time?

EL: One step at a time. If you try to solve everything in one fell swoop, it's too frightening. The idea of writing a movie and having it all solved ahead of time, it's too much.

JE: Do you work from an outline? What's your process?

EL: The process is thinking a lot, mulling and thinking.

JE: While driving, sitting, shaving?

EL: Anywhere. Just going to bed. Making notes wherever I am. In movie writing there is a lot of despair, being alone in an office with a problem—namely, how to write that particular scene. You know where it starts, you know where you want to get to. But how do you do it? I'd lie on the sofa, and the hours would go by, with apparently nothing to show for all this thinking and mulling. *It's going to be six or six-thirty, and I'm going to be driving home. I'm going to be feeling lousy when I get home, because, Jesus Christ, all I got done today was a page and a half. I haven't solved the goddamned scene.* My two sons would see me pacing up and down the kitchen with a midnight snack. What I was doing was trying to solve a problem. Writing is solving problems; that's what it is: How do you do it so you think it's right? In *North by Northwest* I was painting myself into corners. The problem was always to figure out how to get out of the corner.

JE: Can't that be a good process? Isn't there something about the cornered mentality that works for creative problem solving?

EL: I think it forces the writer and the character into solving a challenge.

JE: And makes for a more interesting character?

EL: I think so. No matter what the genre—drama, action-adventure, comedy—if things are easy, if there are no problems, if there's no force for the character to work against, the less interesting the work. Clint Eastwood trying to find the assassin, John Malkovich [in *In the Line of Fire*], has a problem. The better the heavy, the better the picture. The implacable foe. Sometimes the foe is just a situation. In *West Side Story* it was society. You have to make it difficult for your character.

JE: In an original script, do you begin with an idea for a story, or an idea for a character, or both?

EL: I'm ashamed to say how mechanical it is. The whole story of *North by Northwest* came together bit by bit. What happened was, MGM had bought *The Wreck of the Mary Deare* [a novel published in 1956 by the pseudonymous Hammond Innes] for Hitchcock, and he requested me to adapt it. I turned him down. That was a terrible thing, to turn Hitchcock down. People didn't say no to Hitch. He'd finally decided to make a film at MGM, and I'd turned it down. I said, "There's no movie here. Thanks, but no thanks." Good old Ed Henry came to my rescue. He said, "You know, Hitch is quite upset. I want to get you two guys together. I think you'd hit it off very well." Actually, [composer] Bernard Herrmann had introduced us a few years before, when I was at Paramount and Hitch was making *Rear Window*.

We had lunch at the Polo Lounge. We had a good time. Maybe we talked a little bit about one scene in the novel that's a movie, in which the ship is drifting on the English Channel and there's no one on board. After lunch, I went back to my office and called Ed Henry. I said, "Look, maybe Hitch knows how to do this movie." So I said yes. Every day I would drive over to Hitch's home on Bellagio [in Bel-Air] and we'd spend the day together. But I noticed that every time I brought up *The Wreck of the Mary Deare,* he changed the subject; he'd talk about something else. It was as though it produced anxiety in him to have to face the project. I used to drive home every night thinking, *He really doesn't know how to do this.* I'd make a few notes and force him to talk about the picture. Then it became apparent that he really didn't have a clue how to do it; no ideas whatsoever. And I know I didn't. I didn't believe in the picture, and I didn't want that discomfort to continue. So I arrived at his house one morning and said, "Hitch, I've got bad news for you. You have to get another writer; I don't know how to do this picture." He said, "Don't be silly. We get along very well. We'll just do something else together." I said, "What'll we tell MGM?" He said, "We won't tell them anything." We didn't. They thought I was writing *The Wreck of the Mary Deare.*

We used to sit around, Hitch and I, chatting, trying to come up with an idea. One idea after another. Finally, I said, "I want to do the Hitchcock picture to end all Hitchcock pictures." He said, "What's that?" I said, "I want it to have wit and glamour and movement and changes of locale." One day he said, "I've always wanted to do a chase across the faces of Mount Rushmore." That's what he said. I said, "Gee, that's exciting," and wrote it down. But who was chasing whom? That's the way it all started.

I wanted to do a modern-day Grace Kelly type of picture. A "movie movie" I used to call it in those days. There are pictures that are movie movies, like *The Fugitive.* Boy, is that a movie movie.

JE: Meant to be seen on a big screen with other people.

EL: *Virginia Woolf* is not a movie movie. A movie movie is a big experience. You're really taken on a ride.

Okay, Mount Rushmore. Hitch would come up with some ideas. I'd come up with some. He actually came up with a lot of very interesting ideas which we didn't use and which no one but Hitch could do. He said, "I always wanted to do the longest dolly shot in history. You'd start on an assembly line where they're building a car. There's nothing. On comes one part, and another. You keep dollying along the several miles of the assembly line, and, finally, there's the finished car. And somebody actually gets in and drives the finished car off the line. And there's a dead body in the backseat." I said, "Great," and wrote it down. So then it was, *Okay, Detroit. We're going to go to Detroit.*

One day he said, "I always wanted to do a scene in which two sworn enemies are in Alaska. You see them walking toward each other on ice. They put their arms around each other. There's a hole in the ice. A hand comes up through the ice." Don't ask me what it means. I just wrote it down.

Another day he said, "I've always wanted to do a scene near Lake Louise [in Alberta]. At a family gathering, a twelve-year-old girl takes out a gun and shoots somebody." He said, "I've always wanted to do a scene in which a delegate is addressing the United Nations General Assembly. He suddenly stops speaking and says, 'I will not continue until the delegate from Peru is awakened.' The page boy goes over and taps the Peruvian delegate, who falls over; he's dead. The only clue is what he was doodling—the antlers of a moose." Isn't that crazy?

I wrote all these down. *We wind up at Mount Rushmore, then we're going to Alaska.* There was no story, but these ideas—United Nations, Detroit, Lake Louise, Alaska—meant that we were moving in a northwesterly direction. That was the first working title, "In a Northwesterly Direction." Then I used to make notes to myself about whom I wanted for a protagonist. There was a list:

famous sports announcer, Frank Sinatra–type entertainer, Madison Avenue ad executive. I had about ten people listed. I liked the idea of a Madison Avenue type because I liked the kind of repartee and the superficiality. This was the day of the huckster.

It was all very mechanical: *Why were people going on Mount Rushmore? Why would there be a chase? Because there's a hunting lodge near there, and that's where the heavies are bound for—whoever they were.* I went to New York and spent five days at the United Nations, to get the feel of what goes on there; what it's like.

JE: You were just absorbing information.

EL: Yes, information and research. In those days, in the fifties, if there were heavies, they were obviously on the other side.

JE: The Cold War.

EL: Of course. I asked about the Russian delegation. They lived in Glen Cove [New York]. I went out there. [Columnist] Army Archerd knew a judge there. I told the judge that I was thinking about a drunk driving sequence and asked him to put me through it so that I could understand it. I'd never been through anything like that. I wouldn't have known the first thing about it. He did. So now I had a Madison Avenue executive who's going in a northwesterly direction. And, meanwhile, I'm being saluted at MGM because they think I'm writing *The Wreck of the Mary Deare*. They'd say, "How's it going, skipper?"

Eventually, there came a time when I realized that I had to have a fragment of the first act outlined, because one day Hitchcock asked me when I was going to tell MGM what I was doing. I said, "When am *I* going to tell them? When are *you* going to tell them? I'm not going to tell them." He told them: "Ernie and I decided it would take too long to do *The Wreck of the Mary Deare*.

We've decided to do another picture first." He used the word "first," so that they thought they had Hitchcock for two pictures. Then he bullshitted them for our first act, looked at his watch, and excused himself for another appointment. Naturally, whatever he said they thought was terrific.

At the time Hitch was busy preparing *Vertigo* at Paramount. I had to go there to talk with him whenever I had an idea. But he didn't want to talk about our picture. He was busy. I used to drive home at night from Paramount, which is thirty minutes, wondering how I was going to get out of this catastrophe I'd gotten myself into. *This is never going to be a movie.* Finally, there came a day when I realized that Hitch was going to go off and shoot *Vertigo,* which meant that I was going to have to go to my office at MGM and start writing this movie. I'm alone. It's anxiety time. I never wrote a movie like that before, making it up as you go along: *How do you get from here to there? How do you get to Chicago? How do you get the girl into the movie; she doesn't come in until late. Oh, I see, the girl is really the agent.*

JE: These things were just occurring to you one at a time.

EL: One at a time, and not by the hour, either. Nobody knew how to solve this problem, but I goddamned well had to, because they were counting on me. I had to get to that lonely office. By this time MGM knew I was writing something under the working title of "In a Northwesterly Direction." One day the head of the story department said, "Why don't you call it *North by Northwest?*" I said, "Okay." That became a working title; obviously that wasn't going to be the real title.

JE: Yeah, that would be a terrible title for a movie.

EL: Terrible. At one point it was also "The Man on Lincoln's Nose." I was grinding out a page or two at a time.

JE: How long did it go on like that?

EL: Four or five months. Finally, Hitchcock finished *Vertigo* and went to the British West Indies on vacation. I had the first sixty-five pages and sent them to him. I still have his four-page handwritten letter in which he said how much he loved it; that it was amusingly written; that Lew Wasserman [head of then artists agency MCA] was there with him and had said the only trouble with it was that it was too good for MGM; that Oscar Hammerstein and Senator John F. Kennedy and his wife were there, too. That was very encouraging.

JE: There was no one besides Hitchcock you trusted to help you work things out?

EL: Who? Who am I going to?

JE: Another writer.

EL: That isn't done. What do you say, "Please read this and give me an idea"? No. Most of my friends were writers. You just didn't do that. It was my problem to solve. Hitch helped me by being there if I needed him. I'd ask, "Is this terrible?" His way of putting it, when he didn't like it, was, "Ernie, that's the way they do it in the movies." That was the worst he could ever say. It kept you on your toes: *Hey, you're writing a picture for Alfred Hitchcock.*

JE: When you sent the first sixty-five pages, did you know what the next, say, five pages were going to be?

EL: No. I don't think I ever knew that far ahead.

JE: At some point you confided to Hitchcock that you didn't have any idea how to get the film to Mount Rushmore, and he said that he was going to bring in a spy novelist.

EL: What finally happened was Hitchcock began setting up shop at MGM, bringing his art director along. It was obvious that, hey, we were going to be making a picture and we're going to find a title for it. Little did he know that at the other end of the building, I didn't know what was coming next. I'm supposed to be coming up with it, preproduction has begun, and I'm scared because I'm not coming up with it. He's storyboarding, for Christ's sake.

How do we get to Mount Rushmore? I'd been there, by the way. I'd climbed halfway up with a forest ranger and stopped when I realized that I'd have been killed if I slipped. I gave him a Polaroid camera and said, "Find out what's on top because I want to do a scene up there." Turns out, there ain't nothing up there. It's a sheer drop. We had to create it at the studio. The National Parks Service barred us when they found out that there were going to be killings on Mount Rushmore. Hitch was furious with them.

We were in production. The picture was cast. Both Jimmy Stewart and Cary Grant had been wondering which of them was going to be in Hitch's next picture. They used to call him. I told Hitch, "There's a lot of dialogue in here for [protagonist] Roger Thornhill, and with Jimmy Stewart, it'll go on forever." He agreed with me. So I wrote this for Cary Grant, which is a big advantage. There were things he could do no one else could do. What an advantage for the writer, to know that he's writing for Cary Grant. Nowadays you write the picture for Sly Stallone, and it turns out to be Eddie Murphy. *Beverly Hills Cop.*

Finally I broke it to Hitch that I didn't know where I was going. He said he'd bring in a spy novelist for plotting. To me, that was going to be the grossest humiliation, not because a writer was coming in, but because Hitch was going to take all the blame himself and say that he should have been able to help me. So, it suddenly popped into my head, the solution. We know that "popped in my head" is just an expression. The problem was being solved during the weeks of nonproductivity. Maybe I thought of forty-eight thousand reasons why the professor needed him at Mount Rushmore. I had to cover up that whole explanation by having the engines rev up on the plane so that the audience didn't have to hear everything that they already knew. That was a neat trick. Boy, was that an involved bit of exposition to have to get across.

JE: Are there inviolable rules about exposition, development, and resolution?

EL: My rule is that an audience should never be in mystery unless you want them to be in mystery. There are times when you want them to know more than the protagonist knows, and there are other times when you want the audience to find out with the protagonist. It all depends on the particular story.

Hitch had the same problem in *Vertigo*. He asked me to please watch the rough cut with him, because he didn't know where to put the scene that explains the whole thing of Kim Novak.

JE: The flaw with *Psycho* was the psychiatrist's expositional explanation at the end, after Norman Bates has been captured. It's a dead epilogue.

EL: That was terrible. It's anticlimactic. I guess that's why the picture was such a huge flop. I was there, in Hitch's office, when he got the first check for the first quarter—$2,400,000. That picture made a fortune. He shot it with his Revue television crew for $800,000.

JE: The scene in *North by Northwest* when we see Leo G. Carroll and the other CIA agents explaining why Roger Thornhill is in the trouble he's in could have been in several different places in the movie.

EL: I had to figure out where to put it. Cut to an intelligence bureau. Do you put that scene here or here? Where do you want to get the audience ahead of Cary Grant? Eventually, you have to bring him up to speed. Who knows how you make the decision? You just have a sense that, even though the audience knows something he doesn't know, the movie is working. In fact, it's working *because* the audience knows.

JE: How do you know that when you're writing?

EL: I don't know. If I knew . . . You hope you're right, or that you get lucky. The only obvious rules you don't break are, you don't confuse an audience deliberately, and you don't have a character do something that that character would never do, just to make the plot work. And yet, I'm sure both of those rules have been broken successfully time and again. As long as it works. That's the only rule.

JE: Was William Goldman right, that nobody knows anything?

EL: There are some people who really don't know very much. There are some people who know a lot. And there are some people who are very bright. It's true that nobody knows everything, but to say that nobody knows anything is ridiculous.

AMY HOLDEN JONES

I asked Amy Jones to participate for a couple of reasons. One, I was intrigued by the fact that a woman had written Indecent Proposal, *a high-concept, glossy entertainment with big-name stars that was savaged by the critics, many of them feminists, who were appalled that Robert Redford could "borrow" Demi Moore, a married woman, for one million dollars. It seemed to me that there might have been a good story behind the movie's birth, and that she would probably have some interesting responses for her critics.*

The second reason I asked Amy was because of her apparent versatility. She'd also written the family comedy Beethoven *(with Edmond Dantes), and the character-driven* Mystic Pizza.

We met over lunch at a noisy Mexican café in Malibu.

JOEL ENGEL: Most writers have a burning passion to become writers. You didn't.

AMY HOLDEN JONES: I was a documentary filmmaker, and got into the film business because in 1973 I won the AFI Western National Film Student Film Festival, which at that time was the biggest student film festival in the country. One of the judges was Martin Scorsese, so when I got out of college in late 1974 I wrote him a letter. I had tried to work in documentaries, but there was no money in it at all. I mentioned the film and asked him what I should do. Ultimately, he gave me a job as his assistant on *Taxi Driver*. Then I moved out to Los Angeles and worked for Roger Corman as a film editor. Then I got into the union and became a film editor for a couple of years. One of the films I was supposed to edit was *E.T.* The deal was actually signed, sealed, and delivered. But the film had a really long preproduction period, because they were doing *Poltergeist* at the same time; they kept falling behind. Well, I'd always wanted to direct, so while waiting around, I called Roger Corman. Roger's great. He doesn't care whether you're male or female, as long as you can get the job done. He said, "If you want to direct, show me you can." So I took a horror script right off his shelf, which had been written by Rita Mae Brown. It had a prologue of seven pages, which I rewrote. It had suspense, it had dialogue, and it had action—all in those seven pages. I put together a UCLA acting group. My husband, who's a cinematographer, shot it on thirty-five millimeter. And since I was an editor, I cut it. When I gave it to Roger, he said, essentially, "Finish this movie." It's not the script I would have chosen, but I ultimately did that instead of editing *E.T.* I started my career as a screenwriter by directing that picture, which was released as *Slumber Party Massacre*.

That was about 1980 or '81. Women were not directing very many films, so it really didn't get me anywhere, even though the movie was extremely successful for Roger. Also, no one seemed to be looking for young directors; they all wanted established directors. I was a twenty-eight-year-old female director. So I wrote a nonexploitation film, which I think is the only nonexploitation film Roger has ever financed himself and made, called *Love Letters*. It starred Jamie Lee Curtis and Amy Madigan and James Keach. That was my first original script. After that I wrote *Mystic Pizza* for myself to direct. That got buried in the morass of the Samuel Goldwyn Company, and I did the comedy *Maid to Order*.

JE: *Mystic Pizza* may not have launched your career necessarily, but it sure launched Julia Roberts.

AHJ: Well, I think it did launch my career. It was very successful, and I had written it. In the late '80s, when the recession hit, I was still directing low-budget movies. Studios narrowed the number of movies they made and tried to use only established stars, both on the screen and behind the camera. The independents receded for a while. I had a picture at Imagine Entertainment that I was supposed to direct, that I had co-written, with Ron Howard and Brian Grazer producing. The budget was ten million dollars, but in the middle they got cold feet. Funny thing was, they already had an actress cast—Julia Roberts. But they wouldn't pay or play her, because they didn't think she was a star. The movie folded, and I got discouraged with directing, because I felt I didn't have the power to get done what I needed done. Looking around, I recognized that *Mystic Pizza* was successful. I didn't direct it, I wrote it, so why don't I try to write a big-budget movie with big stars that someone else would direct? I thought maybe that would get me some currency, some power. That's how I came to write *Indecent Proposal.*

JE: What year?

AHJ: The first draft went in, believe it or not, in 1991. It was caught up at the studio [Paramount] for a long time because the studio changed heads twice. The first regime liked it and was ready to roll when the second group came in and replaced everyone who'd liked it. The second draft sat around a while before falling into the hands of [director] Adrian Lyne, who wanted to do it. That's when it became a movie. It never went out to directors; he just got hold of it.

JE: So if Adrian Lyne wants to make a movie, the movie gets made. I didn't realize he was in that select group.

AHJ: *Fatal Attraction* made four hundred million dollars worldwide. It's also a kind of icon. People refer back to it as a touchstone of thrillers. *Flashdance* was an enormous hit as well.

JE: Didn't he do *Jacob's Ladder*?

AHJ: He did. That wasn't a big hit, but was critically successful for the most part.

JE: Growing up, you had absolutely no aspirations to write? None at all?

AHJ: Never thought about it. I was a still photographer on the high school yearbook, and went to MIT to study still photography, and there got involved in filmmaking—documentary filmmaking. I never thought I could write. I wrote because I had to write to get a script to direct. Ultimately, it's become more important to me than directing. In fact, if I never directed again I'd be unhappy; if I never wrote again, I'd be truly miserable.

JE: That's a pretty startling turn of events.

AHJ: Well, you're not a woman in Hollywood. One door closes, you have to pry open a window and crawl through it. You just have to keep finding a way.

JE: Because you were determined to stay in the industry.

AHJ: Yes. If you weren't related to somebody, and you weren't sleeping with somebody, at that time period at least—I don't know whether it's true anymore—it was hard. Sleeping with people made a difference. People don't think this happened, but it did, during this horrible time period in the '80s when I was a director. You'd be sitting there with three credits and be asking, "Who is this woman who's directing this movie at Fox? What has she done? I've never heard of her." They'd say, "Well, she's a famous girlfriend." Think about how many wives of big producers have directed.

Penny Marshall is a terrific director who stands on her own, but I think it was helpful to her that she was an actress, because she could bring stars in who were her friends. You have to admire people like Martha Coolidge who didn't have those connections but forged through anyway. I'm not saying they don't exist, because they do. It's not easy. Martha has just beat her way on her own. So has Randa Haines.

JE: In the same way, you made a conscious decision to write what would become a big-budget, glossy film.

AHJ: I should also mention that I started doing rewrites. Because of my background as an editor, I was good at them; they're very similar.

JE: Editors know what works.

AHJ: As I said, along the road to directing I discovered I really like writing. If you do direct, it takes a year to a year and a half for each project. I actually write constantly, and haven't had many dry spells. If I get dry, I can do a rewrite, which is easier. I can do two or three things in a year, and try to have more stuff out there than I would if I directed. The year of *Indecent Proposal,* which was an unusual year, I have to admit—many aren't like that at all—I had that: *Beethoven,* and a pilot for a television series, *Jack's Place.*

Then I had an older script that turned into a Showtime movie. None of those would have been possible had I been directing. That's some compensation, anyway.

JE: Back to *Indecent Proposal,* so I can get a sense of what, in your estimation, constitutes a big-budget script to which big stars will be attracted.

AHJ: I wrote in a way I'd never written before. When I wrote for myself to direct, I purposely wrote movies that could be made for four million dollars. That's all I assumed I would get; that's all I did get. Once I knew I was going to try to write a big movie, then the world opened up. I tried to write on a different scale.

JE: Did you think of situations, people, what?

AHJ: In that particular case there was a book from which they derived strictly one line, that was all: "A couple goes to Atlantic City and meets a man who offers them one million dollars for a night with the wife." That's what often happens if you write for hire. Producers or studios come to you with a take like that and then you dream up the characters and the story.

JE: So it was not an original idea.

AHJ: No.

JE: Is that the kind of idea you might have dreamed up?

AHJ: I think I was lucky because I'd been doing those low-budget films. Learning to think of those high-concept ideas is one of the very hard things that screenwriters do. Maybe the hardest. So this concept both attracted me and scared me when I originally took the project, because I knew how hard it was going to be. They didn't want a dark movie, and it was a concept that inherently lends itself to darkness. They wanted the couple to end up together in the end. So how do you have them bargain with the devil, as it were, and yet come out with their souls intact? The way I dealt with that in the first draft was, she didn't sleep with him. They were a working-class couple. She went there without her husband's knowledge, then couldn't do it once she got there. And the rich man fell in love with her because of her integrity. That worked.

JE: Did she get the million anyway?

AHJ: That was the hook of the script. Because he falls in love with the wife, he pays the million anyway. Then, because she got paid, the husband has to rely on her word that she didn't sleep with him. It was more a script about trust. It worked, definitely worked.

JE: I like that; it's not so heavy-handed.

AHJ: Well, yeah. You see, these things get molded by the studio. I actually liked the working-class couple better. He was a contractor, she was a waitress. They were more like the people in *Mystic Pizza*.

JE: You may be less likely to get multi-million-dollar stars to play working class.

AHJ: Maybe, maybe not. They were good characters. But the third act really didn't work. It needed another draft, and rather than just work on the third act, a whole new set of studio executives came in. Though they weren't ultimately the ones to make the movie, they insisted that she had to sleep with the rich guy; they have to truly make the deal with the devil.

JE: Was that because they thought sex would sell the movie?

AHJ: I don't know. Their position was, and I think it's legitimate, if that's what it's about, that's what it's about; you shouldn't make it about something else; truly make it about having made the devil's pact. They also demanded that they be middle-class, and that the husband be an architect. That was given to me. From that point I almost quit, because I liked the first draft, and it was almost a total rewrite. There's also very little money in it. You have steps in the deal, and the second draft gets you considerably less than the first draft. I thought about it and thought about it, because I only take assignments I believe I can nail. Finally I took a trip, and while on the plane I made an outline.

I was going to visit my husband on location. I gave myself that long weekend visiting him to figure out how to solve the script problems. I had been looking at the films of Billy Wilder. Almost all of them have something to do with people selling themselves, making some horrible compromise. Think of *The Apartment*. Think of *Sunset Boulevard*. And yet, you still care about those people; they're just human. I started to think, "Yeah, flawed people, flawed people. We're all flawed. We all make mistakes. Maybe this is much more complicated and interesting." I came up with the new outline, went home, and wrote it. Indeed, that was the draft, not the earlier one, that attracted Adrian Lyne.

JE: You have to remake the characters, even if many of the incidents are the same?

AHJ: If you write for any studio, even if it's an original script, you have to be prepared to change it. I think that's one of the biggest problems that stops a lot of screenwriters: They can't change it. I can really sympathize with not wanting to change something you really believe in. But the vast majority of time something can be changed and made better—if you stick with it. You can remake it and remake it, making it better each time, over and over. And you can change a script a whole number of ways—I learned this the hard way—as long as you hold onto the theme of the movie and hold onto characters you care about. You can still make it work for you. You're going to have to make it work for the director, the studio, the stars. It changes again and again. Ultimately, *Indecent Proposal* changed in ways that perhaps I might not have changed it.

JE: You're extremely pragmatic.

AHJ: I am, yes. I have the temperament of a film editor. Film editors work alone in the dark, over and over and over again. They have to take input from the director; they work with the director. A really good film editor doesn't just cut a scene, he or she takes the entire movie and helps the director make it into the best film it can be. Usually, there's more than one film in those dailies. There are more performances than one. You start lifting and moving lines and scenes in a way that's not too different from rewriting. You have to open your mind to that kind of flexibility—to being able to tear things apart—to be really good at film editing. Same with writing.

JE: It's interesting to hear someone speak in mechanical terms about the process of screenwriting.

AHJ: I'm not an artist. There are probably other screenwriters whom you would consider artists. I'm not one of them.

JE: Why not?

AHJ: I don't consider myself a very hard worker—almost more a rewriter than a writer.

JE: What defines an artist?

AHJ: I'm not sure there are that many in the film business, because it is a *business*. There may be more in the independent film world. An artist would put his own vision ahead of the project, and I try to fit my vision into the project; I try to make them work together. I also truly believe that once a director is on it, if you can't make the director feel that he's part of it, he won't be thoroughly behind the script. So you have to incorporate his vision in your own for him to feel viscerally behind the movie. It's a community effort more than most arts, which are more singular.

JE: How much did the *Indecent Proposal* characters change?

AHJ: They were all essentially remade, except for the rich man, who didn't change as much. Though by the end, when Robert Redford was cast, there were some changes from the script that Adrian committed to. There were some changes in the montage, which Adrian did himself, of the third act. That act was somewhat taken away from the female lead and given more to the Redford character.

JE: Why?

AHJ: Because of who Redford is. He does not do anything that is unsympathetic.

JE: That's an edict?

AHJ: Yes. For example, he can't be left. There was always a scene in which the girl dumped him for her husband. That had to be rewritten so that he graciously and magnanimously gave her up, because he doesn't get dumped. I think the result is interesting, but I preferred it thematically when she dumped him. Another example would be in the third act. Originally she went through a process of coming to understand that the rich man was a person, besides being rich, who had many drives and qualities that are inherent to billionaires; that he was a complete person, not just an icon, and he actually wasn't the person she loved. The person she loved was her husband. And that involves him doing and being things that are perhaps less sympathetic than her husband, and Redford wouldn't do those things. A classic example, and one I've never completely understood, comes during a long speech in the movie that I didn't write (I believe Marshall Brickman wrote it). He talks about how he saw a girl on a train many years ago and this girl was wonderful and he never spoke to her. It apparently is derived from *Citizen Kane*. Anyway, it replaced a scene I was very fond of and, I thought, crucial to his character. The scene was also sympathetic to him but had to do more with the complexities of his nature as a billionaire. It was a scene in which he showed her a whole row of buildings at night and said, "I own five of those buildings." She says, "You're still trying to buy me." He says, "No, I'm trying to make a point, that when I want something I get it." And he tells this story about how, when he was a child, he was with his parents in Monaco. He says he watched a woman feeding francs into a slot machine for an hour and losing and finally walking away. Then he walked up, snuck a franc in, pulled the handle, and hit the jackpot. The point was that he was lucky, that he was always in the right place at the right time, and that he was in the right place when he saw her, and that it was meant to be between them. Now, that's not an unsympathetic speech, but it is a kind of controlling and overwhelming speech. It's more about him as a billionaire. So for Redford they wrote in a very soft and humanistic speech about how he wants to change his life by finding a woman. I don't think that's an uninteresting take, though that particular speech being a rip-off of *Citizen Kane* was not thrilling to me, especially since I was attacked for ripping off *Citizen Kane,* and I didn't write the speech.

JE: That wasn't the only thing you were attacked for. Feminist critics were vicious.

AHJ: Yes, well, had she been able to leave him, I might not have been attacked as much either. That wasn't my choice. It's just a different way to go—not the way I would have gone, but I live with it because Redford is who he is, and you get a tremendous amount when you get Redford. If you'd had Michael Douglas play that part, it would have been totally different. The third act would have been much different, because Douglas would have been willing to do stranger things that made you understand he has a dark side. After all, a man who offers a woman a million dollars should have a dark side somewhere, shouldn't he?

JE: Would it have been a more interesting film with either Jack Nicholson or Paul Newman or Douglas?

AHJ: It's interesting to watch a director mold a script through the casting. A good director does, and Adrian is definitely a good director. For a long time he wanted Tommy Lee Jones. Now that's a very different movie. The studio didn't want Tommy Lee Jones; the studio wanted Redford. And eventually they wore him down. I'm not sure he wouldn't say they were right, because I don't know how he feels about it. Directors have to make people think they're all powerful, but even powerful ones like Adrian Lyne have to make compromises, just the way screenwriters do.

JE: Nick Meyer told me that it's not interesting whether Demi Moore sleeps with Robert Redford. What would be interesting, he said, is whether she sleeps with Danny DeVito.

AHJ: That movie was made, wasn't it: *Honeymoon in Vegas*. Nick Meyer has an essentially comedic sensibility. What he doesn't really understand when he makes that joke—at least, I suspect he doesn't—is something that was intended in the script and may have been unclear. That is, I saw the movie as a metaphor for adultery. To me, it was not about buying someone; it was about crisis in a marriage, where one person is tempted and then actually does commit adultery. How do you get back together? To my mind, it was about how some marriages survive and some don't. That's what the script was about, anyway; I don't know about the movie. They survived because of forgiveness. The notion was that she does this, they can't deal with it but eventually come to realize that they have to be together and put the past behind them and forgive each other. Had it been Danny DeVito, what's the question then? Of course, she'll go back to her husband. If it's Danny DeVito, the movie's over once she sleeps with him. There is no moral question. The whole issue is, did she do it for the money or because she wanted to sleep with the guy? If you take away the issue of her maybe wanting to have slept with the guy—well, the reality is, she did it because she wanted to sleep with the guy. Some rabid feminist somewhere who criticized the movie perhaps didn't understand that, on some level, the first time she sees the guy in the dress shop she wants to sleep with him. That doesn't mean she would have acted upon it otherwise, but given the best excuse in the world, maybe she will. A lot of people miss the point that she talks her husband into it. He doesn't talk her into it. It's a kind of fantasy: I get to sleep with Robert Redford, my husband needs money, I have a perfect reason for why I did it; I can say I did it for him. It all sounds so right, and in the end it doesn't work.

JE: I guess it's too easy to forgive your wife for sleeping with Danny DeVito.

AHJ: The husband would be urging her to do it, saying, "What do I care?" There's no moral issue if she isn't attracted to him. Whereas, with someone like Tommy Lee Jones, both sides of the coin are represented; he's attractive, but also has a dangerous edge. The script was not written with Woody Harrelson in mind as the husband. It did not read intellectual. He was supposed to have been an intellectual and an artist. I probably would have cast an unknown, because a good-looking, complicated, intelligent, interesting unknown against a superstar would be very interesting. Had I been there when Harrelson was cast, and I wasn't, the proper thing to do would have been to rewrite his part: Once you've got it, use it.

JE: When you're creating character from scratch, what do you visualize? Do you write down a description of the character?

AHJ: I free-riff on them. In *Mystic Pizza,* for example, I started with the title. I'd seen a place called The Mystic Pizza and thought it was the best title I'd ever seen in my life. At the time, I really wanted to do a female *Diner.* Originally, *Mystic Pizza* was about four girls. So I just sat down, wrote down the title *Mystic Pizza,* and started riffing on who these characters were. On some level, all characters are part of your self, if you're really good at it; your worst side, your best side, your worst impulses, your best impulses. They're you when you were thirteen, you at twenty-five. You can project yourself onto any character, pretty much the way an actor does. There was nothing about any of the characters in

Mystic Pizza that was autobiographical—I never lived in Mystic, never had a sister; none of that. But the story comes from imagining what could happen, essentially to yourself, and from themes that are important to you. *Mystic Pizza* has this theme that I've written over and over again. It was intended to be in *Indecent Proposal* as well, which is how you can only rely on yourself, how you can't rely on men. You can love men, but you can't expect them to define your life. Men aren't the answer; they're part of the question. Half the things I write have that theme, that men aren't the answer. That's not to say anything against them; I love men. It's just that I think there's a tendency for some women to think that whomever they're with is going to solve their life.

Anyway, so when I start a script I begin by thinking of characteristics of the characters and write paragraphs on each.

JE: Do you visualize them physically.

AHJ: Sometimes I think of an actor, and often I'll visualize them physically, but not always. I'll usually think what type of person the character is. For example, the comedic lawyer in *Indecent Proposal* I wrote with Jason Alexander in mind. I couldn't convince Adrian to cast him, but that's whom I thought of. I often have one character somewhere who's comic relief, because I think audiences need and like to laugh, and you can often get that in a drama just by having a comedic character. Sometimes I think of an actor type, but usually what they are is some permutation of myself; and that can be anything, including a murderer.

JE: The best and the worst in all of us.

AHJ: For anyone who wants to write fiction, especially screenwriting, the best thing to do is to take an acting class.

JE: How so?

AHJ: I can't act at all, but when I began directing I took an acting class, and that enabled me to write. I started doing scenes, being the person who read the scenes. That enabled me to understand what actors look for in scenes and what they have to do in a scene—internalize a scene—and how an actor has to be any number of people; really walk in their shoes and understand them from the inside. That's exactly what a writer does, exactly the same thing. And understanding what an actor looks for in a scene enables you to write. It also teaches you a lot about subtext instead of just text. Really bad writing is like text, over and over again.

There was a terrific exercise we did in acting school. We were given a scene with totally amorphous lines, like "It's a beautiful day" and "I love your shirt" and "Why did we get up so late?" Nothing lines. Then the exercise would be to say these lines as, for example, a Nazi and a concentration camp survivor; or an estranged mother and daughter. You take the same lines and get at what's underneath them—what the character is thinking rather than what he's saying. That's a great exercise for a writer, because often people don't say what they're really thinking; they say something else.

Probably the best scene in *Indecent Proposal* is the scene around the pool table when the rich man makes the offer. It's very simple, written quickly and simply. It's so obvious to me that he's like a puppeteer, controlling. He's luring them in with the bait. The biggest moment on the page, which I think is still somewhat there on the screen, is a pause—a pause, not a line. It's the moment when the rich man says to the husband, "What would you say if this were a real offer," and the husband doesn't answer for a heartbeat. Then the wife would have to jump in and say, "He'd say no." The rich man says, "I didn't hear him say no." Finally, the husband says, "I'd say no." It's all in that pause; the door is open. Feminists attacked that and said, "Why are they asking the husband? They should be asking the wife." Well, didn't they understand the whole point of the scene? The point is that the rich man is humiliating the husband in front of the wife by asking the husband that question, not her. He is proving to her that he will not immediately answer no. If he asks her the question, he proves nothing. Of course she'd say no. The whole point is: *Your husband would be tempted—are you? Your husband is temptable and human—are you?* It's crucial that he ask the question of the husband. Whether or not that's politically correct, who the hell cares? It's human nature. If you have to write politically correct, you may as well throw human nature out the window. Then you can't write, or at least not well.

JE: Some feminists apparently don't like human nature. Actually, what they don't like is men's nature.

AHJ: They don't like men. The National Organization for Women is not run by people who like men; not anymore. It's very sad. I've been a feminist all my life. I've beaten my way—beaten my way!—into some sort of existence into a business that is overwhelmingly male. For twenty years I've been doing that, having doors closed in my face and opening windows. And to end up sitting next to some twenty-year-old representative from NOW, who went right out of Smith to a job at NOW, and she's telling me how to behave, is a pretty amazing experience.

JE: Where did that happen?

AHJ: I was asked to be on a local public broadcasting program, to talk about women in the industry, not about the movie. I said I'd be thrilled not to talk about the movie. So I agreed. But it was a setup. The other woman was not in the industry; she was with NOW. She spent the whole half hour trying to dress me down as being a sell-out and a creep.

I'll never write just politically correct. What does that mean? Women can be villains as well as heroes. What does that mean—that you can't write Lady Macbeth? Would Shakespeare be told that he can't write Othello, because he's black? Please! Blacks and women, we're complete humans, with good sides and bad. We make mistakes. If you cannot write the complex human being who happens to be any one of those things, then you're not a writer; you've been hobbled.

JE: There's a parallel with *Beethoven*.

AHJ: Feminists attacked the fact that the wife didn't want to work. That was an element of the first draft, which I did not write, but I did rewrite to try to make it work better. In the original script I was given, the notion was that the kids have to go into daycare, Beethoven has to save them from a bad daycare person, and the wife wants to stay at home. I did some subtle work on the plotline, besides some action work. I believed strongly that the woman was expressing a choice. She says, "I don't want to work; I want to be with my children. That's the most important thing to me." The husband says, "Forget that, I need you at work." "No," she says, "I want to be with my children; it's more important." Feminists say that that's a politically incorrect choice. They attacked me for it. I say that they can stuff it. That woman is making her choice. To me, the issue was whether she gets her way and does what she wants to do. The answer was yes. I admire women who choose to stay home with their kids.

JE: As a working writer, you have to live with critics and criticism.

AHJ: It really bothers me that reviewers are writers, and yet they seem to forget that a movie is a script. They will not mention a movie writer's name very often, and they will not make any distinction between what's on the page and what's on the screen. I think reviewers should read the script of every movie they see.

JE: When a reviewer likes a film, he credits the director. When he doesn't, the writer often gets the blame.

AHJ: Exactly right. I can't tell you the number of times I've wanted to ship the script out and say, "Why don't you read this before you rake me over the coals, to check whether what you see there is really what I wrote."

JE: When you do have to change your conception of who the character is, how do you save the story and yet make the necessary alterations?

AHJ: You can open a dialogue where you don't just close a door and say nothing. You see, there's a line you can't cross. You can't, I don't believe, alter the theme of the movie; you can't alter what you're trying to say with the movie. But any writer would be surprised to see how much can be changed without losing those things. Every scene, if it's good, is going to advance the character, advance the plot, address the theme. A scene that's not doing those things isn't doing what it's supposed to do. But it can do it a number of ways, and characters can change in a number of ways.

There are, however, some things that are completely repugnant. I have a script now that I love very much. At the moment it's called "When She Was Good," nominally a remake of *Niagara*. Once again, it's back to the themes that I work on all the time. There's a happily married young couple in it. The wife's a doctor, husband's a cartoonist. They end up in a resort cabin next to an ex–football player and his wife, who is basically a sexpot—a gorgeous, tough, strong woman who married for money; a woman who married a man to advance herself and who has tired of the man, and he's lost his power and has all of the ingredients of a wife beater. He is trying to hold on to this woman sexually—not emotionally, in a normal human way, but physically. So, side by side are the good and bad examples of marital relationships.

If someone were to come along and say to me, "I want you to rewrite it so that this husband"—who I have as the classic example of a wife beater who ends up killing his wife and being the villain of the piece—"is absolved. We want everything to be that woman's fault, and we want him to be just a victim." I couldn't do that. And I'd fight it to my dying day. I'd give up the whole thing. But I would try very hard to convince them. I'd say, "Look, we can shade him. We can try very hard to make what he does more comprehensible. We can see that they're both wrong, that they're both bad, but he's going to end up killing her. And if you say that he's justified in doing that, that is repugnant and disgusting. There is nothing that justifies that man ultimately killing his wife, no matter how badly she behaves. You can't say that that's right. Doing so would attack the whole theme I'm trying to get across in the movie, which is about good sex and bad, good love and bad; ways that two people torture each other; ways that two people support each other. That's what the movie is about. And if you just say that the husband is blameless, it's the wife who's at fault, the whole thing falls apart.

So, they could say to me, "Move it, set it in a different place." They could say, "We want this movie to be played by Susan Sarandon instead of Jennifer Jason Leigh, so we're going to change the whole age thing." They can ask me to rewrite the third act in any number of ways. They can say any number of things, but they cannot ask me to absolve the husband and have me still be on the movie. There's a line, and you have to fight as hard as you can on that stuff. There are times you're not going to win, so you have to leave. What's really horrible is that, once you leave, they'll hire someone else who will do it.

JE: Where did the humor in *Beethoven* come from?

AHJ: Well, it's a pet movie, which is one of my favorite genres. *E.T.* was the most successful pet movie ever made: An alien comes to live in my closet; I have the best pet in the world. The humor comes from the exaggeration of the animal's size. He's a huge Saint Bernard. It wouldn't work if he were a dachshund, for example. It comes from that fact that he's a dog whom the children and mother will love, but will also drive the father crazy. I think the reason it works is that adults can understand Charles Grodin's character, can understand his frustration at having a huge slobbering dog in the house who's driving everyone crazy. At the same time, everyone knows what it's like to be the kid, to be the wife, who adores this pet whom the dad in the house doesn't really want around. A lot of the humor comes from exaggerating a normal situation. There's a big difference between having a new poodle and having a new Saint Bernard. A very big difference.

Before I came on the movie, the movie did not begin as it ultimately did. I added an opening that I think was very important, because it made the viewer identify with the dog—a puppy in search of a loving home. You are the dog who's in the store and wanting people to take you home, and they're not taking you home. Then you as the viewer are with the dog the whole rest of the movie. It's his movie right away, because he has a problem. Any interesting character has a problem. He wants a family. Once you know that, you want him to succeed from that moment on.

One of the other things I did was to give the kids problems. When I came on the script, they didn't really have personalities or problems. Children truly identify with pets, and believe that the pets think and feel. It's a fantasy come true, getting this big, wonderful dog who does save everything and Daddy ends up loving him after all. That's a basic child's fantasy.

JE: You've written *Mystic Pizza,* which falls into one genre, *Indecent Proposal,* which is in another, and *Beethoven,* still a third. Are you capable of writing, say, a *Die Hard*?

AHJ: I could, but I don't know if I'd enjoy it that much, because films like that don't have any thematic subtext. They only have "I'm a superhero against impossible forces." I should think that that's an easy script to write. Anyone who wants to make money writing scripts can probably sit down and write that pretty easily. It's almost formulaic. All you need is a hero who's gifted in some unusual way; he can do just about anything. Usually he's disillusioned at the moment they bring him in to solve some amazing crisis, which they set in some locale it's never been in before—say, a tunnel, maybe a ship, maybe a bus going fifty miles an hour. Then you have a horrible villain who has no complexity, no light side. And by the way, the hero has no dark side. You pit them against each other and come up with one formulaic scene after another.

That wouldn't interest me very much, though I can do that with the horror genre. Give me a mother or a child, someone I care about, who's being chased by a monster, that I can get into, because you're talking about primal fear; that, I can get into. But that hero's fantasy of killing everyone, I think that's more of a male thing. It doesn't interest me; it doesn't have any subtext at all.

JE: Subtext seems to dominate your writing thoughts.

AHJ: Subtext, theme, and metaphor. Most of my movies are metaphors, too.

JE: Do your original ideas begin with character or concept?

AHJ: Often they begin with a title, like *Mystic Pizza*. If I don't have a title, or can't think of a title, I don't take the job. Someone recently offered me a very interesting script, but for the life of me I couldn't think of a title. I walked away.

When She Was Good. I had that title for years and was looking for the proper story for it. Another original I'm writing got its title from a quote in the Bible that I really loved, *Kisses of an Enemy*. To me, that's about men and women. The people we fear are often the people we love.

JE: So titles are your window into the story?

AHJ: After that, I usually work from character; character and situation. It depends. After I got the title, *Mystic Pizza* came exclusively from character, because it's a multiple-character piece. *Kisses of an Enemy* has two very crucial characters and a huge plot twist that sets everything in motion. But it's also thematic: a woman who depends too much on a guy and gets in horrible trouble.

JE: Do you have any hard and fast rules that by, say, page thirty-one, this or this has to happen.

AHJ: Oh, yeah, I do. By twenty-seven, something has to happen. Usually a big plot turn. Usually something you don't expect. That's not necessarily the end of an act. The end of an act can be anywhere from thirty-five to forty. I always sense very strongly where the ends of the act are.

JE: You work from three strong acts.

AHJ: Right.

JE: Exposition, development, resolution.

AHJ: With a horrible crisis coming at the beginning of the third act. Like, for example, *Indecent Proposal,* with the couple splitting up at the beginning of the third act.

JE: What else, rulewise, do you look for in a script?

AHJ: A script's problem ought to be apparent by page two. If you're still reading and you don't know what the problem is by page five, you've lost me. The problem has to be there from the very beginning.

JE: Why can't the setup take longer?

AHJ: It can take a while, but you have to know what the problem is very early. An audience wants to know what a movie's about pretty quickly. There are a lot of rules of screenwriting. Don't mix tone; that's another. People make that mistake all the time. If I were advising beginning writers, I'd say to stay within a genre for your first couple of scripts. Study it, learn about it. I often tell people to do what I still do: Go to a library that has scripts, and study the classic scripts of that genre you've chosen. When I had to write comedy, I went to the Academy [of Motion Picture Arts and Sciences] library and read some of my favorite comedies. Reading a script is not the same as seeing a movie. You have to read the script. It also starts you off aspiring to the best. A lot of people are too lazy to do that. They think it can just pour out of their mind. Think about it, though: You wouldn't try to write a novel without reading a novel. You can't just go see a movie adaptation of a novel. You have to read what's been written.

Also, understand the market. They make a very narrow range

of things now. You have to write a kind of movie that will get made. I try to write something that will interest me, but still fall within the boundaries of what will get made. Pragmatism has a way of working. To this day, I have only one unproduced script.

I was talking to a friend recently who wanted to start writing scripts. She wanted help from me. After reading a bunch of samples, I told her that she needed a class, that she had to sit down and write examples from the genre she wanted to write, that she needed a tutor to go over her writing. She said, "That sounds too much like work." I said, "That's where the rubber hits the road. It *is* work."

NICHOLAS
MEYER

Interviewing Nick Meyer is not unlike watching a one-man play. He is among the most captivating of storytellers. His green eyes gleam with the extraordinary pleasure he seems to take in telling a story well—in entertaining his audience. He peppers his stories with references to history, philosophy, and music. He also manages to make smoking a cigar look like the most civilized and pleasurable of activities.

Meyer is the author of one of my favorite screenplays, Time After Time, *in which H. G. Wells travels to modern-day San Francisco in order to capture Jack the Ripper, who has fled to the future in Wells's time machine. In addition to being romantic, witty, and exciting, it is also the only time-travel movie I know of not to violate the parameters of logic set up by the premise.*

We met in his office on the Paramount lot in December of 1993— several days after his wife Lauren had died of cancer. When I suggested that we postpone the interview, he insisted that he needed to keep working.

NICHOLAS MEYER: I was always a filmmaker before I was anything else. The first movie I ever made was my own version of *Around the World in Eighty Days,* which I started when I was thirteen and finished when I was seventeen. If I was always anything, I was a storyteller, and it never really made much of a difference to me what medium I worked in. In the age of specialization, I have never been terribly interested in specializing. It usually seems to me that a given story will work better in one medium than another. Some stories seem to be plays, some books, some movies. It's only the commercial element that makes them interchangeable.

JOEL ENGEL: *The Seven Percent Solution* was both book and movie.

NM: But it was first and foremost a novel, an homage to Doyle. And I guess I've always been equally in love with pictures and words. I think of myself as a storyteller in the generic sense.

JE: What was the first real screenplay you wrote?

NM: The first one I wrote was at seventeen, based on a Jack Finney novel called *Assault on a Queen*. I didn't own the rights to this movie.

JE: It was made into a movie in 1965, starring Frank Sinatra and Virna Lisi, written by Rod Serling.

NM: Terrible movie. But my screenplay followed the book. I was seventeen—what did I know? I just followed page by page. I was at the University of Iowa, reviewing movies when this movie came out. I sat there watching it, stunned by how bad it was. I assumed that they really screwed it up because of whatever endless demands Frank Sinatra was making.

JE: The mechanics of screenplay writing—

NM: Self-taught. I got hold of some screenplay, just so I could see the proper formatting. As the years went by, the only change

I made was to eliminate the words "cut to," which always seemed redundant. I just write "interior" and "exterior," and no one ever had any trouble figuring out what was happening. The only time I ever write those things in is if I visualize an optical—say, "dissolve" or "fade out." Otherwise, why bother? They just take up space on the page. If there's a specific effect, I indicate it. The other one I always found funny in a script was "smash cut." I always wondered how the hell is a smash cut different from any other kind of cut? I don't know. What they mean is, abrupt.

JE: "Just when you least expect it, we cut to—"

NM: Right in the middle of the scream that turns into a train whistle.

JE: How similar or dissimilar are the mechanics of novel writing and screen writing?

NM: They are about as unrelated as English and French. English works well in German; German can be translated into English. But English doesn't fit with French. Anyway, there are no mechanics to novel writing. The mechanics are called prose, grammar, syntax, spelling—all things that have no bearing on a screenplay. A screenplay is not a finished product; a novel is. A screenplay is a blueprint for something—for a building that will most likely never be built, but it's still a blueprint.

JE: Unless you direct your own screenplay, it most likely won't look the way you envisioned while writing.

NM: That's another topic, that's a topic of collaboration. We're talking about novels and screenplays; they're completely different. A screenplay, like a play, is a form of drama. As such, there are dramatic laws, or certainly inevitabilities, the first probably laid down by Aristotle in the *Poetics,* to which dramas must conform—and if they don't conform, they'd better have a good reason why not. A novel is much looser. It may or may not be dramatic; there's no time limit. A novel is a finished entity. It makes very specific demands on the novelist; a screenplay doesn't, necessarily. An army of people are going to go over it on its passage to an answer print, second-guessing every comma. The actors will rewrite your lines, the director will cut it differently, the producer has a different idea. It is in fact a blueprint that's handed off to the builders, of whom you may or may not be one.

JE: When you direct, do you allow the actors to change their lines?

NM: Sure, if they can make it better. As a director, I merely reserve the right to say no. The director is a bit analogous to the conductor of a symphony orchestra. It's a collaborative adventure.

JE: What upsets screenwriters is the sense that their vision is taken from them.

NM: Now we're talking about collaboration. This is a big topic, and not always well understood. You begin by accepting that movies are collaborative ventures. If you're not prepared for the perils, pitfalls, and joys of collaboration, then movies are probably not a very good venue for whatever it is you want to do. There are good collaborations and bad collaborations. In the best of them, somebody understands you better than you understood yourself. I return to music, which helps me to analogize properly. When I was in college, CBS released several recordings of Stravinsky conducting Stravinsky. I got real excited and blew some of my money on these records, thinking, *Yes, these will be definitive—*

back in the days when I thought that there was such an animal. I thought I would hear how the composer wanted it. Well, Stravinsky conducting Stravinsky was bad. Boring. Mediocre. Uninspired. By contrast, when I listened to Leonard Bernstein or Antal Dorati or Pierre Boulez, who they called the "French correction," it was much more exciting. Now that's collaboration. Stravinsky wrote down the notes—the script, if you will. Bernstein got hold of it, and the result is a revelation. Stravinsky would have to be an idiot not to realize how terrific Bernstein's take on it was. Great composers, great writers, are not necessarily the premier interpreters of what they've done. And in a great collaboration, and I have intermittently experienced this myself, you look at something that somebody did with what you wrote, and your jaw drops open with a kind of happiness that says, "My God, he understood me better than I understood myself." He brought out meanings and colors and ideas. Parts of *Sommersby,* parts of *The Seven Percent Solution,* parts of *Star Trek IV*—all of which I wrote but didn't direct—where I said, "Ah, he really grabbed something I didn't know was there," made a moment out of something. It may be that the first time Holmes is in Freud's office in Vienna [in *The Seven Percent Solution*] and deduces everything about him, and the camera kind of goes around while he's ticking off the various things—I marveled at that. So in the event of a successful collaboration, you may find that you did better than you knew. And by the way, successful collaboration is not necessarily collaboration between friends. Gilbert and Sullivan did not get along. They had the same sense of humor, and that was it. Gilbert wrote the words, mailed them to Sullivan, who wrote the music, which he mailed back to Gilbert; Gilbert staged the show. The tendency, in fact, may be to look for a collaborator you like, who may be a form of yes man. I ask you, Billy Wilder and I. A. L. Diamond—now there were two great movies, *Some Like It Hot* and *The Apartment.*

Then what happened for the next twenty years? They made a lot of movies, but where was the edge that Charles Brackett brought to Wilder's work. They didn't like each other at all. Brackett was able to say to Wilder what Diamond never could: "Billy, no."

Then there's the nightmare scenario that's much more common, which is to be misunderstood rather than understood. You go, "Get me a gun, 'cause either I'm gonna shoot him or I'm gonna shoot me. I gave him gold and he turned it into lead."

JE: Both of these presume a kind of objectivity that many writers don't have. They think everything they write is gold.

NM: There's the point of view of the collaborators, and the point of view of the audience, and of posterity; they're not the same. I would be the first person to agree with you, that the artist is not necessarily, or even likely, to be the most objective or useful judge of his own work. Or of his implications, or what he was trying to say. I think they're kind of dumb in that way. When people come to me and say, "Why did you put in X?" I always say, "Why do you think I did it?" I'm not the answer to a bunch of equations in a math book that you can just flip to; I don't know. You do things on instinct. There's the story of the man who went up to Margot Fonteyn after a performance and said, "Oh, I so enjoyed your dancing. Tell me, what were you doing up there?" She said, "I'm sorry, I explained what I was doing while I was doing it. If you didn't understand me, then I failed." There's a lot one can say about the whole subject of objectivity, and I'm sure that you're quite right. I will tell you, though, that I don't think everything I write is gold. I think I know more or less when I've fulfilled what I set out to do, in terms of my own parameters, which may not be anyone else's. I thought *Sommersby* was a terribly mixed bag for me. Overall, I thought they blew it, in terms of what it was supposed to be; I was real angry. Sure, someone can point out that the picture was a hit. If we're gonna use that yardstick, all bets are off.

JE: Ultimately, I suppose, this all gets to how you know, as the screenwriter, when the script you're working on is done.

NM: Warren Beatty said that films aren't finished so much as abandoned. Go see a movie called *The Mysteries of Picasso*. Somebody put a camera behind a plate of glass and got Picasso to paint on the glass, so you can watch him paint. He works on this one painting and won't leave it alone. A dozen times, a dozen times, you know that it's finished. Finally, he says, "I've wrecked it." And he has. He's screwed up eleven times, saved it ten times, but the twelfth time it goes down the tubes. The only thing more remarkable to my mind, watching the film, was his reckless willingness to keep on fooling with it, to radically rethink it.

The movie *Julia* is not one I particularly liked. But in it, Julia turns to Lillian, who's supposed to be Lillian Hellman, who wants to be a writer, and says, "Be very bold." That may be advice for life, maybe for art, but for an artist it's very important—to be bold. Lear says, "Nothing will come of nothing." It's true that you may never get a bloody lip if you don't lead with your chin, but you may never get anything else, either. The hardest thing for me, as an artist, is to be bold, is to be out there. And it's particularly hard in a conservative, commercial environment like Hollywood. I was complaining to someone the other day about my frustrations in this business. I said, "Look, let's talk food for a second. What I want to do is make charcoal-broiled steaks. And I want ears of corn and a big salad. I'm not talking about frog legs, I'm not talking about escargots. That's what I want. All American—whatever. And what I'm getting offered is Chicken McNuggets, and I can't do them; I'll throw up. I could do Fatburger. That at least is real junk food." I suppose that's what *Star Trek* is. I can get behind that. But don't give me *The Beverly Hillbillies* or *The Flintstones*. No.

JE: How does that sense of outrage and ambition translate to your characterizations? How do you create character for a screenplay that is going to be accepted?

NM: My screenplays, by and large, are not accepted. I have stacks of unproduced scripts—some on commission, some spec— that everyone says, "Gee, Nick, this is so well written."

JE: Damned with faint praise.

NM: Right, it's the kiss of death. "You're such a great writer, Nick. Wow." See ya. Because I keep serving up the charcoal-broiled steaks, and they're considered too sophisticated. I remember I wrote the ultimate swashbuckling movie. I did Arthur Conan Doyle's *The White Company* for Zoetrope and Paramount, and everybody loved it, but it was just too expensive. It went off to a company called Savoy and was returned with a comment that went, "If we did a movie like this, we would like it not to be so intelligent."

JE: What is it that makes these screenplays unproduceable? Is it the characterizations?

NM: They're too sophisticated.

JE: Define that.

NM: I would say that they are best appreciated by people who know how to read. And most people no longer know how to read. I think that's true of most of my work. I write for people who read, whether it's a movie or anything else.

JE: Is it the sense of character that separates the sirloin steak from the Chicken McNugget? Maybe my favorite film of the last several years was *Enchanted April,* not because the story was anything to recall, but because the characters were people I wanted to spend time with. That movie ended too soon for me. I just wanted to be in their company as much as possible.

NM: I'm not really sure whether it's simply the degree of complexity or the person's psychological makeup, or the subject matter. I think a lot of times it's the subject matter. People will say, "It's period. I don't want to do it."

I have an idea here for a movie, which is worth mentioning because of why it was turned down. After Napoleon was defeated at Waterloo, they sent him to Saint Helena, an island in the South Atlantic. Once Napoleon saw it, he knew he'd never get off it. That's it. His lodgings weren't yet finished, so he was billeted with the quartermaster, who had a high-spirited, thirteen-year-old daughter named Betsy, who was in many ways as much a prisoner on this damned island as was her new playmate, math tutor, all-around pal—the former master of Europe. She was the only one who wasn't afraid of him. For three months, she pulled his sword and chased him around the room. I thought of making a little family film—just sit on this island—about this thirteen-year-old girl and the forty-six-year-old emperor. When they heard about it in Europe, they said, "Oh, his mistress." They're so decadent, they didn't even get it. It was just a friendship, and about how you can learn to be free when you're in prison, and lessons back and forth. Someone wrote a novel about this. At the end there was a horse race, and Betsy rides Napoleon's horse National Velvet-style to victory. Finally, the three months are over and he's taken up to his house where he's going to live out the last six years of life. I thought that this was a family film I could do. Interesting, offbeat—that's what I would have brought to it, an offbeat sensibility. And Sherry Lansing [head of Paramount production], a woman I like, said, "I don't want to do period." End of movie, having nothing to do with the merits of the film. I mean, what does she do anyway but make R-rated television movies: Would you sleep with Robert Redford if he offered you a million dollars? What kind of choice is that? Would you sleep with Danny DeVito? Now *there's* an interesting movie.

JE: That's a funny take. Did you say that publicly when the film came out?

NM: Being outspokenly honest has not been great for my career. Remember that line, "You'll never work in this town again"?

JE: Let's talk about how you go about constructing a blueprint.

NM: Yes, it is a blueprint. You're writing a play, a play for the screen—a screenplay. What are the elements that make a play? I was trained by Howard Stein at the University of Iowa Writers' Workshop. He said that everybody had to read Aristotle's *Poetics,* which we did, in the Francis L. Ferguson translation. These are my antecedents. When I taught screenwriting, I would point out that in writing drama for the screen, we first decide what drama is, then worry about how to put it on the screen. That sounds deceptively simple.

According to Aristotle, who in fact was only offering his observations, not setting them down as rules, the skeletal structure of a drama means that a question is asked at the beginning. The process of asking that question is known as exposition. I formulate the problem. Act One: The ghost tells Hamlet, "I was murdered by my brother, your uncle, and I want you to get revenge." So here's the question: Will Hamlet kill the king? The job of the dramatist is to raise as much suspense as possible as to the outcome of that question, and when the question is answered the audience goes home. End of play. What will happen if? That's dramatic structure.

Aristotle also seemed to say that character is fate. We learn about a character from the decisions he makes or fails to make. Hamlet sees Claudius praying and doesn't kill him. Through every decision we keep learning about Hamlet's character; he seems to be indecisive, and yet people can argue for four hundred years about why he's indecisive. Everyone has a theory.

If you put those two things together, the question and the behavior of the character, that is the skeletal structure from which I would derive drama. Now you talk about putting it on the screen, to translate as much as possible into pictures. There are things only movies can do. I'll tell you my favorite scene in movies. It happens to be from a terrific movie, but it's not my favorite. It's my favorite scene. A Fred Zinnemann movie called *The Sundowners*. It's about sheep drovers in Australia. One of the great assets of movies is that they can make you interested in things you would not otherwise be interested in. This goes back to my three rules that studios don't want to hear about movies. Number one: It doesn't make any difference what the name of the movie is. You can save all that money you use to research titles, 'cause nobody, frankly, gives a damn. A movie can be called *I Am Curious, Yellow*. A movie can be called *Sommersby*. A movie can be called *8½*. It doesn't make a difference. Number two: Nobody cares what the movie's about. It can be about women's baseball during World War II. It can be about Reconstruction. No one will care. And, finally, number three, nobody cares who's in the movie. The only people who care are the executives who answer to the stockholders when it fails. "What do you mean I did it wrong? I had Robert Redford and Paul Newman." Nobody cares. They care only about one thing: *Is it good? Is it really terrific? Do I have to see this? Does it have a scene so memorable, like the guy falling out of the bottom of the boat and everyone screams?* That's all they care about. The rest is a waste of time, what the title is, what the movie is about, whether it's period.

So *The Sundowners* is about sheep drovers in Australia, not generally the most compelling of topics. Just try getting that one by now. It's about a family—father, mother, son. Their job is to herd the sheep from where they're raised to where they're shorn. Screenplay by Isobel Lennart, who also did *Funny Girl*. The family is very happy, except for one thing: The wife doesn't want to do it anymore. She's been on the trail for more than a dozen years, running the chuck wagon, or whatever. And now that her boy is of a certain age, she wants to have a house with a picket fence and the whole nine yards. The husband, for reasons which are not too hard to understand, is rather obscurely but definitely threatened by this entire prospect. That's the situation when we get to the end of this particular sheep drive. Picture a screen with nothing on it but a set of railroad tracks going from left to right. Upstage of those tracks is the station. Downstage across from it arrives the buckboard. The kid is not in this scene, just the father and mother. The buckboard stops opposite the empty set of railroad tracks, and the husband turns to the wife and says, "You stay here." He leaves. Wife sits there. Train pulls into the station, stops right in front of her. Sitting in the train right across from her is a woman about her own age, a city woman, wearing a silly hat; she's doing something with her compact. Suddenly, she looks up over her compact and sees sitting in the buckboard a woman about her own age, and instead of rice powder on her face she has the dust of the trail. And instead of a silly hat she's got flyaway hair under a straw hat. And for one frozen moment, these two women find themselves staring into each other's lives. Then the train gives a jolt, begins to move off, the city lady is called back to her compact, train leaves. Now the husband comes back to the buckboard, sees his wife sitting there, tears running down her cheeks. Second line of dialogue: "What's the matter with you?" "Nothing, dear." Man puts his arm around his wife and they drive away.

That's my favorite scene in movies, because only movies can do that. It's about editing, about photography, about three lines of dialogue, about acting.

JE: That's a well-constructed scene.

NM: Well, now I'll tell you something more about the scene. I'm having dinner at [writer] Faye Kanin's one night in about 1987, and happen to mention this scene. Faye says, "I'm so glad you mentioned that scene, because my friend Isobel Lennart wrote the screenplay, and she couldn't get Fred Zinnemann to understand how it was going to work." That night, I mentioned to Lauren, my wife, as we were driving home that I'd always thought that it had been Zinnemann's conception, not the screenwriter's. A few months later, we're living in Spain, and we become friends with Peter Viertel and his wife, Deborah Kerr, who happens to have been the woman in the buckboard. We're having lunch, and I say to her, "You know, in addition to the fact that I am so thrilled beyond words to meet you from all the happiness you have given me in a million movies, you also have the distinction of having appeared in my favorite scene in all of moviedom." And I tell her which scene. She says, "Oh, I'm so happy that you said that. Because that scene was really my idea." I said, "It was?" She said, "Yeah, there was a lot of dialogue originally, and I asked Fred why we couldn't just do it with looks."

That afternoon I'm driving home with Lauren. I turned to her and said, "Isn't that interesting that you can go to a writer's house and you find out it was the writer's idea. You go to an actor's house and find out it was the actor's idea. One day, all things being equal, I'll meet Fred Zinnemann, and we'll get another version. Sure enough, six months later, I'm in London, having tea with Fred Zinnemann. I told him the story. He says, "Hmm. I can't quite recollect. Isobel Lennart was a lovely woman, but she didn't know anything about sheep drovers, and I think we just cut out all of her dialogue and just used the dialogue from the book, but Deborah may be right that it was her idea."

So the point is, there's collaboration. Here's this amazing scene. Was it the screenwriter? The actor? The director? Who the hell knows? It got there somehow, and that's all that really counts, unless we're talking egos.

JE: But it brings up an interesting point for screenwriting. In a novel, you would miss the emotional impact that comes from simplicity, because you would have to describe what's going through both women's minds.

NM: Henry James would take six pages.

JE: Hemingway might do it in a few lines, but it would similarly lack the fullness of the moment on screen. So the question is: In screenwriting in general, how do you get the most from the least? How do you tell a movie, as opposed to a play?

NM: My attitude toward screenwriting changed enormously once I started directing. It is impossible to convey an experience to somebody if they haven't had that experience. I could stand here all day and try to describe to you what beer tastes like. Well, if you've never tasted beer, we could talk for a year, but it still wouldn't substitute for one swallow. You'd go, "Oh, that's beer." I could tell you about the death of my wife, could tell you for a year, and you'd say, "I can't imagine what you're going through." You'd be right—and you'd also be lucky. Unless you have an analogous experience—and I don't mean the death of a pet, either, though that may be as close as some people can come—you're not going to know. If you haven't directed, haven't found out what that process is about, then you are very likely to be far more rigid and vest what you've written with greater importance than it deserves. "Oh, Christ, don't cut that line. That's the heart of the movie." Maybe it is and maybe it isn't. Maybe the movie, when you put it together without that line, will still have enough of the rest of what you have written that you don't need the line. In fact, a very common phenomenon, not just with screenwriters but also with playwrights, is you get an idea for a scene, around which you're going to build a whole story, say, what happens when a guy comes home and finds himself in bed with a French poodle, or whatever it is. From this you construct a whole story. At the end of it, the one thing that no longer seems to belong is the seminal, catalytic scene that inspired the whole work. A certain kind of amateur refuses to pull that scene out, out of some slightly misguided sense of I don't know what, an abstract concept that was inspirational but now doesn't fit. You outgrew it, you dispensed with it. You fight and argue. But there's only one rule in show business. If it works, leave it in.

JE: You're arguing against, in an ironic way, directing your own screenplay.

NM: How?

JE: It's possible that the director will be so married to the words he wrote, that he won't notice that the seminal scene is now extraneous. Another director may see in an instant what you can't after working on this screenplay for three months or six months or a year.

NM: That is the nature of collaboration. There are people who write and direct their own material. Remember what Henry James said, that "life is hot but art is cool." If you are the puppet-master, you cannot be out front sobbing at the performance. You have to remain clearheaded backstage and make sure that the strings do not get tangled. There are two kinds of objectivity we're talking about here. One is creative objectivity, which is while you are working. Any artist who doesn't have a degree of that probably can't amount to much. That's different than objectivity about evaluating what is finished or when it's finished, which is more problematic. It's always difficult to say when it's finished.

JE: When is it?

NM: I don't know. You either know or you don't, or you get exhausted with it. You say, "I can't do it anymore," or, like Picasso, you say, "I've wrecked it; it's beyond me now." Occasionally, you dot the *i* and zing your pencil across the page and say, "I've nailed it." Beverly Sills has said that there were nights when she came offstage and went into her dressing room and absolutely knew that she was the greatest. On the other hand, there was the night that Olivier came offstage having done the most brilliant Othello of his life, and was in a terrible temper, a foul mood. Somebody said, "What are you so pissed off at? You were great tonight." He said, "Yes, but why?"

The point is, when I'm writing I go into a kind of trance—slightly disembodied. By the way, I have found working on a computer to be very useful, because the business of writing is rewriting; going over it again and again and again, and fooling around. A computer encourages you to do that. I don't have to use the Scotch tape. I don't have to use the Liquid Paper. I don't have to use the scissors. And now, if it's the matter of one comma, it's nothing. "Go ahead, add the comma, switch these paragraphs around, switch this actor, this line of dialogue." So in that sense, yes, you have to be very objective. You want some consolation? Save everything. Save every line you ever wrote; you'll use it again. I had stuff I cut out of *Time After Time* put in *Star Trek IV*.

JE: I loved *Time After Time*.

NM: The studio [Warner Bros.] hated it. Just hated it. Until it went through the roof. Anyway, in the blueprint-screenplay for that movie was a scene in which H. G. Wells is wandering around San Francisco still looking for Jack the Ripper. Having caused one traffic accident already, he comes to see a sign that says "Don't Walk." He stops at the curb, and a Chinese boy with a ghetto blaster comes up behind him playing acid rock. And Wells is looking down at this thing playing the most awful sound he's ever heard. There's that little scene. Later, he's at dinner at the girl's house. She says, "What kind of music do you like?" He thinks a minute and says, "Anything but Oriental." Well, when we previewed the movie, nobody got it. Nobody. It took me a while to realize that the reason nobody got it was that the setup, the boy with the radio, and the dinner were two and a half reels apart. They'd forgotten about the boy already. So I had to cut it. I hated to do it because I dislike rock and roll so horribly that this was my chance to trash it. I cut out the punch line. I figured that I'd just leave him in with the boy and the radio; that would be enough. Then I realized that I hadn't shot it very well. It was my first job as a director, and a lot of things aren't in the movie because I shot them badly. This was one of them. I had to cut the whole thing out.

Now I'm writing *Star Trek IV,* which is the same plot: time travelers in San Francisco. I even asked whether they have to be in San Francisco, whether they could be in Paris. I'm always trying to get to Paris. Answer was no. So I put the punk kid with the ghetto blaster on the bus, and Spock gives him the Vulcan nerve pinch. Recycled. Save everything. It'll come back. You'll use it. There's a line of dialogue I keep trying to work into a movie. I've put it into three screenplays, but it never makes it into a finished film: "Great men are seldom good men." It's been a casualty every time.

JE: I hear there's a good story behind your unproduced *Don Quixote* screenplay.

NM: Some years ago, David Foster, who produced *McCabe and Mrs. Miller,* said he really wanted to work with me. "Let's do something." I said, "You don't want to do anything with me; I'm impossible." He pleaded, said, "Come on, let's do something. What do you want to do?" I figured I had a way to stop him. I said, "Did you ever read *Don Quixote?*" "No." Well, he read it and loved it. So we had a story conference with Ned Tannen, head of Paramount. "Well, boys," he said, "what's this about?" I said, "We want to make a movie of *Don Quixote.*" He said, "Yeah, and?" "There's no and. I don't want to put music to it. Don't want to update it. I just want to do the first buddy comedy." That's what I said. The first road picture. For some reason, maybe his kid had been studying it in school, he said to go ahead. I told him that maybe I ought to go to Spain and look at La Mancha. He said to do it. So I went.

Eventually, I realized that this was really grownup stuff. I knew

I wouldn't be able to write it sitting in my office at Paramount with the phone ringing. I decided to stay in Spain to write it. I wrote it. Everybody loved it.

JE: It must have been a long screenplay.

NM: Actually, it was about 130 pages, normal size. What I did—this is the way I adapt novels, same with *The White Company*—I got a notebook and reread the book, putting down a sentence for every page. I turned a thousand-page novel into a hundred-page outline, with a page number next to each sentence. That way, you learn the book real well. Then you can read the book in outline form and say, "That I like, this I don't like, this I need, that I don't need." Sure, you can make dumb choices, but not because you don't understand the material well.

JE: Why wasn't it made?

NM: I suppose that when Ned commissioned it, the studio had had a good year, was riding high, and so forth. After I finished writing it, which was June of 1987, I went off to make *The Deceivers* for Merchant-Ivory in India. Ned said not to worry, that it would be here when I got back. A year later, Paramount had had a terrible year. End of story.

JE: Do you have any particular insights on the process of thinking visually in order to have the story told in as many pictures as possible, rather than entirely or primarily through the mouths of the characters?

NM: In many ways I think it helps to be illiterate as a screenwriter. The best of them think in pictures, not words. What makes Steven Spielberg great is that he thinks in pictures. That's not pejorative. For me, coming from a verbal and playwriting background, I have to go through a double process. First, I think in dramatic terms about what's going on, and I wind up thinking about words and dialogue and so forth. Then I have to think about ways to get rid of words and dialogue and make it into pictures. When sound first came to Hollywood, they brought out all these playwrights, because they needed help with the talk. They tell this one guy to write this one scene of a marriage breaking up. He did—ten pages; brilliant dialogue. They gave it to Billy Wilder, who allegedly solved the problem with one scene, no words: Man and his wife get into an elevator, the man is wearing his hat. The elevator stops at another floor, an attractive young tootsie gets in. Cut to the lobby: elevator doors open, man has removed his hat. End of marriage. No words.

For me, it has been a torturous process. First of all, I learn everything slowly. I'm the last person to understand anything, I promise. The good news is that when I do understand it, I probably understand it better than anyone. But I can tell you that my screenwriting career, internally, has consisted of my trying to learn to think in pictures. I've gotten good at it. But I began by having to make rules for myself: no speech longer than ten lines long.

JE: Have you reduced that?

NM: Oh, sure. I've also now gotten confident enough to allow myself a twenty-line speech, if I want it. I've come out the other end of this process.

JE: What works.

NM: Yes. It's been very involved, and I will still probably never be as good as people who think directly in pictures. It's the differ-

ence between learning to ride a horse when you're five years old
and learning to ride when you're twenty. I'm a good screenwriter—better than ninety percent of them. That's enough to
make me mediocre.

JE: Do you have any particular rules pertaining to how and
when you get the words down on the page?

NM: I used to make a rule that I would have to write ten pages
a day, no matter what. Ten pages, seven days a week, no excep-
tions, no holidays, no sickness, no excuses. They could be terrible,
awful pages; doesn't make any difference; you just do it. And, by
the way, there seems to be no correlation between how well you
think it's going and how it's really going. There are days when I
am really struggling, unhappy. And then later I read it and say,
"There's nothing wrong with this. In fact, it's pretty good."
    The converse is also true. You think, "Geez, I'm really cook-
ing." Later, I read it and realize, "Wow, you were kidding yourself. This is self-indulgent, stupid stuff." I spent a night with Artie
Shaw, the great musician. He told me about the time he jammed
on marijuana with his guys and recorded the session. They were
brilliant, he said, playing amazing stuff. Then they played it back
when they were straight, and there was nothing there. Nothing.

JE: When you write, are you constantly thinking structure,
structure, structure? Or do you just let the story tell itself, whatever way it comes out, as long as you're true to the story? By, say,
page twenty-five, does something have to happen? By page fifty?

NM: I'm vaguely aware that if nobody has been killed, it's probably not good. Really, the most important thing I tell beginning
screenwriters—or even beginning novelists—is: Get a first draft
down on paper; keep going; don't look back; don't stop; don't
reread it.

JE: Don't reread when you write?

NM: No, just keep going. Go, go, go. Once you have a first draft, then the work begins. Then you start to play. You can play forever. It's like carving something out of a block of marble. Let's say that the object is to make a statue of a man. If you obsess about the fingernail on his right thumb, you are wasting time; it's going to be wrong. First get the shape of the man. See how big his hands are going to be, then you'll know more about his fingernail. Get the guy out there so you can see the idea of it. Get the first draft down so you can see the idea of it. Then you can say, "Oh yeah, I want the head to be smaller" or "That knee should come up a bit." Then you can fool around, but you can't fool around if you've got nothing there. Just keep going. Don't show it to friends. If it's two hundred pages, fine. Three hundred? Fine. Keep going. Later on, you'll pull where necessary.

JE: What's the best screenplay you've written?

NM: I don't know.

JE: Which one are you happiest with?

NM: I tend always to be happiest with the most recent. I will tell you that I am embarrassed now with the screenplay for *The Seven Percent Solution*. Too much talk. Even in the editing room I was trying to get [director] Herb Ross to eliminate some of the cease-less chatter. And I'm now embarrassed by that.

Maybe the screenplay that could have won an Academy Award and wasn't even nominated was *Time After Time*. That was terrific screenwriting, and I'm very fond of it.

JE: What was the origin of that?

NM: Somebody showed me fifty-five pages of a novel he was writing, inspired by *The Seven Percent Solution*. I acquired the rights to that material and wrote my own thing. I gave him the screenplay, which he turned into a novel. I loved that script, in terms of a finished piece of work. I'm not, however, very enthusiastic about my direction. I'm as embarrassed about some of the things I did directing it as I am about *The Seven Percent Solution* screenplay. Maybe it's time to remake the film. I know where to put the camera now.

TED TALLY

The short answer to why I asked Ted Tally to participate is, of course, the Oscar he won in 1992 for adapting The Silence of the Lambs. *The longer answer is that I'd read the Thomas Harris novel on which he based his screenplay and was thoroughly impressed by how he'd retained the quintessence of the labyrinthine story and its characters. Because of the complexities of adaptation, people usually say of a movie made from a popular novel, "It's not as good as the book."*

Months later, my appreciation for Tally's work was ratified by no less than Ernest Lehman, who told me that Sam Goldwyn had once offered to buy The Silence of the Lambs *while it was still in galley form—if Lehman would agree to adapt it. After reading, he said, he returned it to Goldwyn with the admission that he hadn't a clue in the world how to do it. Tally, Lehman said, "did a fantastic job."*

Tally spoke with me by phone from his Pennsylvania home.

JOEL ENGEL: You went to Yale Drama School, but not to learn to write.

TED TALLY: I really wanted to act; acting and directing is what I did as an undergraduate. Though I did begin writing plays in high school, writing was not as interesting to me as acting and directing. I kept on writing as an undergrad, but it didn't become a real focus until graduate school. The summer before my third year in the Drama School, I was lucky enough to write a play that they really liked. It was called *Terra Nova,* about the race to the South Pole. It got me a professional production at Yale Rep. Robert Brustein, who was then head of Yale Drama, arranged a grant for me and a part-time teaching position, so I never really had to struggle to become a professional writer. It happened right out of school. I was very lucky. I've never really had another kind of job.

JE: You never had to wash dishes or wait tables?

TT: No. I had no idea what I was going to do if I couldn't do this, because I have no employable skills. I got an agent then, a good theater agent, Helen Merrill. She never really had an interest in movies or TV; to the contrary, she usually discouraged her clients from pursuing that. She was old-fashioned—thought that we'd lose our souls or something. I think that probably inhibited my Hollywood development for several years. I wrote plays that were done off-Broadway or in regional theaters for about eight years.

JE: Any I might know?

TT: Probably not. None was very successful in New York, though *Terra Nova* had about thirty regional presentations and was done all over the world. In England it was produced by the BBC for television. It opened a lot of doors and led to my first screen-writing job, which was with Lindsay Anderson, the British director who did *Oh Lucky Man!* and *if. . . .* He had been born and was raised in India, and wanted to make a film about India, a sort of British western, as it were. He's an expert on John Ford, having written books about him. He loved the genre, but couldn't see himself making an American western, though because he knew the terrain, he could do one in India. After reading *Terra Nova,* he got me hired to write this project for Orion pictures about the Sepoy Rebellion in India in 1857. It was like getting paid to learn how to write a screenplay. When I was hired, I didn't even know what a screenplay looked like. I'd never even seen one. In those days, 1977, 1978, they were rarely published. Today, it's much more common. Lindsay, who supervised the writing, said, "Don't worry about it. It's no big deal. Form is not that important to me. I just want to work out the story."

In some ways, Lindsay can be a difficult man—irascible, gruff. He liked to bark a lot. But he was a good teacher of movies. He really began my education in movies. I learned a lot in the year we worked together. The only sad thing was that the project never got made. It would have cost a zillion dollars: *"Gone With the Wind Goes to India."*

JE: This is in Orion's early days?

TT: It must have been very early. I couldn't believe these guys were paying me, though it wasn't much, to work with Lindsay Anderson and learn how to write movies. He supervised every page of it. He may as well have had a credit, though he didn't want one. We never edited that script at all. It just got longer and longer and longer, until finally it was about 190 pages. It would have had to be a miniseries. We named it "Empire." I glanced at it about a year ago and thought it really didn't look too bad.

JE: In what ways didn't it look bad?

TT: That it wasn't embarrassing is probably a better way to put it. It didn't look like a first effort, except for its incredibly grotesque length. It didn't look amateurish. It moved. I'm sure that's all Lindsay's doing.

JE: What happened professionally after that?

TT: I wrote some other screenplays, one for United Artists called "Hushabye," a thriller about black market baby adoption; an original idea. There were others as well, all unproduced. All that time I continued to write plays, too, but after about eight years I decided that I really wasn't getting anywhere in the theater; I'm getting productions, but they're closing in three weeks. And by about 1985, it was no longer gratifying just to get paid for screenwriting and not see anything for that work except money. I decided that I either had to get serious about the movies or stop doing screenplays. I wasn't living completely in either of these two worlds, theater or movies. You can call it an early midlife crisis—thirty-five years old and wondering. I decided I'm going to get a new agent, go to a bigger agency, buy a computer, get serious about screenwriting and quit condescending to it. I think I'd felt a little bit that I could do it with one hand tied behind my back. Coming from that Yale Drama School background, I may have believed a little that movies were the work of the devil; that sort of thing, that everybody in the business is greedy and stupid, and that real art only happens in theater and books. So I decided that I'd have to get more serious about the work. I have to take a few trips to California and meet some people, get some better contacts. That's when I switched from my theater agent to ICM and got a computer.

I did get more interesting things to write, but they still weren't getting made. Then, finally, an actor who'd been in two of my plays, Griffin Dunne, offered me a job doing an adaptation of the novel *White Palace*. The producers were Griffin and Amy Robinson, whom I'd known a bit from New York, and Mark Rosenberg and Sydney Pollack, who really impressed me. In the meantime I'd had a few things produced for television, a BBC adaptation of one of my plays, and an NBC movie of the week I shared credit on, *The Father Clements Story.* So things were happening, but not in feature films.

I wrote six drafts of *White Palace* over two years. It was a stormy relationship in the script's development, because there were four producers who had trouble agreeing on a lot of things. I felt pulled in many different directions.

JE: Who were you taking most of your notes from?

TT: I guess I took most of my notes from Mark Rosenberg and Amy Robinson. Occasionally there would be a meeting with Sidney, who was very shrewd. But he was really involved in other things. They could never decide whether they were happy with the shape of the script. Universal kind of liked it, but not enthusiastically. It was real development hell. Finally, when everyone thought the script was in pretty good shape, they began offering it to directors. Nobody wanted to direct it. Nobody. They went through the entire Directors Guild of America roster and came up empty. I sometimes suspected that it was because no director wanted Sydney Pollack looking over his shoulder. Or no director wanted to have to answer to four producers with four different opinions. Or maybe the material wasn't good enough; that's also possible. But anyway, when they weren't getting anywhere with directors, they began offering it to actresses. Susan Sarandon wanted to do it right away. That was very exciting, and seemed to move things along a little faster. Universal showed great patience, I must admit. I kept expecting them to throw it away when eight or ten directors didn't want to do it. But they hung on, and finally they got Luis Mandoki, who had directed only one other movie, *Gaby,* which was quite good.

Now they had a director and Susan Sarandon. My understanding is that the studio greenlighted production at that point. They said, "We'll find an acceptable younger male actor, and we'll make this movie—definitely." But shortly thereafter, the producers decided to bring in a more experienced screenwriter. I was devastated, because here we were so close to production and I'd put two years into this, and now I was going to be robbed of personal involvement in finally getting a movie made. And they had a lot of trouble casting the man's part because, again, four producers and a director and now a female star couldn't agree on anything. Finally, Susan agreed to James Spader. I learned a whole bunch about Hollywood thinking. When it doesn't take any originality to see something, then it will happen. I'll bet his name had already come up and been rejected. They would not have accepted James Spader before the success of *sex, lies, and videotape*. All of a sudden he's kosher to everybody. I was frozen out of the making of this movie, which was particularly devastating because I'd decided after all the ups and downs I'd been through that I couldn't really dismiss being a screenwriter until I finally got one made, because I wouldn't even know what that's like. I thought, It's not fair to give up on this because I might really like movies if I ever have one made.

JE: What else would you have done?

TT: I don't know, write a novel; anything. I didn't get that far. I didn't want to give up until I had a movie made. You know, I wouldn't have known anything about being a playwright unless I'd had plays produced. You don't learn anything until something gets made.

JE: You get a sense of what works and what doesn't.

TT: Right. You also need the exposure in order to get more interesting collaborators.

JE: Playing devil's advocate, I would say that many if not all filmmakers bomb from time to time, despite their experience. Haven't they learned what there is to learn about the relationship between the script and the screen?

TT: That's fair. I suppose you do have to learn a new set of rules for every movie. It's not like you ever learn and now you've got it. You hope you make a different set of mistakes from movie to movie. The bigger thing about being shut out of *White Palace* is that I'd been working and working, and I was looking forward to it actually being fun. It's not fun unless it gets made. And unless it gets made, you're never going to feel legitimized. An unproduced script is not publishable, and you can't get a bunch of your actor friends to put it on as an Off-Broadway show. A film script is good for only one thing. Otherwise, it's dead. And in many cases you don't even own it.

JE: All right, so now Spader is aboard, and they're going to get a new screenwriter.

TT: They brought in Alvin Sargent, whom I've never met. As it turned out, he did a terrific job, except for the ending. But that wasn't his fault. That was the producers.

JE: How much of your work did he change?

TT: A lot. It was so interwoven that it's finally hard to separate. The structure was basically as it had been, and some scenes were almost word for word. What he brought was this wonderful humor and earthiness. When I finally saw it at a screening, I went expecting to hate this man's guts. But I came away realizing what a terrific job he'd done. Whatever problems the flow of the movie still had were not, I think, his fault. The ending never worked.

The producers rewrote Alvin's ending and reshot the last scenes before releasing it. In my opinion, the ending of the last script I did worked better than what they ended up shooting. That was the producers trying to be writers. They were fatally influenced by *Pretty Woman,* and they wanted a sweep-her-off-her-feet, fairy tale, romantic ending. Given these two very unlikely lovers in *White Palace,* that kind of ending is inappropriate. They wanted that quick, snappy, romantic, commercial flourish, and they were roundly panned by the critics for it. Even so, when I saw the movie and looked objectively at it, I thought that it really was much better than it had any right to be. Susan Sarandon was wonderful. Spader was good too. It had some very, very credible, unusually adult sexuality—some real passion and honesty and fire. But by then the whole thing had been way overtaken by *The Silence of the Lambs,* which I got because of *White Palace.* It just goes to show that, no matter how dark things get, they may be serving some greater purpose.

JE: Tell me the story behind how you got *The Silence of the Lambs* job.

TT: The author of the novel, Thomas Harris, was an occasional client and a friend of the owners of an art gallery in New York City where my wife was the director. So I had met him socially a couple of times; we'd had dinner, and he knew that I was a fan of his work, that I'd read his first two books. I asked him one night if he was writing another novel and he said yes, as a matter of fact, he was just about finished with one. I expressed some enthusiasm, and that was the end of it. Then, out of the blue, he sent me an advance copy of *The Silence of the Lambs.* I'm not even sure he knew I was a screenwriter; maybe vaguely aware. Clearly, he had no ulterior motive in sending it to me. It's just that he was a friend of my wife's and knew I liked his work.

When I read it, I instantly thought it was a great yarn and recognized that it was going to be a phenomenal movie. I was sure that William Goldman or someone like that was writing it, because the book was about to be published and had been floating around Hollywood for a long time. I would probably have left it at that except that my wife said to find out for sure. "Who knows?"

JE: Smart woman.

TT: She's been taking credit for the entire experience.

JE: The unaffectionate but ambitious husband in *Enchanted April* leans down to his wife and says, "A man could go far with a clever girl like you for a wife."

TT: Sure enough, she kept saying, "Call Arlene [Donovan]," my agent in New York, "and just find out. You never know." So Arlene made a few phone calls, and lo and behold, Orion was negotiating to buy the book but there was no screenwriter. A lot of studios had passed on the book; they just thought it was a slasher movie. Either they hadn't read it or it had bad coverage. Whatever reason, they were passing on it on behalf of the directors in their stables. It was like, "Well, we'll buy it if Brian De Palma wants to do it." "Oh, he doesn't? Then we pass." That sort of thing. So Gene Hackman, who'd done several Orion films and had for years been looking for a project on which to make his directorial debut, said that he liked the book. Orion said that it would buy it for him. They actually bought it for Gene to star in and direct.

JE: He was going to play Hannibal Lecter?

TT: He couldn't decide whether that was going to be too much to take on, given that he'd never directed before. He was wisely cautious. He said, "If I have the nerve I'll do it. Otherwise I'll play the FBI guy, Crawford. If I don't do it, I'd like to get Bobby to play him." And I thought, Bobby De Niro? Bobby Duvall? Bobby Redford. I couldn't ask, because it would have been too uncool. I never did find out.

The next thing that happened, Arlene said that there was no writer yet but that Gene Hackman not only wanted to direct and act in it, but also wanted to write it. Orion told her that Hackman wanted to do the screenplay, so we should wait a month and then call again. They knew how it would turn out. Sure enough, about a month later either Arlene called them or they called her back and said that Hackman had given up on the screenplay. Thirty pages into the book he already had thirty pages of screenplay. He asked to see a writing sample from me. We sent *White Palace,* which could not be more different from *The Silence of the Lambs.* I couldn't imagine how he'd be able to extrapolate anything from *White Palace,* but it was all I had currently, and we could say that it was about to be made. That made it look like something; and, in fact, Hackman liked it and invited me out to Santa Fe to talk. We spent a couple of days together. I'd prepared as if I was about to take my SATs. I mean, I knew that I had to go out there and sell, sell, sell. He didn't know me, the one sample he'd read was not really apt, and I thought that I had to go out there with an entire vision of the movie in my mind. I didn't want to bore him, but I'd taken copious notes. My plan was to wing it, to see when I got there how patient he was. So we had dinner and talked, had breakfast the next morning, more talk. At the end of that time, he seemed satisfied. His friend Bob Sherman, who was to be the producer, drove me out to the airport and said that I'd gotten the job. Bob told me, not Gene. Hackman is inscrutable. He's a brilliant man, a very gifted actor, but he's secretive, almost brooding.

I never quite knew where I stood. He said, "You won't be offended if I ask you to do a treatment, will you?" I said that I'd always planned to write a treatment, because I'd have to do it for myself anyway. I wouldn't know where I was without a scene by scene breakdown of the adaptation.

I went back and did a detailed treatment, expanding on the things we'd talked about. When I do these things, they sometimes end up twenty-five to thirty pages long, a paragraph for each scene. If it's a montage, just a sentence to indicate the gist of each scenelet. Basically, it's a description of every scene in the movie. If it's from the book, then referring to where it is in the book. If it's using parts from two or three chapters in the book, then I give those references. If it's not in the book at all, I would say that it's a new scene.

JE: You did that for *White Palace,* too?

TT: That's how I always approach these, so that when I'm actually writing, I'm working from that as well as from the book. It'll just kind of very roughly indicate where the scene is set, who's in it, what happens, and maybe a few notes about the feeling it needs to convey. It's just a blueprint, and I often throw out huge chunks of it when I'm writing. Still, it makes me feel more secure to have it. What sometimes happens is that I come to realize that scenes in the treatment don't need to be written because they're extraneous.

The next time I met with Gene, in Chicago, I talked for about four or five hours straight, going over this treatment, scene by scene by scene. Occasionally he would interrupt me to ask a question or to make a suggestion. He was very shrewd about the book. He'd done his homework; really knew the novel. He impressed me with how smart he was. Some of his ideas seemed a little odd, and I wasn't sure they would work. But on the whole, I was very impressed by his grasp and how he wanted to do it. And he seemed pleased with what I had come up with. He gave the okay to go to script.

When I went back to New York I began work on the first draft and didn't hear a peep out of him for weeks and weeks. About halfway through the first draft, I got a call from my agent: "Gene has quit the project." She said that either he got cold feet about directing or was afraid the story was too violent and he'd done too many violent movies, or whatever. "And," she said, "it gets worse." "What can be worse?" "Well, Orion hasn't actually signed the book yet." It turns out that their financing was all kind of waiting for their deal with Hackman, and because he was gone they hadn't signed. "Even though they're supposed to pay half a million dollars and buy it," she said, "they haven't. It's negotiated, but there are a few sticking points." So all of a sudden, I've been working on this thing for two and a half months and I might not even get paid. I'd been paid some fraction of my startup payment; not what it should have been, because they were holding us up over the deal with Hackman. It looked like I might not get any money, any movie, any *thing*. This was not long after I'd been replaced on *White Palace,* so needless to say I didn't take the news very well. It was just about the worst twenty-four hours of my life. I can't even describe it.

Then I got a call from Mike Medavoy [head of Orion], whom I will love until my dying day. He'd given me my first job all those years ago on *Empire,* and he was the one at the studio who had to approve me getting *The Silence of the Lambs.* You know, he gave the job to someone who'd never had a screenplay produced, and he was paying half a million for the book on which the screenplay was based. That's a lot of confidence without any real good cause. I thought he was either the dumbest guy in the world or he had truly amazing faith.

JE: Maybe he sensed your passion for the project.

TT: I don't know, but he called me up, which was stunning in itself: I'd never before been called at home by a movie mogul. He said, "You know what's happened with Gene. It's all right. Don't worry, don't panic. Keep writing. We're going to make this work. We're going to finish signing the book rights. We have faith in you, and partly because you're writing this, we're going to keep going. We'll find another director. Don't worry." That made me feel better.

JE: Not terrific?

TT: Well, I didn't think I was completely out of the woods yet. *What if they can't find a director or they hire someone I can't get along with?* But at least I could keep writing. A few weeks later, just before I finished the first draft—and I'm a slow writer, so I probably spent five months or more on it—I got another call from Medavoy saying, "Do you know Jonathan Demme's work?" I said yes. He said, "I'm thinking of offering this to him. What do you think?" He was actually asking me. It probably didn't matter what I said, but the fact that he was asking me stunned me all over again. However, I thought that Jonathan was *a horrible* idea for this. I liked his movies, but he'd never done anything vaguely like this, not that I knew.

JE: How about *Something Wild*?

TT: There were some similar elements of *Something Wild*. But I thought of him as a very funny, quirky director. I'd been thinking that surely they'd get John Badham, or one of those guys. So I told Medavoy, *"That's* an interesting idea," because after all, what else can you say? And he said, "I think maybe he needs this project, and it needs him." I guess he meant that maybe Jonathan had never had anything commercially successful, and certainly he knew that Jonathan would bring a kind of humanity to this, make it more interesting than just another thriller director. And that was Medavoy's genius. Because I don't think that one executive out of ten in Hollywood would have thought of Jonathan Demme for this expensive, by now best-selling thriller.

JE: It may have always been in the script, but this became a movie about character with Demme at the helm. Without him, it may not have.

TT: I hope that it always was that in the script, and actually I finished the first draft before Jonathan was hired. But Jonathan honored that direction. He shared an obsession with me that this movie not try to exploit violence. We didn't want to add to Hollywood's trend toward desensitizing violence. We found that we hit it off immediately. We had lunch and I thought, This guy is so cool. I couldn't believe that I'd met a human being in this business who didn't talk down to me or treat me like a piece of used Kleenex to be thrown away when the script is done. It was just magical from the beginning. I told him about my recent history in Hollywood, how horribly unsatisfying and frustrating it had been. He laughed and said, "Ted, you're just going to have to get used to being successful, because we are going to make this movie." I said, "Oh, sure, I've heard that for the last eight years." He said, "No, you don't understand. We start shooting November seventeenth." This was May. I said, "Are you kidding?" He reassured me and said, "We are absolutely going to make this, and you are absolutely the only writer who will ever work on it. I promise you I will never ask you to live with anything in the movie you don't like. Now let's get to work." I thought I'd gone to heaven. He meant it, and he was as good as his word. That's the way we worked from then on.

JE: How many drafts?

TT: The draft before we met, then two more quick drafts, and a polish. That was it. A blindingly fast process. Even with all the foul-ups, we ended up shooting less than a year after my first meeting with Gene Hackman.

JE: Orion sat on the completed film, didn't they?

TT: Yes, because they didn't want it to compete with *Dances with Wolves,* which they believed was going to be very successful.

JE: When did you get the two wonderful actors, Anthony Hopkins and Jodie Foster?

TT: Once Jonathan came on board and it was greenlighted and a start date was set, then everything began happening at once. While I was rewriting, we were also talking about everything else in the world, including casting. Jonathan is generous with all his collaborators. He treats writers as a resource, as if they might know something about this material they've been living with for a year.

The very first meeting we had he said, "Who do you see playing [FBI agent] Clarice?" I said, "Jodie Foster." He said, "Yeah, she's a good actress. What about Michelle Pfeiffer?" I said, "Well, she's really good, too." What I was thinking, of course, is that, good as she is, she's all wrong for the part—too pretty, in fact distractingly beautiful, and kind of fragile-looking—but you can't say that at your first meeting. Jonathan had just done *Married to the Mob* with her. He always wants to use again the people he just worked with, because he creates such a family feeling. He actually was in negotiation with Michelle Pfeiffer when she dropped out. The upshot is that every time there was a hiccup in the road to getting this movie done—with Hackman, with Pfeiffer, whatever—it always led to something better. It's like that with the rare, charmed moments in your life: Even the accidents are good ones and turn out for the best.

JE: What about Anthony Hopkins?

TT: We talked about him almost immediately. Jonathan based a lot of his feelings for him on *The Elephant Man* [in which Hopkins played the kindly physician]. I liked him because Lecter's language is almost theatrical—very epigrammatic. I couldn't think of a single American actor with whom I'd have been comfortable speaking that language.

JE: Bobby.

TT: Yeah, Bobby could have. Dustin Hoffman could have. But apart from language, I was obsessed with having an actor who was great but not that well known.

JE: To distract from the role.

TT: I didn't want all that baggage. If Hoffman plays him you say, Yeah, he's brilliant, but that's Dustin doing a star turn.

JE: You can't lose yourself in the fantasy because the actor on screen is bigger than the movie.

TT: And sometimes it's worth it, because he's so good. But that's an age-old problem in the movies. I just thought that, for

Lecter, the audience has to believe he's this genius-cannibal-lunatic. How are they going to believe that unless he's played by an actor they're not all that familiar with? Even though Hopkins was one of the best actors in the world, and had done a lot of movies, he really wasn't that well known by American audiences.

We weren't sure who was going to play Crawford, and Jonathan even met with Robert Duvall, but he decided he didn't want to do it.

JE: It's not that crucial a role anyway.

TT: Well, in the script it was a bigger role. There were a lot of scenes between Crawford and Clarice that were edited out, because they were largely expositional. I was afraid that the audience wouldn't be able to follow the case without them, but looking at it, Jonathan decided that you mostly get the stuff even though it's not laid out on a platter.

JE: As you tried to synthesize Thomas Harris's vision from the novel into the script, what was the one thing, if there was one, that you tried to keep in mind?

TT: The key to the adaptation to me, and it's hardly earthshaking, is that it's her movie entirely. The one thing the book does that I did not want to do is go into multiple points of view, sometimes in Lecter's head, sometimes into Crawford's head; it allows itself a little universality in point of view. And to me, it was her movie absolutely. It had to live or die with her. She's our guide through the movie.

JE: She's literally our eyes.

TT: Yes. We should experience these events emotionally and physically through her. That was the plan. She interested me more than Lecter. He's a great, great character. In fact, I think that he's the greatest villain in recent popular fiction. But Lecter had already been in a book and a movie [Michael Mann's *Manhunter,* based on Harris's *Red Dragon*], and very well done at that. So she was the one who really interested me—as well as Jonathan. Jonathan says he's a heavy estrogen director. It's true. He loves women's roles, loves to work with actresses. I think what attracted each of us was the idea of a strong central female character who was nobody's girlfriend and nobody's sidekick, who really would carry this story by herself. So my guiding principle was: If she ain't in the scene, can I lose it altogether?

The risk of that, and I do think the movie suffered from it to some extent, is that if you're so locked into her, the murderer becomes something of a cipher. If we only know what she knows about him—if we're experiencing this world through her eyes, and she doesn't know much about him—then we the audience don't know much about him, either. I even toyed with the idea of never seeing his face, until she sees it at his door. That was too hard to bring off, though, because there's so much that goes on with the kidnapped girl. He interested me less anyway, but he did suffer some for the fact that it was Clarice's movie, and from the exclusivity of the POV. You do have to have some scenes with Lecter where she's not there; that was unavoidable, as with Lecter's escape. So, late in the movie she's missing from the screen for about fifteen minutes, which always worried us: How can you have the leading character out of the action for that long so late in the movie?

JE: Chilton, the psychiatrist who was essentially Lecter's tormentor, the one Lecter sets out to devour at the end of the film, was the one part of the movie that didn't work for me.

TT: In the book, he's older and more out of it. He's a petty bureaucrat, prissy and proud about his turf; sort of a petty sadist to his staff, and certainly toward Lecter.

JE: In the movie, we didn't get any of the real sadism.

TT: It's reduced to a tiny thing by putting on a loud religious television program outside Lecter's cell, and by turning his lights off. It's one of many areas that's richer in the book than in the movie, just as Crawford is richer in the book; he's got a dying wife and more of a life outside the case than we had time for.

JE: That, I didn't miss. Chilton's backstory I did.

TT: He's jealous of Clarice getting access to Lecter, who's his prize possession. He's horny for Clarice. A thoroughly obnoxious guy.

JE: In some ways it seems he's there just for the last joke, when Lecter says, "I'm going to have an old friend for dinner."

TT: No, he's there probably to give Lecter a way of escaping from that prison. If it were not for Chilton's vanity and interference, Lecter would not be able to escape. Just for plot, that's why he's there. In the book, certainly more than the movie, he provides an interesting kind of foil. He is what Lecter would be if Lecter were not so brilliant. He is a psychiatrist himself, but one who doesn't understand anything. He's almost comic relief.

JE: To write Lecter, do you have to be as brilliant as he is?

TT: No, but it is very difficult to make up lines for him. Fortunately, Thomas Harris writes brilliant dialogue. You could do a lot worse than to get an assignment adapting a Tom Harris novel. He really writes good dialogue.

JE: So then some of the dialogue was taken intact from the book?

TT: Oh, yeah, a lot of Lecter's dialogue is intact. Where I had to make up dialogue for Lecter it was difficult, because he has to surprise you all the time, and he never just says what he means. He has to be obscure and yet the audience has to get it. There were also points when Jonathan said, "I don't think he's mean enough. He has to be meaner." You know, it's squirmy in places. I would come home some days from working on Lecter scenes and be real glad that I had a newborn child. It's not like I had nightmares, but he is certainly a difficult character to live with over the long haul of writing a script. His saving grace for the screenwriter is that he's funny. Yes, he may be perverse, and maybe awful, but he is very witty. That kept it interesting.

JE: Are you writing a sequel?

TT: No, but I do know that Thomas Harris is writing another book that has Lecter in it. Whether it should be called a sequel, I can't say. Tom doesn't feel any obligation whatsoever to buy into Hollywood's agenda. He's very secretive about his writing. No one quite knows what he's doing. You just cannot ask him. It's not done. Even when any of us has talked with him, you can bring up almost anything, but not his work.

JE: What did you do to, in essence, make yourself Clarice, so that you could see through her eyes, so that the screenplay could be written through her eyes?

TT: It's easy to put yourself in her shoes, because she doesn't know what's going on, and she's scared. It's easy to be scared of Lecter and, imaginatively, of a scene in which you have to examine a brutally murdered body for the first time. I found it easy to let her be my eyes and ears and heart. I would work on scenes with her and have tears in my eyes because I felt so sad for her. She was so brave and so lonely. I think I also connected to her on a personal level. A big part of what made her tick was that her father had died when she was so young, and she was left alone. I don't want to make too much out of it, but my father died while I was working on this movie. I think I had a kind of identification with her beyond what you would normally expect to have in an adaptation. And she's from the South and I'm from the South. I just felt that I knew her and cared about her very deeply.

JE: That was a moving scene, the one that contained the "silence of the lambs" revelation.

TT: I could never work on that scene or see it in dailies without tears in my eyes. And I don't even know why. Jonathan said to me once, "What does it matter, really, that some lambs got killed? I like lamb chops and so do you. Why should I care about that?" He was playing devil's advocate. He said, "Isn't it going to feel somewhat reductive that we've gone through all of this endless psychological cat and mouse stuff, and peeling away of layers of her psyche, and what we get down to is that she saw some lambs being killed? Why should I care?" I said, "Jonathan, I don't care about the lambs. I care about her. And it matters terribly to her, and that's why I care about it as a member of the audience or as the writer." He said, "All right, I accept that."

JE: It doesn't at all have the sense of anti-climax.

TT: No, it doesn't. I think that's partly because you're watching two of the best actors in the world. And Thomas Harris is so much more than an ordinary thriller writer. Obviously, there was a whole subtextual level that had to do with loss of childhood innocence, loss of the parent, learning about the problem of evil in the world. It's not overstating it to say that there's a Christ symbolism in the lamb and the blood of the lamb. It's working real deep, and Lecter is a kind of lover, kind of father figure, kind of demon.

JE: Do you have a problem with Lecter being on the loose at the end of the film? And making a joke?

TT: I would have ended the film that way no matter what, even if there were no legal possibility of a sequel. It's been suggested that it ended that way just so that we could set up a sequel. Not true.

JE: That's not what I mean. I'm talking about the righteousness or lack of righteousness of having the murderer go unpunished.

TT: But one murderer is punished.

JE: And the other is not.

TT: Which to me is more true to the world as I know it than a sort of traditional Hollywood ending. To end the story in this kind of open way, evil is still out there. You've won a temporary, a partial, victory. But evil is still there. That's what gives the end of the movie its richness. Plus, it's just very creepy to think, *My God, he's out there, what if he's sitting behind me in this theater?* To have Lecter still on the loose lets the movie continue to work in the audience's imagination and to live on in a way that it would not if it had real closure.

JE: It's the ending *White Palace* should have had.

TT: There's almost never been a movie made that couldn't benefit from its ending being a tentative affirmation. Because what else is there, really? Anything more than that feels too pat. If it's less than that, it feels unsatisfying.

JE: You didn't like *It's a Wonderful Life?*

TT: I adore that film. It's one of my favorites. After an early preview of *Silence,* in which the audience looked like we had stolen their lunch—they just sat there, speechless, motionless, either horrified or grossed out, I couldn't tell—I said, "Jonathan, wouldn't it have been nice if all this power and all this craft had been in the service of *It's a Wonderful Life?*" It's almost unsettling to be able to do that to a group of people, to be able to wipe them out so thoroughly. It's terrifying to be able to do that, and you almost wish you had used that power for something totally benevolent.

JE: What do you know now, since you've made this film that swept the Oscars, including one for you, about screenwriting that you didn't know before?

TT: It's hard to put into words. I learned a lot of lessons from Jonathan, about less being more. I learned to have a little more faith that the audience gets it, that they're always smarter than we give them credit for. They're always quicker on the uptake. I saw Jonathan and his editor, Craig McKay, do just amazing things with the first print of this movie. He shot whatever I wrote very faithfully, but when he got in the editing room, he played with it. The editing room is his favorite place, his favorite part of filmmaking, the most creative part. I learned a lot about the process, because I was finally admitted into the practical side of it. I wasn't excluded just because I was a writer. I learned to never ever make fun of producers again. Because what they do, if they're good, is incredibly difficult.

JE: Do you write differently now?

TT: I think I write with more confidence. I certainly try to write with more briskness. I have a problem with being too wordy, and probably explaining too much.

JE: Because you don't give the audience enough credit?

TT: That may be too simple. Maybe it's my theater background, where it's all talk, talk, talk. You have to work a long, long time to find what you can do without. Maybe I have a bit better sense of that. Mostly, it's confidence.

JE: Does that have anything to do with the Oscar?

TT: That was just icing on the cake. By the time the Oscar came along this movie had already been such a wonderful experience. It sounds odd, considering how dark the subject matter was, but this was a fun film to make. People would crack each other up on the set. Everybody had a great time, partly because it was Pittsburgh in February, and you have to keep laughing to keep from crying. People would say they'd never had so much fun. It came from Jonathan.

JE: You've just finished working on "Before and After," from Rosellen Brown's book, and "All the Pretty Horses," from Cormac McCarthy's book. Any fears that you'll become known as the "adaptation king"?

TT: Well, there is that danger, of course. I spend so much time reading submissions that I don't spend much time thinking up things that I might want to do on my own. On the other hand, I guess it helps to have an identity. I probably get two or three offers a day, when I'm available. And I do enjoy doing adaptations. From a business point of view, it helps to identify a marketable skill that you have. The world is not going to run out of good novelists. Plus, there are other reasons for doing adaptations. They get screwed around with less by studios and producers than original scripts—despite my experience on *White Palace*—because everybody is starting from a common basis.

JE: It's already been given the seal of approval by the guys in New York.

TT: Somebody already published this book, so it must have something—at least, that's what they figure. Even if they haven't read it, they assume there must be something to it; there are at least existing stories and characters. I think the vision of the original writer gets monkeyed with less; therefore, an adaptation is more likely to be made than an original script. And I think the majority of Academy Award best pictures have been adaptations. It's not an accident. Also, I hate to buy into the mentality that more writers is better, but in a sense if you're combining two writers' sensibilities, and if they're not fighting each other, you may get a richer vision than just one writer can come up with.

HORTON FOOTE

Horton Foote is in his sixth decade of prolific writing for the stage and screen. He has won Academy Awards for the 1962 adaptation of Harper Lee's novel To Kill a Mockingbird, *and for his 1983 original script* Tender Mercies, *which gave Robert Duvall the role that won him a Best Actor Oscar. Foote is renowned for creating characters who breathe and bleed and sweat—characters whom actors long to play. He is able to turn ordinary people into archetypes.*

Though our conversation was shorter than any other, I found his remarks especially enlightening. His work is about actualizing a vision— having something to say, and saying it. Writing, to him, is a vehicle for both discovering and expressing a philosophy or world view.

He spoke to me by phone from his Texas home.

JOEL ENGEL: What strikes me most about your work is that almost everything, at its spine, has to do with morality. Is that a fair assessment?

HORTON FOOTE: I'm pleased to hear it, though I can't tell you that I sit down to write a moral fable. I really am not, in that sense, a didactic writer or a proselytizer.

JE: What I mean to say is that a moral sense seems to inform your work.

HF: I'm flattered.

JE: So there's nothing intentional about it?

HF: I would fight that impulse if I had that impulse. I think writing should be free-flowing. Naturally, there's structure to it, and you would be a fool to say that whatever you are as a human being or the things you read or see or the kind of theater you like do not in some way inform your work; it's bound to. But I don't ever try to consciously do that.

JE: *To Kill a Mockingbird* came from the Harper Lee novel, so it wasn't an original screenplay. But in your adaptation, the character of Atticus Finch stands in some ways as a bookend to the Robert Duvall character in *Tender Mercies*.

HF: I hadn't thought about it that way, to tell you the truth. They're both men of goodwill. Both are struggling to find order in a very disorderly world.

JE: In that disorder is some nastiness. How do you go about creating it on paper?

HF: You create what you observe, what you see around you. It's not that you're reporting, but you take that, if nothing more than to contrast. It seems to me that grace, whatever that word means to whomever uses it, is a very mysterious thing. I've known people—people I grew up with—who've had terrible things happen and been destroyed by them; and I've known people who haven't been destroyed by them. I guess part of what I'm trying to figure out as a writer is why do some people survive and some not?

JE: All of those elements go into the making of a life.

HF: It's certainly true of Max [in *Tender Mercies*]. There was a period of enormous destruction and darkness and despair.

JE: When did you first write professionally?

HF: 1940. I didn't think I was going to be a writer. It was suggested to me when I was part of an acting company. We were doing improvisation, helping people from different parts of the country understand each other. [Choreographer] Agnes de Mille had come down to do a production and saw some of the improv I did. Afterward, she asked me if I ever thought of writing. "You seem to be in touch with very interesting material," she said. "You should think about it." Well, I wrote a one-act play with the lead role for me; that really was the impulse. It had some success, which was encouraging, so I went back to Texas and wrote a three-act play, again with the lead for myself, then went back to New York. The company produced it, and Brooks Atkinson, who was then the dean of theater critics, was most appreciative and encouraging.

JE: This was Off-Broadway?

HF: Off-Off-Broadway, though we didn't call it that in those days. Anyway, then I began to switch gears. I was a promising young playwright. To be a promising young playwright is a fate worse than death.

JE: What does that mean?

HF: It means that everybody's expecting great things from you. And since I'd had so little experience as a writer, I really had to learn how to write with people watching me.

JE: In the late 1970s, Arthur Miller wrote a television play that starred Richard Benjamin as a young playwright who was suddenly the toast of the town with two hit shows playing simultaneously. His face was on the cover of *Time,* and he was being hailed. But he kept wanting to hang out at the restaurant where, until very recently, he'd been a waiter and an *aspiring* playwright. Everyone had to tell him that he'd graduated.

HF: Mine was a little different than that. I hadn't had that kind of success; mine was only critical. I wasn't a stupid person; I knew I had a lot to learn.

JE: How did you learn it?

HF: I decided to leave New York. First of all, I went through a period of working with dancers; I mentioned de Mille. I was hired to teach acting with Sandy Meisner, who was head of the Neighborhood Playhouse. When he went on the road, I would take over his classes. They commissioned me to do a work, which they did each year, for all the disciplines of the school—dance, speech, acting. And Martha Graham was head of the dance department. She choreographed, and I directed a piece that I wrote. It was a one-act play to which she added movement and music and a score. I was fascinated by how she worked. Then I became very close to a dancer and wrote a ballet for her—a theater piece, really. Then I became friendly with [choreographer-director] Jerome Robbins.

JE: I'm missing the connection between dance and playwrighting.

HF: Great choreographers are like playwrights. Martha didn't use words, but her sense of structure and ability to tell a story were extraordinary.

JE: That's the point where all art forms meet, I guess: telling a story.

HF: I wanted to experiment. So I went to Washington and started a small company there, taught in a school, and they gave me a theater. I was able to bring some actors down from New York. For about three years I did a lot of experimenting, mostly based on trying to find a synthesis between movement and words. After I got it out of my system, I thought, "Well, this is wonderful; I really have learned a lot. But it really isn't for me." So I went back to a much more realistic form and returned to New York with a play called *The Chase*. Meantime, [producer] Fred Coe had me writing some things for television. *The Trip to Bountiful* grew out of a television play.

JE: At the time you started writing for television, were you considered a successful playwright?

HF: That depends on how you define success. Fred had no money to hire stars, so he decided, very wisely, to go for the play; he went for playwrights. Paddy [Chayefsky] and myself and Tad Mosel—we were all playwrights searching for productions.

JE: Live television drama in those early days was essentially composed of plays performed for cameras instead of live audiences. Spartan sets. Intimate interplay.

HF: It was a medium for writers. We had a lot of freedom. Fred encouraged us to do anything we wanted to do. We had a lot of wonderful young actors to work with—New York actors, since this was New York. And young directors. Anyway, that took a lot of my money, but I also did another play my second year there, *Traveling Lady,* with Kim Stanley.

JE: What was it that drove you to the typewriter in those days? What compelled you to write?

HF: The same thing that has always driven me. I just have this need to figure certain things out in myself. I do it in terms of stories and plays. I'm trying to find things out; a sense of discovery.

JE: That's what I meant earlier. Many of your protagonists seem to be trying to make sense of the world and their place in it: *Baby, the Rain Must Fall, Tender Mercies;* even *To Kill a Mockingbird,* which was an adaptation, is ultimately about a young girl coming to understand her relationship to the world and to good and evil around her.

HF: I think that's a fair evaluation. But I can't tell you now, sitting here in this chair, that that's what I begin to write out of; I don't worry about it. I just find something that interests me. It's like putting a puzzle together.

JE: Do you begin with a character or a theme?

HF: It depends. I just finished something that I'm very pleased with. Here's how it happened: While getting ready to give all my archival material to SMU, I came across about twenty pages I'd written in 1974. I read them and wondered why I'd put them aside all these years. I didn't know where it was going to go or what I was going to do with it, but I saw some life there. That's what you look for—life. So, I began working with it.

JE: Would you agree that character defines story? And are you always aware of structure—always building the proper structure—as you write?

HF: I don't think that way. I don't think in terms of structure or character. I simply try to take a journey. The journey is distillation. A lot of it is imaginative. I usually start with a very specific point, either a moral dilemma I've known about, or an incident, or characters who are involved in certain problems; it starts from many sources. Then the whole thing is how to make that into some kind of final sense. Do you know Elizabeth Bishop's poems?

JE: No.

HF: You should read them; they're extraordinary. She has a poem called "The Moose," which is wonderful. I was interested in it because I just got a copy of her letters. In one of the letters she describes the incident from twenty years before that inspired the poem. That's really what you do. I would think that there has to be something going on that we're not even consciously aware of.

JE: So then a writer is someone who can tap that invisible process.

HF: Well, the kind of writers I like.

JE: As opposed to strictly yarn weavers.

HF: Yes.

JE: I feel silly asking this, but is there a technique? Something you can do to find the tap?

HF: I don't think you're in control of that. I think your technique just comes; you can be very objective, can see other work, read plays, think of problems, etc. But when you're creating, you want this thing to take you over—to take *you* over. Then there is always that point when you have to say, "No, this isn't working" or "This is working." So you do get objective, but later.

JE: Is that first draft, as Hemingway said, written in hot blood— and the second draft in ice?

HF: I would think the first draft is when it takes you over. To the later draft or drafts you bring all the experience you've learned through the years. Not to be a crowd pleaser; I don't mean that. But how to refine the work and make it find a real life for that particular piece.

JE: How do you know when you see it?

HF: That's part of it. Sometimes you don't know until ten years after.

JE: So when you picked up those pages after twenty years—

HF: There was life there. That, I can tell you. I can't tell you why I abandoned them twenty years ago. When I read them again, I knew that I wanted to take that journey. You never know until you get into the journey whether it's going to work.

JE: *The Trip to Bountiful* sounds like it could be the title for the way you work as a writer.

HF: That's not a bad one. Listen to a poem Elizabeth Bishop calls "A Question of Travel":

Is it lack of imagination that makes us come
to imagined places, not just stay at home?
Or could Pascal have been not entirely right
about just sitting quietly in one's room?

Continent, city, country, society;
the choice is never wide and never free.
And here, or there . . . No. Should we have stayed at home,
wherever that may be?

So you see, that's the journey. That's the theme in a lot of my work.

JE: Since you said you write to figure things out from your own life, do you think of your life as a journey?

HF: Yes. And I've come right back to where I started. I've never shared [Thomas] Wolfe's dictum that you can't go home again. I've always come back. I live now in the house I grew up in.

JE: Getting back to the work taking you over, what do you do when it's not taking you over? Do you abandon it?

HF: Sometimes you have to. Sometimes it's wisdom to do that. You can't use your will about certain things, I don't think; you just have to keep quiet.

JE: What do you do on days it's not taking you over but you're not ready to abandon it?

HF: When you struggle. Sometimes I read something, sometimes I walk away. When it gets to be depressive, you figure that if you just go play, then it might work. I've been through this so often, I know that eventually something's going to happen. If it doesn't, I know I'd better leave it alone.

HF: When you first began writing, and were presumably a passionate young man, did the writing always come fast and true?

HF: Well, when I was writing at the beginning I had other problems. I had to make a living. I took jobs that allowed me a period of free time in which to work, to write. Fortunately, I've never had writer's block.

JE: My question really is, What was it that enabled you to continue writing when you weren't yet a professional writer and weren't sure whether you'd ever be?

HF: I never doubted that I was a writer. I also had a supportive wife, which is an enormous help.

JE: How did you react to the criticisms of others when you were showing your work around?

HF: They hurt. But you just keep faithful. The main thing for a writer is to find out who you are. Now, that's not going to please everybody. You have to discover what your real talent is—what really interests you as a writer. That's really the thing. Not how popular you can be. But what really is your métier.

JE: How does one find that out?

HF: That's part of the journey. The answer is in the journey. If I could answer that question directly, I'd make millions by putting it in bottles. I don't mean to be mystical about this, but I think certain things can't be defined. There are writers who I know in my mind are wonderful and I respect them, and yet I don't respond to them.

JE: Such as?

HF: Well I don't think that would be fair to tell you that. But there are plenty. And there are writers who aren't too popular whom I admire very much, and have learned from and continue to learn from. It's just a question of finding out what really helps you.

JE: Are all your screenplays originally conceived of as plays?

HF: *Tender Mercies* was not. That's the only one.

JE: Why did it become a screenplay and not a stage play first?

HF: I just thought of it that way.

JE: Can you define that thing that a screenplay is that a play is not.

HF: They're getting to be closer all the time. I think cinema is affecting the theater a great deal. It's common sense, really. There are things you can do in a film that you can't on the stage. For instance, *Trip to Bountiful* was done on television in the early days when they had no money and three sets at most; you never could take the journey. In the film we can take the journey. That's an oversimplification, but that's really how your mind goes. And then the great problem to me with a lot of the films is, too often, they dissipate themselves by treating them like travelogues. They get drunk with that sense of, I can go here, I can go there. There's no real spine to the story.

JE: As a playwright, you really must explain almost everything through dialogue. Not much happens on the stage that isn't talking. But in a screenplay, often the story and characters are advanced without dialogue.

HF: That's one way of doing it. I still think that words are extremely important in film.

JE: But the camera can do things that words can't or take too long to do. Do you need a strong director to point out that this particular scene may need no words?

HF: You make your own evaluation about that. Of course, you listen and if you agree, that's right. You'd be a fool not to agree.

JE: Of course, unlike in the theater, the writer doesn't really have any control over what happens to the screenplay after it leaves his hands.

HF: Well I do.

JE: How?

HF: Different ways. You can go in the back door. On *Tender Mercies,* I was a coproducer. Same with *The Trip to Bountiful.* I also had final say on the cut.

JE: You're in the minority of writers, maybe even unique.

HF: I make great sacrifices to do that. I take much less money in order to get that, because I think it's important. On other films, like *Of Mice and Men,* I didn't have final cut. But I trusted [director and star] Gary Sinise and [star] John Malkovich.

JE: How much can an actor add to what you've written?

HF: If you're smart, you get the best actors you can. I have been enormously blessed by the actors I've had. The kind of actors I like go after the life of the character.

JE: Have you ever beefed up a role or rewritten a screenplay based on discussions with an actor?

HF: Never.

JE: What did Robert Duvall find in Max in *Tender Mercies* that you may not have intended?

HF: He eliminated many things for me. I don't know that I even had any preconceived ideas about how it should have been played.

JE: How can that be? Don't you see it in your mind's eye, your imagination, while writing? Don't you picture the character in a particular way? Isn't that what characterization is?

HF: I was an actor. I would never impose that on an actor. I don't believe in that. Let me give you an example: *Bountiful,* which I've now seen three extraordinary actresses do—Lillian Gish, Geraldine Page, and Ellen Burstyn. You can't find three more different actresses. They're each wonderful in the same part. It's like three virtuoso violinists playing the same concerto. They have to bring what they can to it. You would just be stultifying them if you said, "This is how it has to be done." That's a mistake many writers make. How do they know how the actor sees it?

JE: I just assumed that a writer conceives of a role in a manner.

HF: If they did something that I believed was absolutely wrong, I would certainly scream and holler. But I leave my mind open. How many Hamlets have there been in this world? There are aesthetic Hamlets, athletic Hamlets, gloomy Hamlets, ironic Hamlets, all saying the same words. There are all kinds of visions, ways of seeing it. Shakespeare doesn't have a single stage direction in the whole of his works. Exits and entrances, and alarms and flourishes, and that's about it.

JE: You share with him having been an actor.

HF: Same with Chekhov.

JE: Actors all love to be in works by Shakespeare, Chekhov, and Foote. What do actors like in roles?

HF: You have to watch them, because sometimes they like to sentimentalize it. They think their characters are all good people. Kim Stanley once said to me, "Watch them like a hawk. They so rarely get to play what they think is a good person, they'll sentimentalize it."

JE: These days, I often hear actors relishing getting to play nasty characters, because how often do you get to play someone who's so evil? What's changed?

HF: I don't know if anything's changed. I can just tell you that in my plays they sometimes latch onto what they think are the good parts.

JE: If an actor likes the character and feels the life of the character, do you give him free rein?

HF: As long as he finds the truth of the character.

JE: What does that mean?

HF: That's the search. Your truth is not my truth, certainly. I would never impose my truth on you, and I'd resist your imposing your truth on me. But every artist is searching for a sense of truth. Great actors just instinctively go for the truth of the character.

JE: That's too abstract for me.

HF: How can I tell you? To get at the particulars of that character will lead you to a sense of the truth of the character. It's a
journey that actors have to take. That's why I can't work with
them; it's their journey.

JE: So it's safe to say, given the sense of journey that seems to
permeate your concept of work, you never feel that by, say, page
thirty-one, something has to happen, or by page eighty-three, this
has to happen.

HF: I never know what's going to happen. I may look back later
and realize that it's getting slow here or dull or whatever, and I'll
wonder what I can do to shake it up. Then your imagination has
to get to work.

JE: Is it laziness—your imagination not being engaged—that
accounts for when a script gets dull or slow?

HF: No, I don't think so. I think you can get self-deluded. The
next day you'll wonder why you were so enthusiastic about this.
You'll see that it's flat as a pancake.

CAROLINE
THOMPSON

I interviewed Caroline Thompson a few days after Black Beauty *opened—and a few days before, she presumed, it might drop out of theaters entirely. Since she'd made her directorial debut on the film (and wrote it as well), she was somewhat upset by the news that, despite mostly good to excellent reviews, moviegoers were preoccupied with blockbuster films. Ironically for me, I'd asked Thompson to participate after enjoying the film a few weeks before at a screening. Seeing it reminded me of her other works, which, because I have a young daughter, are all popular around my house.*

The interview took place in the courtyard of her Los Angeles–area home, where she keeps and rides several horses. The courtyard contains a modest rock and foliage garden, the focal points of which are a trickling fountain and an ersatz hedge shaped into a rearing horse—a gift from the set of Edward Scissorhands.

JOEL ENGEL: When did you know you wanted to write?

CAROLINE THOMPSON: Ever since I was a kid. I was going to be either a writer or a veterinarian.

JE: You combined them.

CT: In *Black Beauty*. I wanted to be a horse vet. But I found in high school, when I was an apprentice to a vet, that I certainly didn't have the physical makeup of a horse vet. I couldn't help a breached colt be foaled in the middle of the night all by myself; I'm just too small. And I just always loved words. To me, words always have had something spiritual. They resonate. I studied classics in college [at Amherst]—Greek, mostly—not because I was clever, but because you got to spend an entire year reading five books of Homer; you got to love each word and to imagine where each word came from. I don't know why I had that love. I don't come from a family of word lovers.

Like most writers, I think, I was always a pathological liar. I would make up stories to other kids, teachers, parents, everybody, then wouldn't remember the details of the stories. I'd get busted for them. Either I didn't have such a great memory or was just trying something on, not knowing I was going to get away with it, so I didn't record it.

JE: Do you remember any of these concoctions?

CT: I always used to pretend that I owned a horse. I was really pathological, lying about everything. Maybe that's one reason why I'm relatively good at functioning in this business. This compulsion to make things up is definitely why I became a writer.

JE: Lying and imagination.

CT: There are failures and successes at lying. I was very good at it, until I got busted; and even then I was great at weaseling out of trouble.

JE: When did you get involved in journalism?

CT: I come from a very practical family. Knowing that I wanted to be a writer when I was in high school, my father urged me to look into journalism because it had a paycheck. While I knew it wasn't what I wanted to do, I thought, *Well, why not check it out?* It was during Watergate, an interesting time to look into journalism, and I grew up in Washington, D.C. So during my senior year of high school, I interned at the Washington bureau of the *Los Angeles Times*—because it's a nonunion paper. I also worked there some of the summers during college. What I learned, very quickly, was that journalism didn't really interest me, despite the excitement of the time.

JE: Too much emphasis on fact.

CT: Actually, it's sadder than that. I wasn't interested enough in other people. I was much more interested in the matrix inside myself than I was in any external matrix. I couldn't get excited about trying to make sense of it. I always just felt sorry for reporters, who were so dependent on their sources. The other thing was, I used to argue all the time with my editors about objectivity and subjectivity. The notion of so-called objectivity was always so absurd to me, and they would never fess up to it. The whole enterprise just seemed to me absurd, manipulative, and somewhat evil. They were creating a version of the world that they presented as completely accurate, based on their beliefs and objectivity. It was horseshit. I could never get over that hypocrisy. I think that's what really did it for me.

My dream, my overriding impulse, had always been to write a novel. So about a year after graduating from college, my boyfriend and I looked at the map on our wall. We knew we wanted to stay in America, but didn't know where to live. Both of us had this strange draw to L.A. I remember having come out here when I was eight years old, standing on top of Mulholland Drive and looking down at the Valley on one side, at the city on the other, and saying to my parents that I would live here when I grew up. So we packed up our car and moved out here. I supported myself while I sat down to write a novel as a free-lance book reviewer for the *Los Angeles Times,* and doing occasional, really terrible, celebrity interviews. The novel was called *First Born,* eventually to be published in 1983 by Coward-McCann, a division of Putnam. Writing it was an interesting experience. My first draft was so bad that, after eighteen months of writing it, I read it and threw it away.

JE: What was the subject?

CT: It's the story of an aborted fetus that comes back to find its mom. It's a really angry send-up of growing up in suburbia, and of the compulsion of people to guard their appearances. I've always loved metaphor, because I think it's more powerful than so-called reality.

JE: *Edward Scissorhands.*

CT: Right. And I've always been drawn to stories of outsiders and isolation. *Black Beauty* also fits that. But the one in *First Born* is the strongest.

CT: Interestingly, after I threw it away, I went back to it right away. I rewrote it as an actual gothic novel, which is to say that it took on the form of a diary, the way the gothic novels of the late nineteenth century were often written; they're either in the form of letters or diaries. I found that with the book having the formal qualities of being written as a diary, I was freed up: Within those boundaries I could really use my imagination better than I could trying to write in a meandering, formless form; a novel can be anything. Strangely, I found that intimidating and overwhelming.

JE: You needed a structure, parameters.

CT: Yes. I think that's what eventually made me love writing scripts so much.

The director Penelope Spheeris, who at that time had made *The Decline of Western Civilization,* which I thought was brilliant, wanted to make *First Born* into a movie. That sounded great to me. I was very disillusioned with the publishing business. My whole life, I'd wanted to be in that world. A bunch of things had changed my mind. Just the fact that I couldn't title my own book was a shock to me. Plus, they were so afraid of what it was that they sold it as something it wasn't, a horror novel. Gothic, yes; horror, no. What I hated about publishing was that they were nice to my face and fucked me behind my back. So when Penelope asked me, I thought that at least in the movie business they fuck you to your face. That's much better.

Penelope, who was writing then, wanted to do the adaptation. I said, "Listen, this really interests me." I was lost then. I'm not a very long-term person. I'd had a dream—to publish a novel—and I'd accomplished it. That's really all I'd wanted to do in my life. So at the age of twenty-five or twenty-six, when it came out, I wondered, *Now what?* Also, I was getting a divorce at that time; my life was emptying out. I told Penelope that she could have the book for a dollar if she let me write it with her. We did. We spent six to eight months adapting the novel, and had a wonderful time. She's a great cook. The deal was, I'd bring my computer over to her house, we'd work on the script and she'd cook our lunch. Perfect deal.

After we finished the adaptation, Penelope's agent read it and was so shocked by it, I guess, he asked me if he could represent me. He sent it around, and everybody wanted to meet me. They couldn't believe that a human being would come up with this story, because it was so shocking. Then, when they met me, they couldn't believe that *I* had come up with it, because I seemed so innocent.

JE: How old was the aborted fetus and what shape does he take?

CT: He was aborted at twelve weeks; a quasi-formed human. If I had to describe it in Hollywood terms, I'd say that it was a cross between *Eraserhead* and *E.T.* I was writing it about the time those two came out, and when I went to see them I felt a real kinship, especially *Eraserhead*. I think of it as a perverse autobiography. It was funny and ended up in tragedy. I like things that seem funny and end up tragically.

JE: What happened to it?

CT: We set it up at a couple studios. It got nowhere. But Tim Burton, who'd just made *Pee-wee's Big Adventure,* was also represented at William Morris. They didn't know what the hell do with him; he's such an anomaly. Nor did they know what to do with someone of my sensibilities. They'd ask me if I were interested in writing this or that. None of it appealed.

JE: They could have brought you work that you refused?

CT: I suppose so. There were a few things. But I've never been able to do anything that I either didn't understand or didn't feel deeply. So I couldn't say yes. They encouraged me to come up with stories. I came up with one I really loved, called "Distant Music," again about a freak. It was like *Beauty and the Beast,* a freak and a girl. I sold it to Frank Price at Universal. A very interesting experience. I'm offered this opportunity and said, "Gosh, I'll join." I was asked to come up with stories. I did. I sold one. I got an office on the lot—one I could bring my dogs to. I put a down payment on this house.

JE: All on that one sale?

CT: I was just insane about it. In fact, I'd asked Tim Burton, "Am I insane?" He said, "No, you'll be fine." How would he know? But it was nice to have a friend say that. So I sat down to write that script. Unfortunately, they liked the premise of what I was doing—but wanted something completely different. I tried to please them and was totally miserable and lost, and never understood anymore what I was doing. After that initial understanding, after it got warped by the studio's desire for it, I swore that I would never again put myself in such a position.

JE: Square peg, round hole?

CT: Exactly. Obviously, I'm really flexible, and I like working with people. But if I'm talking *here,* and they're talking *there,* we have to be honest about it and say, "This isn't right." But I wanted to join in, so I did. And suffered greatly for it, even though I started to have material things I'd never had before. That was a good lesson.

JE: When did Tim Burton enter the work picture?

CT: William Morris hadn't known what to do with either of us, so they introduced us to each other. They wondered what each of us was about, decided we were weird—that was always the adjective—and put us together. We got along immediately and became close friends, and wanted to work together. I credit Tim completely with the primary image that became *Edward Scissorhands.* One night at dinner, when we were yapping about what we might do, he told me about this drawing he'd made in high school of this character named Edward Scissorhands. He said that he'd always wanted to make a movie about it but had no idea what the story would be. Immediately, I thought that it was really stupid, but it's so stupid that it's brilliant—dumbly obvious. At that time, having grown up in suburbia [Bethesda, Maryland] and still being obsessed with suburbia, I immediately realized that this was an obvious metaphor for being an outsider. Edward can't even touch anything; he destroys everything he touches. It brought up to me that feeling from childhood of not belonging.

Tim's initial impulse—and since it came from him I was inclined to respect it—was that he wanted to try it first as a musical. At the time, he was having problems during preproduction on *Beetlejuice,* getting so many questions about reality and unreality. He thought that if it was a musical that everyone would accept the unreality of the character in this situation. That sounded fun to me. I came home—immediately knowing what the scenes were, what the characters were. It was scary.

JE: How did you know those things so suddenly and effortlessly?

CT: As I said, the metaphor was so clear to me that the simplicity of finding ways to express that metaphor was immediately obviously clear. I can't explain it.

JE: How about the Dianne Wiest character, the mom?

CT: She's based on my mom, and Alan Arkin was my dad—always saying these enormously trivial things in a ponderous manner.

JE: In that same kind of preternatural calm?

CT: No, that was imagined. Just the trivia being expressed ponderously. Bizarre. Anyway, for whatever reason, I just knew what to do with this story. So I came home and sat down in front of the computer. Having a much stronger background as a prose writer, I just wrote the story out. And wrote lyrics for songs—hilariously silly and, I'm sure, terrible. There was one called "I Can't Handle It." Another called "Everything I Touch Turns to Tatters." Just terrible. But it helped me through from one place to another. I actually just spun through it; wrote a lot of dialogue, too. After just a few days I ended up with seventy-five pages, which I gave to Tim. He said, "This is really great. I don't want to do it as a musical anymore. It works as it is." I was delighted to hear that.

In the meantime, Scott Rudin, then head of production at Fox, was after Tim to do something. He would have made a deal to do the phone book with Tim. Tim wanted creative control, so the deal we made was that Fox would pay us comparatively little up front—though it was still more than I imagined ever making—and after we turned the script in, they'd have a week to say yes or no; if they said yes, we'd be in preproduction within three months.

JE: So Fox was buying the right of first refusal for less than they ordinarily paid, but with the understanding that the script couldn't languish; it had to be made soon.

CT: Yes. It was a great idea. Tim's agent's idea. A good one to remember. I wrote the script very quickly and gave it to Tim, who must have been in the middle of shooting *Beetlejuice* then because I didn't hear from him for four or five months. That was a bit frustrating, knowing that I'd done this script that I'd really loved and hoping that he would, too.

JE: You did love it?

CT: I did. It had come out so easily, it was almost as though I was chasing it. The best things are like that for me, where I'm rushing to keep up with the story; not that I'm inventing the story, but that it's inventing itself.

JE: Do you have a specific process to get to that point?

CT: The way I work when I'm writing is that I get up and into my office by eight-thirty. I write five pages. And when I'm finished with those five pages, I leave. It can take an hour; it can take seven hours. I believe in making the work situation really simple, so you can go in there and work and not worry *about* working. It's such a deep habit that I don't even think about it. I just go in there and do it and leave—and go horseback riding.

JE: You get a first draft in about six weeks?

CT: On *Edward,* it came out much faster than that—four weeks, I think. When Tim finally read it, he loved it, and that was it.

JE: You shot a first draft?

CT: Yes, but we didn't shoot it for years. Tim went to do *Batman* after *Beetlejuice.* I thought, *Shit, he'll never make our movie after* Batman. But, bless his heart, Tim's the real thing; he's an artist and makes what he loves, not what he thinks *they'll* love. In the interim, other people became interested in my work based on that script, which got read a lot. During that time I went to Disney, because I had loved *The Incredible Journey* as a kid, and said that I'd like to write a remake of that. They agreed. And the next thing I knew I was writing that. Eventually, I was taken off it, because I wasn't as cooperative as they wanted me to be. And, eventually, I was brought back on, only to be fired and rehired three more times.

If I love something, the basis of something, I'll try to stand by it and help it be what I think it can be—personality and personal trauma be damned.

JE: Passion.

CT: It's all about the work for me. It's all about surrendering the self to the work.

JE: If you love the work enough—

CT: The rest will happen as it should.

JE: Falling dominoes.

CT: A romantic idea, isn't it? But it's stood me in good stead. The thing is, I'm a very cynical person in my public life. In terms of my life with myself, I'm anything but.

JE: There's such a childlike quality in your work, that to hear you say you're cynical is a surprise.

CT: Only because I'm so romantic, I suppose; I'm always disappointed. That's obviously the root of cynicism.

JE: Joni Mitchell said in a song that all romantics "meet the same fate someday: cynical and drunk and boring someone in some dark café."

CT: I suppose that's true. I always hate falling into a category, but there's a comfort in it. It's funny, people have asked me where this stuff comes from. I wasn't, particularly, an outsider as a kid. If you looked at my life you'd never think that I was a freaky little kid. I didn't have any real problems, as I assume Tim did.

JE: No doubt.

CT: And yet, I carry a lot of those same internal things that he does. Where that comes from in me is that my overriding sensation on the planet is of disproportion, which is to say that I remember so vividly being tiny, sitting in a chair and my feet not touching the floor; or reaching for something on a table and having the table be too high. I just have this nauseating relationship to the proportions of the world: Everything is out of proportion to me—physically, mentally. That's where my own feelings of being an outsider are grounded. For some reason, that overriding sensation informs everything that I do. My stories may not ostensibly connect to the others, but if you look at what I do, every story is about creatures or people whom the world doesn't welcome or for whom the world isn't made, or they can't communicate in the world. They are inevitably in disproportion to the world.

JE: So you mine your childhood, even though it may not have any palpable relationship to your adult life.

CT: And it may not have any ostensible relationship to my childhood. But I am still completely informed by that feeling; that's what seems to drive every piece of work I do. I don't even think of it consciously. I'll somehow find myself in the middle of something and say, "Wow, this is the same thing again."

JE: It's thematic.

CT: It fits into why I wasn't interested in journalism. People would say in these grave voices, "Well, you've got to go research your stories." It never occurs to me to do that. I just write out of this feeling. That's all I work out of.

JE: How do you match that feeling to a new imaginative world each time?

CT: Sometimes I do it better than others. I really don't think about it. And I don't try to pin it down. Well, here's one example: In college and after, I had this magnificent dog who was the most alive creature I've ever met. She seemed more aware of what was going on around her than anyone else in the room; and more sensitive and more understanding, more sympathetic, but more hurt by it. It was really from my feelings for her that I drew the character of Edward Scissorhands—this kind of sweetness that wasn't prepared for the horrors of what was going to hit him.

In some sense, Black Beauty is the same character. Anna Sewell wrote such a wonderful book, but I sort of nudged the character to be more like the innocent. What happens in an adaptation is that I get into a dialogue with the work I'm adapting. One thing I really want to get back to is the original work that I haven't done in four years. Even *The Nightmare Before Christmas* was an odd enterprise, because I wasn't the first writer hired on it. Tim had written a treatment for it ten or fifteen years ago, so that the trajectory was clear: The king of Halloween wants to take over Christmas but fucks it up. And Danny Elfman had already written all the songs. They had built this entire animation facility in San Francisco. But gazillions of dollars and emotions into this, they still didn't have a script. In fact, the screenwriter turned in the script while they were actually in production on one of the songs. Talk about pathological liars. What he did was, he took all of Danny's lyrics and reformatted them to look like dialogue, and turned that in as a script, hoping against hope and I don't know what. It was ludicrous.

It was summer, they were in production on one of the songs— and Danny's songs, ten of them, were extremely narrative—but no script. What do you do? Finally, Tim called me and asked if I would write something. I was free right then and also was kind of pissed that I hadn't been asked to do it in the first place. I went up to San Francisco to look around their facility. I saw some drawings of additional characters and didn't like the way the character of the girl was created. I don't know what gave me the confidence to do this, but I said, "Look, I'll be back in ten days."

JE: With a script?

CT: Yes. I only needed to have fifty pages or less. It was a seventy-minute movie, and there were so many songs.

JE: What sparked or synthesized while you were there?

CT: I saw that there was a big gap, that the story of the girl character and her dilemma could be something; but they'd given her nothing to do. As awkward as it became, which is to say that Jack's story is told in songs and hers is told in narrative form, I was pleased to see a hole and then fill that hole. Tim was relieved and delighted. They took it into production and that was that. Needless to say, if we'd had more time we could have made the balance between them much more rich.

JE: What happened and how in those ten days?

CT: I just wrote the story of Sally and the scientist. It seemed clear that Jack had these things he wanted, and she didn't have anything she wanted or anything in her way to what she wanted. That was a story I understood, wanting to get free of a circumstance.

JE: By "nothing in the way," do you mean no complications?

CT: Right. No complications. The character of the evil scientist was my contribution to the story. Without it she had no past from which to move forward. When I went up there, I saw Sally, who is sewn up. Immediately, I had two images; they just floated into my head. One was of her throwing herself out the window and completely dismembering and sewing herself back together again. The second image was with the Oogie Boogie character: She's impelled to go help Jack, so she's impelled to go free Santa Claus. Because she can take herself apart, she leaves her leg in the door-way, then can use her hands separately.

Those two things floated straight into my mind right away, just like that.

JE: That's a wonderful facility.

CT: Well, if stuff like that didn't happen, believe me, I'd be doing something else altogether. Obviously, you can't make yourself have ideas. You either have them or you don't.

After those two images floated in, I saw a drawing, on a com-pletely different board of miscellaneous characters they weren't using, of this guy with his head open and his brains exposed. He was sitting in a wheelchair, scratching his brains. I loved that image. Automatically, it made sense to me to make him Sally's creator, and he wants to possess her and she wants to get away. It happened in a snap, so when I said I'd be back in ten days, I had those three things in my head.

So far, when people have asked what I'm planning, I've been able to get away with saying "I don't know, but let me give what-ever's in my mind a shot—I'll be back real fast, so you'll see." I hope I can continue to do that. The joy for me in working with Tim is that he never asks what I'm going to do. He knows I hate to talk about it as much as he hates to talk about it, because I think it denudes things. When you start to describe it with your mouth, you either get through it so far that you don't need to write it ever—it's too boring; or, it's so false because inventing verbally has nothing to do with writing.

JE: Do you ever talk it out with anyone?

CT: I don't like to, no. You know how, in school, you had to write an outline and then an essay from that outline? I couldn't do that. I would always write the essay first and then the outline off the essay. My mind isn't logical; it follows a different path. I don't even know what you'd call it.

JE: Nonlinear, that's for sure.

CT: Right. It follows an instinctive path that you can't delineate.

JE: It's a gift.

CT: I guess. But, believe me, for a long time it felt like a great burden that I couldn't think the way other people thought.

JE: When you go to your office, do you ever lay down on a couch and space out and think?

CT: No. I just sit down and put my hands on the keyboard.

JE: No note-taking in advance?

CT: Sometimes if I think of something coming up, I'll quickly scribble it down. But that's rare. If you don't sit down and ground yourself to it, it's never going to happen. I just go in there every day, sit down, and do it.

JE: Are there periods when you sit there, just contemplating?

CT: Not really.

JE: It's just constant productivity.

CT: Pretty much. I once read something Hemingway said: "Don't leave the desk until you know where you're going tomorrow." So as I'm writing my five pages, I'm always thinking about where I'm going, where I'm going, where I'm going. I do have a sense of where I'm going. I don't leave that room in a panic over where I'm going tomorrow. I also find that I work out an awful lot in my sleep. I love to sleep. I work on my work while I'm sleeping.

JE: How do you know that sleeping should get the credit, and not just the hours away from the project?

CT: Because it's too regular. When I leave the office, I know *what* I'm going to do the next day. I don't know *how*. But when I wake up, I know how. Is that scientific? No. But, to me, that means I've worked on it in my sleep. Very often when I used to get stuck—I don't do this much anymore—I'd take a nap and be somewhat unstuck.

JE: When you walk away from those pages every day, do you just consign the work to an unused compartment in the brain, not to be accessed consciously until the next workday begins?

CT: As a writer, yes. I've always been able to put it away and go horseback riding and not panic about it or obsess about it, have my evening, go to sleep thinking about the work, then get up and work the next day. What startled me about directing [*Black*

Beauty] is that I was obsessed by it twenty-four hours a day. The most frightening thing was, I'd shoot the movie during the day and dream about shooting it at night. Sometimes I couldn't remember what we'd actually shot and what I'd dreamed we'd shot. I'd have to ask my first assistant director.

JE: After directing a film, Milos Forman waits until he's bored to tears before going back to work.

CT: For the first time in years, I'm taking a breather. I've been working really hard the last five or six years and haven't had a chance to just sit back and see what's inside of there; it's time to do that.

JE: A sabbatical.

CT: A breather. I know some people who, the more they put out the more they have to put out. Other people, like me, put out and put out and put out, then feel exhausted and have to fill it up again. I have emptied out so much that I just have to let what's in there show itself to me again.

JE: What is it that empties?

CT: I think of it as physical, though of course it's not. I think of it as coming from the solar plexus, but that's just a metaphor. I've always been a voracious reader, and for the past five or six years, I haven't had a chance to go to that source of myself in a passionate way. I just want to go to read books and watch movies and daydream again. I haven't had the space in which to daydream. Daydreaming is key. Maybe nothing will happen; maybe something will happen. I just need a little unpressured time. I actually have a couple of scripts in a drawer that I want to go back to. I want to see what's there. I don't even remember at this point.

JE: You may find just a page or two that sparks something else.

CT: Or, I may find that they're perfectly fine. I don't even want to know yet. At this point, I really need to go, in some sense, to my own bottom—let myself just fall there and come up from there. Actually, I did do that in 1984, after working hard. I let myself just go there, found that I had plenty, and came back with lots of energy—as opposed to driving myself with willpower all the time, which is my other resource.

JE: Sheer discipline?

CT: Yes. Sheer stubbornness and sheer willfulness. I have those in spades, and they keep me going through some things, but it's not where I like to work from.

JE: What was the story behind *Addams Family*?

CT: That was another lesson for me. *Edward Scissorhands* was in preproduction. Scott Rudin, who was by then an independent producer, approached me about doing an adaptation of *The Addams Family*. I reacted like he was crazy, like, "Are you kidding? Why would I ever want to write a big, commercial, stupid movie like that?" Well, saying that to someone like Scott Rudin, he only gets more excited about you. He kept after me. I said that I loved Charles Addams's drawings, but that I didn't want to make some campy television series movie out of them. He said, "No, no, no. You can do what you want. You're the only writer for it." I'd said that I didn't want to make a big studio movie; I didn't know how to do that. I'd also been honest and said I didn't think I could do it, that I wasn't capable. Meanwhile, Larry Wilson, who had written *Beetlejuice,* was actively pursuing the gig. Scott woke up one day and got into his mind that he should introduce us, that writing comedy is better with two people, because if both of you think it's funny then it probably is.

JE: Sounds theoretically true.

CT: It stands to reason, anyhow. So he asked me if I would come in and meet this guy. To be honest, I didn't know what I wanted to do at that moment. Nothing else was being offered to me, because *Edward Scissorhands* hadn't been made yet. I felt so happy with *Edward,* I'd really expressed myself for the moment; there was nothing in there dying to get out. My agent kept saying that I should see what it was like. So I agreed to meet Larry. We immediately liked each other. He's very funny, very charming. So, little by little, I got this job. Backing into it. And I began to think it would be interesting to see what a major studio commercial release would be like, despite how little I really wanted to do it. But the closer we got to production, the more panicked everything got, the more bland the script got, the closer we got to being fired, and eventually we did get fired.

JE: I guess the lesson is that some people have the temperament to be guns for hire. They can go in there, take the assignment if they choose to accept it, and suck it up. And you're not one of them.

CT: No.

JE: But even if you're not writing huge, commercial studio releases, you essentially still have to deal with the same people.

CT: The thing that makes me crack up about people I've met in this business, and by and large I'm talking about agents and executives, is that they don't live their own lives. For instance, they'll go home on December 18, and someone will have decorated their house for Christmas while they were at work. Or, my favorite is this one executive I had a meeting with who will remain unnamed. He said, "I'm so excited today." I asked why. He said, "Well, when I get home my house is going to be completely different. When I left this morning it was Southwest. When I get home it's going to be Country French. I can't wait." I asked if he'd picked any of the furnishings. He said, "Oh God, no."

The same guy, on another occasion, said, "You know, I really like this girl I'm with now. But we're having problems. She's accused me of not being flexible. I was thinking about it the other day, while I was in my kitchen. I opened up my beverage refrigerator and looked inside. I saw nothing but Diet Coke. I thought, 'You know, maybe she's got a point. I like a lot more soft drinks than Diet Coke. I like Sprite. I like 7-Up. I like root beer. I like Dr Pepper.' So, you know what I did? I restocked the thing, and I feel so much better now."

JE: Would you ever use an incident like that in your work—just extract something from real life and drop it into a script?

CT: I've never done it. When I said I based the characters of Peg and Bill in *Edward Scissorhands* on my parents, that was true. I based the *characters* on them, not the incidents. Attitude and perspective. My mother was always bringing people into the house. So when I'm sitting there thinking that this woman Peg meets a strange person—how could she possibly get him home?—it was easy to imagine that she just brings him home because that's the kind of person my mother is.

JE: Were you happy with the way *The Secret Garden* turned out?

CT: It was an interesting experience. It was one of the few times that the text was shot as written, meaning that the English [the film was shot in England] respect the text so much more than Americans do. They didn't play with the lines at all. My only problem was with production design. I felt that the garden should have been more like this garden here—more fathomable. Maybe it's that way for me because I love boundaries, but to me, that metaphor is all about freedom inside boundaries and being able to come alive inside boundaries. As seen in the film, the garden had no ostensible boundaries. It was limitless.

JE: Eden.

CT: I thought it undercut the metaphor, because the metaphor is a sexual metaphor—developing your box. That was my emotional problem with the film. It ties into why I went into screenwriting—besides being kind of confused and disappointed in the world of publishing: I fell in love with the formal aspects of it. It's got specific boundaries. Even though I never took a screenwriting course, the rhythms of film are very deeply in me from having watched tons of movies all through life. I found that, given those boundaries, my imagination could come alive. Whereas with fiction writing, where there are no boundaries, I was so overwhelmed by the infinite possibilities that my mind would shut down more.

JE: Screenwriting is about problem solving: having this space to solve that problem. A novel is creating the world in six days.

CT: My mind shuts down at infinity. I panic. I find I come alive within the boundaries of the screenplay. What I do when I'm writing a scene is ask: What is the feeling? What's it about? What's the purpose? What does it feel like? What does it feel like? What does it feel like?

JE: How do you know when you've gotten it right?

CT: It just feels right.

JE: Do you keep rules in mind as you write—tension and drama and conflict?

CT: Not, per se, as rules. I don't approach anything, ever, intellectually. If it feels right, it feels right. If it doesn't, it doesn't. I don't know how else to describe it. The hardest thing for me as a director [on *Black Beauty*] was that I couldn't walk away after my requisite six or so hours. I had to keep alive for eighteen hours a day, seven days a week, for ten weeks. There were times when my own instincts would be too tired to speak to me. I would have to go and sit by myself and just relax; let them come back.

JE: How did you learn the screenplay form?

CT: One reason Tim wanted to work with me is that I wasn't stuck with all these rules, like, "The first act turns on page blah-blah." On the other hand, I did have instincts for the form—internalized. A prose writer learns to write by reading books; a screenwriter learns by watching movies. You don't learn by being told, "Here are the rules. Go home and make something up that fits them." The nice thing about rules is that they're there to be broken. That's why I love screenwriting. There they are; there are the boundaries. What can you do within those boundaries that messes up their hair? What can I do to play with it? It's an internal feeling, not something somebody told me. I hear it in my head. I feel it inside. I see it in my mind. It either works or doesn't work—for me.

MICHAEL MANN

I'd interviewed Michael Mann in 1992 for a New York Times *story on the historical research he'd done for* The Last of the Mohicans. *Even then we strayed into the subject of storytelling through words and pictures—screenwriting—when I expressed my sense of appreciation and wonder at the way he'd told so much without impeding the narrative.*

There is some irony to the fact that Mann's greatest fame seems to have come from his creation of the landmark television series Miami Vice *(he later did* Crime Story *as well). Television is known as a talky medium, and yet I consider Mann to be masterful at telling his stories without extraneous dialogue.*

We met one afternoon in his Los Angeles offices.

JOEL ENGEL: What's the best screenplay you've written?

MICHAEL MANN: Two that come to mind right away are *Thief* and "Red Dragon," which was released as *Manhunter.* I'm working on something that I like a lot. But since it's not done, I can't include it.

JE: Your next movie?

MM: No, now I'm trying to cast a movie about James Dean. If I find a cast I like, I'll make the picture. It doesn't have to be an exact match, but you can't put somebody in the role who's observably not James Dean. A guy who's six-four, two hundred and fifty pounds—John Goodman is not James Dean. Other than that, it really gets down to acting skills. The screenplay, written by Israel Horovitz, is about acting. It's about making acting as observable a challenge as climbing Mount Everest or guarding Michael Jordan.

JE: Why is *Manhunter* a better screenplay than *Mohicans*?

MM: *Mohicans* is an excellent screenplay, but you asked me about ones that I wrote. At least a half to two-thirds of the plot—not the story, not the characters—comes from Philip Dunne's 1936 screenplay. That's why I made sure he got credit. When he wrote that it was before the Writers Guild. So the studio was under no obligation to give him credit. He was a great writer, and it's a wonderful screenplay; it reads like it was written maybe two or three years ago. There's a huge jump between James Fenimore Cooper's novel and Dunne's screenplay. He made a major contribution regarding how to deal with the material. The novel was not a terribly good book. It's not *Moby Dick*, not a classic. Hawkeye is not anything like the Hawkeye that I imagined or Dunne imagined. So that's why I answered *Manhunter*, because there's nothing in that screenplay that I didn't do.

JE: *Mohicans*, I think, is an excellent screenplay; it's a real *screenplay*. There's so much that advances the story and our knowledge of the characters without having to take ten minutes to tell us what you're telling us. There are no dead moments, no sense that there's too much exposition.

MM: That's the trick: to encode the education and the orientation into a different period. Not only is it a different period, the screenplay also had the job of disabusing you of what you thought the eighteenth century was, because it was not that. The screenplay had a lot to do without going sideways into horrible exposition.

JE: You write screenplays that can tell a lot without extra pages of expository dialogue.

MM: I write cinema.

JE: But even the television you write is written cinematically. An economy of words.

MM: It's a very conscious decision. I'm writing a screenplay that's a blueprint for a motion picture that I'm going to direct. And imagining the cinematic experience completely is a requirement—part and parcel of the writing task. Consequently, since I load that on myself, it will cause me to invent solutions to certain problems, *Mohicans* being a case in point: How am I going to express the fact that the American Indians in 1757 were commercially, militarily, and culturally equivalent, if not a dominant force, to the settlers in upstate New York and Pennsylvania; they weren't this minority that was on its way to being disenfranchised. I didn't have time to footnote the motion picture: "Ladies and gentlemen, for your information, the leadership of the Mohawks had been to Europe; the Mohawks dominated sixty-five percent of the world's fur trade; and the only reason the Europeans were at all interested in North America was because of one commodity—fur."

I looked for ways to do that without footnotes. The solution, in this case, tended to be visual. The posture. The dress.

JE: It seems more often than not that it's visual.

MM: Not always. I very consciously choose whether I'm going to reveal something in dialogue or encode it in visual information. For example, I chose to encode visually the fact that the French had a more successful foreign policy with the American Indians than the British. I did it by having a variety of five different looks for the Indians who were allied to the French. If you take somebody aside who's seen the picture and say, "Did you get the sense that there were all different kinds of Indians associated with the French but only one kind associated with the English?" they'll say, "Yeah." You get a feeling about the French, that they had a better foreign policy. The research that went into coming to the conclusion can't possibly be fit into the screenplay. But one of the screenplay's objectives is to convey that information, because of the French versus English conflict, one of five conflicts depicted in the film.

JE: When you direct, how closely do your screenplays resemble the finished product?

MM: If you read one of the screenplays and then looked at the picture—*Manhunter, Thief,* and *Mohicans*—there's very little that's not described on paper. That's for two reasons: One, I've figured it out ahead of time; and, two, as things change during preproduction, I usually update the screenplay. But the writing process is really how I prepare myself for directing. The orientation, the fragile nature of Graham's psyche, is set out in the beginning of *Manhunter* in dialogue.

JE: It happens very fast.

MM: That's right, because the staging of the scene supports the dialogue. I usually ask myself in a given scene, What's the critical path? How am I making the story point here? Physical action or visual sensibility or dialogue? If it's dialogue, is it conflict? Is conflict expressed in dialogue? And sometimes I'll choose different modalities to deliver that scene's story point. In the opening scene of *Manhunter,* it is in the dialogue between Graham and Crawford. It's very strange dialogue. It's as if you've dropped out of an airplane and accidentally dropped onto this beach and entered, midconversation, between two guys talking about you don't know what. Very strange dialogue.

JE: That's my point. It's expository without seeming to be.

MM: Drop you right into the middle. I want people to get the feeling that they're being dropped right into the middle of a rapidly flowing stream. They didn't tiptoe in from the bank; they're just—boom!—in it. The stream's moving. That's a very conscious way that I want us to enter. But sometimes I will come in with a beginning, middle, and end.

JE: The structure of your screenplays appears to have less fat. We come in at the last possible moment and exit at the first possible moment.

MM: Not always. Think of Hawkeye and Cora in *Mohicans.* They embrace, kiss; stay there and dwell on them. Then it ends, and then there's a coda to it.

I wouldn't agree that the stuff I write tends to go from essence to essence to essence. I try to be conscious about the rhythms of storytelling, which means that in a film's component scenes I'm either going from essence to essence for a reason, or I'm doing an incremental lead-in, or I'm entering midscene and then giving you an exit to set up a pattern. Sometimes I'll enter midscene, give you an exit, midscene, exit, midscene, exit.

JE: How do you access the storytelling rhythm?

MM: It's artistic function. It's not intuitive. It's a function of what I'm driving toward, which is the act end. I'm working backwards from the end of act two, for example. I've got fourteen or fifteen scenes in act two; I'm telling the story of act two. As I'm driving toward that objective, I may want the illusion that things are calm, because when danger enters it's going to be a shock and a surprise. Therefore, I don't want anything that the audience already knows are suspense-generating devices. They see forty-four hours of story per week [on television]. They don't know it consciously, unless they're students of it, but they really understand storytelling; they have all kinds of archetypal plotting and plot mechanisms already in their brain. That's their environment. You can't ignore it, so you have to deal with it. Sometimes you'll use it by leading an audience into a clichéd plot development to lead them into an expectation of danger coming from over here—set them up. Then you bring in something unexpected that completely violates their expectations.

I ask myself these questions: Am I generating suspense? And what kind of suspense? If you're generating suspense, you're informing an audience that there's danger in this environment. Where's the danger going to come from? Is it going to come from the darkness around the corner? As the writer, you have to ask yourself those questions. To me, the subject of *Manhunter* is terribly frightening. It's true murder, true homicide; it's not cheap shots of a young girl walking past a dark wall where you leave a lot of space behind her head—you know, profile shot, she's walking right to left, you put her in the left side of the frame, leave all this space behind her head for something to enter, and add in scary music. That is not how I wanted to make *Manhunter*. I didn't think of it that way and didn't want to shoot it that way. Actually, there is one episode in the film when I did fall into horror-movie genre, when Molly is awakened in the middle of the night. But that was to set you up for something bad happening. It turns out to be a bunch of cops at the door. I did exactly what I just said, I had that eerie fish tank—aquarium—in the foreground throwing strange colors up on the ceiling. She walks in left to right, a lot of space behind her head, scary music playing. She goes to open the door, we don't want her to open the door; cut to the door handle and her hand comes in. I set you up for there being nothing there. When real homicidal, psychopathic horror is going to come at people, it's going to be a shock, a surprise, like the sudden abduction. Knock you out of your socks.

JE: Are you a good verbal storyteller, and, if so, were you always?

MM: I'm not. Only under very special circumstances can I do that, and I have to really work at it by preparing a presentation. If I'm completely comfortable, then I can just fall into it.

JE: Were you a gifted writer as a kid?

MM: Not particularly.

JE: Were you noted for your imagination?

MM: I had an exceptionally good one.

JE: When did you know you had it in you to be a writer?

MM: I never did. After I went to film school and tried to work in films, I thought that movies suffered from the tyranny of writing, that there was too much of it, too many words. I started writing as a necessity, because I couldn't get a gig directing when I first came out here. The early work I did was in Europe, which didn't translate here. So I started writing in the hope of putting together a screenplay that people would want to make, and I could impose myself as the director: "You're only going to make this if I direct it."

My first script was terrible; maybe it had a couple of interesting bits of dialogue. The rest was horrendous. I was lucky, though. I had a mentor, a television writer named Bob Lewin. He did this thing that happens among writers out here. You're an established writer and you meet a guy who's got a lot of talent. You see that he's making mistakes you made back when. He's struggling to walk through a wall, so you show him where the door is. "Walk right through." He really helped me out—taught me the basics of structure. I couldn't figure out how to think about story. I had all these great scenes in my head, and a real ear for dialogue. I thought I knew of exciting ways to shoot things. It's not that I didn't know story, it's that I didn't know how to think about it. There was no program in my brain to structure thoughts so that I could arrive at a story.

JE: Is there a way to be more specific about that?

MM: No. The more specific you get the more meaningless it gets. All right, let me try an example: A story about a guy who's been a bootlegger and a gunman who's retiring to a rural part of the Midwest. There were some political conflicts in this area; an interesting alignment of forces between the KKK and mine owners on one side, and organized labor, immigrants, and bootleggers on the other. This guy found himself caught in the middle, became a reluctant gunfighter, and killed a man who was the leader of the Klan in his region. He himself was wounded and died in the skirmish. True history. Now, go make that into a story.

Well, how? Where do I start? If you do it the way I just told you, it's like any number of bad screenplays. This is a linear biopic: this happened, that happened, this happened, that happened.

That's not a story. A story is, he dies. We don't want to do a linear biopic, so let's have an investigation. In the process of investigation with multiple detectives, I can break down into its component parts the true history of Hearst—call him "Kane"—and I can arrange the sequence of all these encounters without regard to chronology. I don't have to move through time in a linear fashion. I can cut to either investigator investigating whatever aspect of his life I want to reveal. I can go present, I can go three weeks ago, twenty-six years ago, back to four years ago; put it in any fashion I want. I've liberated myself from the tyranny of chronology by inventing the narrative. How do I want to tell the story? What's the end? What's the act-three curtain? What's the act-two curtain? What's the act-one curtain? How should I arrange it? All of that is the art of constructing a narrative. But when I began I didn't have the most rudimentary tools to know how to discipline my mind to think about a program. A good analogy is a computer. You put a program in, say, WordPerfect. You can type whatever you want, and it'll sort according to its built-in programming. A writer needs a program, or a number of programs, in order to comprehend a story.

This presumes, by the way, that you've got a good idea. How to tell it is the question. I got a real basic education in that, for which I will be ever grateful, from Bob Lewin. He was very generous, not just to me, but to others as well. During the 1988 Writers Guild strike, when I was doing television [*Crime Story*], a number of us were in a room together. We were all executive producers, running television shows, but our sympathies and support were with the writers. Steven Bochco was there, Stephen Cannell, a number of others as well. We began talking about how we got started and all, and every single guy could remember who'd acted as his mentor. Every single one. Some guy to say, "Here, kid, here's how it's done. You got some good dialogue here, this scene stinks, here's how to fix it. I know you think this is brilliant but it's shit." That kind of thing.

I also had a second round of mentoring or tutoring from a guy named Liam O'Brien, who was a hell of a playwright; wrote *Trapeze* and wrote *Police Story,* which in the '70s was the premier piece of writing on television—the *N.Y.P.D. Blue* of its day. Liam ran it with Ed Waters. It was the show to write for. Joe Wambaugh was still involved as executive producer. That was a real collegiate kind of atmosphere.

JE: What did Liam add to your body of knowledge about writing?

MM: How hard you have to be on yourself, from a critical perspective. When to spot indulgences. "Yeah, you think this is marvelous? You're deluded." When you're writing something and you get that little glow—the second you start imagining the accolades—you've just at that moment had it. You cease to be in a channel. You've actually blown your concentration, and you don't know it yet. Somebody once said to me that, in order to do great, great work, there are two things you don't want ever to receive: someone saying you can't do it, and accolades. You have to maintain a purity of perspective and motivation.

The other thing that Liam said better than anyone, though people have been saying this for centuries, is that drama is conflict. That fit with my bent at the time, which was to see dialectics anyway. I view a lot of phenomena in that way.

JE: A good example of that, ironically, is in the musical *Oklahoma.* The hired hand character played by Rod Steiger in the film is there only and entirely as a catalyst for conflict; he's the engine that drove the train.

MM: Musicals and comedies sometimes have admirably precise story construction. Good situation comedy has tremendous construction. You see it in Billy Wilder and I. A. L. Diamond. Terrific stuff. Brilliant.

One of the things I got from Liam was a great articulation of how and why and all the manifest ways in which drama is conflict. The moment in which one reminds oneself of this is when the middle of act two is suddenly too large, and all the energy goes away, and you thought it was working when you wrote it, then you read it the next morning and it's Sominex. What's wrong? When I ask myself what's wrong, I then look for where the conflict ought to be. What happened to the conflict?

By the way, this comes up in directing actors, too. I'll tell you what Elia Kazan said: "What's the guy want?" Kazan thinks he's summing up his entire approach to directing actors by making that statement. That's like saying, "Picasso has a brush stroke." It doesn't mean that you don't have to study hard and train to be good because all you have to do is think about what the guy wants, what his motivation is. You could reduce it to that understanding only by taking into account the complexity of his films. When he says, "What does the guy want?" he means, when you're talking to an actor, you may say, "She's a waitress, she came to your table to bring coffee and is ignoring another table. What does she want from you?" That's the director talking. That's something to put into an actor's head. You can say to the actress, "This is your station, you've got eight tables you're working, but this guy's looked at you three times already and you're curious. He wants something. What? You'd better bring his coffee first, because you have to find out what he wants." That's a way of thinking about two characters colliding in a scene in which something is going to happen. You're setting up something.

JE: Does something that goes bump in act one have to crash in act three?

MM: Not necessarily. There are no rules. That's rule one. It's context. Because the whole of a screenplay, the whole of a motion picture, if it works, is a consensual dream. It's a relativistic universe that you create. It's a good idea, when you're creating that universe, to invent some consistent laws by which it operates; and to be cognizant of the fact that this motion picture is going to move through time, approximately two hours of it. There are certain rhythms by which we perceive a flow of events and a story. So it's a fairly good idea to have four acts or three acts. But it's relative in the sense that you establish what the expectation is.

JE: How long will the audience allow you to create the rules of the universe and set up the expectation? What's your window of opportunity?

MM: I have a completely unscientific theory that you can mesmerize an audience with things other than content and its development for about seven minutes. The most staggering, explosive cinematics get you about seven to eight minutes of attention; that's it. After that, I don't care what you put up there, they're tuning out, getting passive. Now, I don't recommend that you take all seven or eight minutes.

JE: So they'll forgive anything for that long?

MM: That's poor construction. I don't know about the word "forgive." I wouldn't want to, but if somebody wanted to vamp they could do it for about seven to eight minutes.

JE: So, as a filmgoer, my willing suspension of disbelief after the lights go down lasts about seven or eight minutes?

MM: According to my completely unscientific observation. After that you say, "What the hell is happening?"

JE: So if you violate your cinematic universe's laws of physics sometime after they're established, I'm probably going to hate, or at least resent, the movie.

MM: You'll register the inconsistencies.

JE: When you're writing, do you have to know at the beginning what the ending is?

MM: I do. Because I want to know where I'm going before I know the most interesting and exciting way to get there.

JE: How often do your endings change?

MM: They've never changed. How I execute the ending, however, may change, as it did in *Mohicans*. The ending was to be that these three people—Hawkeye, Cora, and Chingachgook—had persevered; they'd survived this terrible attrition. I wanted to get across this sense of frontier toughness, with them standing before the unexplored mountains in front of them, though not impart the idea that everything was going to be rosy and happy. I wanted a real high point. In fact, the movie drives to this high point. This was by design, in the writing. It begins almost underground, in the sense that you're in the forest, in the trees. Then, through the progress of the movie, you end up with the climactic conflict at high elevation. The ledge on which the fight takes place is the highest locale of the movie.

What I shot for the ending was a big speech by Chingachgook and some dialogue between Hawkeye and Chingachgook and some dialogue between Cora and Hawkeye. But it felt like it was overdone to have the words there, too. I thought that the people just there by themselves, without the speaking, was more effective in the cinema. I don't know if it is on the television screen; it may not be. But in the cinema you get the experience. So I threw away all the dialogue; marvelous speeches. Chingachgook says that this new world is for whites. He says that his people are no more, that it's the end of the frontier, that not just the American Indian but the entire frontier culture is vanishing as well. Chingachgook finishes this long speech—and it was a great performance by Russell Means—with the line "Will there be anything left to show the world that we ever did exist?" That was to be the last moment of the film. After that, the three of them stare out into the wilderness. I guarantee you, there wouldn't have been a dry eye in the house. It was terribly moving and thematically very important; real tough to lose. But I lost it, because there was a sentimentality to it I didn't want. I think the feeling came across without it.

CHARLES FULLER

Charles Fuller won a Pulitzer Prize for his play A Soldier's Play, *on which he based the film* A Soldier's Story *(the screenplay received an Academy Award nomination in 1985). I come back to it probably once a year for the engrossing characters, whose lines were written by a man with a playwright's ear for dialogue.*

Before we began the interview, Fuller had been reading a newspaper account of the deal that paid screenwriter Shane Black four million dollars for a spec screenplay. Soft-spoken and amiable, Fuller said he believed that the movies were on the verge of a renaissance in storytelling; that studio executives would soon be spending more time trying to find great stories instead of "stars" whose presence is often intended to dress up mediocre stories.

The interview took place in his Los Angeles home.

CHARLES FULLER: After *A Soldier's Play* I decided that I would try to do something different, like write movies. Writers ought to be able to do more than one thing; they ought to be able to write whatever they choose to write.

JOEL ENGEL: Who says?

CF: I do. This country is so tied up with specialists: playwrights write plays, screenwriters write movies, essayists write essays. I went to college, I learned English, and I think you ought to be able to do as many things as you think you can do.

JE: You used to write short stories, didn't you?

CF: Ages ago. I wouldn't go back to that. The next thing I'd like to do is write essays. I think I should learn to write essays before I give up the ghost.

JE: Who are your favorite essayists?

CF: My best friend, Larry Neal, who died years ago, was my favorite. He used to write the best essays I ever read. We grew up together and became writers about the same time.

JE: How old were you when you knew you wanted to be a writer?

CF: Fourteen.

JE: What did you read that inspired you to write?

CF: Larry and I decided that it would be a good idea to become writers, if for no other reason than to fill the library with books written by black authors.

JE: How important is it, as a reader, to identify with the race of the author?

CF: All writing that involves human characters is tied up with the race of the writer.

JE: And the gender and the age.

CF: Right. It's all connected. Ernest Hemingway never wrote a story in which the protagonist was a black man—not that I can recall. There's no reason to assume that he should have.

JE: On the other hand, many of his protagonists weren't specifically white.

CF: That's no reason to think that black writers shouldn't write black protagonists, or a Puerto Rican writer a Puerto Rican protagonist, or a woman writer a female protagonist. It's very natural for them to do that. When I began writing, there were very few stories. *Invisible Man*. The work of James Baldwin. Richard Wright. Lorraine Hansberry [*A Raisin in the Sun*] had written a few plays. There had been short-story collections written by blacks. In all, only a handful of material, when you compare to the body of Western literature; it was minuscule. But if anyone was going to describe me, I wanted it be me.

JE: Had you seen yourself described poorly?

CF: When I went to the movies, Mantan Moreland was a star. Stepin Fetchit was a star. Rochester [Eddie Anderson] on Jack Benny's show. We were maids and butlers and porters. And that needed to change. I wanted to change those images and describe black people in different ways. That was my motivation for wanting to become a writer. I wanted to change the way we were perceived.

JE: Why do you think so few of the millions of other black children who must have seen the same thing didn't think to take up the literary fight themselves?

CF: Writing is a difficult occupation. At the "end" of learning how to write, there's no guaranteed income. You can learn how to be a mechanic, and you're going to get a job. Take a business course of study, and you're going to get hired somewhere. But learning how to write does not necessarily equal pay for it. In the city I came from, Philadelphia, very few people I knew wanted to write. The only other person was Larry. I ended up writing for the theater. In the theater, you got a faster response to your work. People see it, and they like it or they don't.

JE: How did you get it produced so that it could be judged?

CF: The first play was at Princeton's McCarter Theatre. John Lithgow's father, Arthur, was the director. They were opening their fortieth season and wanted to do it with a brand-new play. Arthur asked if I was willing to write a play to open it with.

JE: How did you know him already?

CF: I had been writing skits for a community theater some friends and I started—satire, social commentary: blacks and Puerto Ricans living in the same community, finding it hard to get along with each other, arguing. While they're arguing, some-one comes along behind them and steals their televisions.

JE: Nice metaphor.

CF: Arthur came to see the work and afterward asked if I'd be interested in writing a full-length original play. I wrote it—*The Village, A Party*. And we agreed that we could bring along com-munity people I was working with—actors, craftsmen; people who needed to learn how to operate a theater, do the lights, build the sets.

JE: What a great opportunity for everyone.

CF: It was a good exchange. It helped the people in the community and also helped Princeton.

JE: What year?

CF: 1968. That's when I started writing plays.

JE: Including *A Soldier's Play*. I assume you were in the army.

CF: Yes.

JE: Was it based on reality?

CF: Only in the sense that World War Two was real. The story wasn't exactly built on anything I'd encountered. *A Soldier's Play* was written as a kind of personal memory to my friend Larry, who died in 1981. Larry would write poems that were connected to American literature, and I would write plays that were connected to American literature. *A Soldier's Play* is really a reworking of *Billy Budd*.

JE: There's an extraordinary line in *A Soldier's Story*, said by the doomed sergeant, that I think is someday destined to wind up in Bartlett's. He says, "Not having is no excuse for not getting." Wonderful. Whose voice is that? Your mom's, your dad's, an uncle?

CF: Relatives. I grew up in a family that stressed that nothing was to overcome you. I didn't grow up thinking that circumstances would ever get the better of me. My father said, "You were born black. Now what are you going to do?" It was a fact of life; you accepted it, and everything that goes with it, and went on from there. That doesn't mean you don't do anything, that you just stand there and say, "That's what I am. Oh, woe is me."

JE: You internalized those lessons.

CF: Racism is something you can't overcome if you assume that the person who is racist is smarter than you are. That's ridiculous.

JE: You're fifty-five. When you were growing up, there was a lot more racism than there is today.

CF: True. But I didn't let it paralyze me, so that I couldn't accomplish anything.

JE: Exclusive of the writing itself, how much deal-making and schmoozing and back-slapping and glad-handing do you have to do to succeed? Gamesmanship.

CF: The truth is, there aren't that many games that black writers can play.

JE: Why does the race of the writer mean anything at all? What does race have to do with gamesmanship?

CF: The content of the story. Generally, black writers write black protagonists.

JE: The Writers Guild has a black writers' roster. That's surely a terrible thing; a huge step backward.

CF: I'm not on it. I refuse. It's nonsense and isolationist. We are a union. Besides, how many movies get made in a year with black protagonists?

JE: Any movie Denzel Washington wants to be in.

CF: That's not true. But even if it were, the industry knows who's black and who isn't.

JE: *A Soldier's Story* had everything to do with being black. On the other hand, it also had everything to do with being a human being. These were complex characters who were motivated and believable. I think that counts more than their color.

CF: Not true. It took Norman Jewison [the director] forever to get that movie made. Every studio turned that movie down, except Columbia. If it was just complexity, I don't think that would have happened.

JE: But the question has more to do with your abilities as a writer. I believe that you would be able to write a complex, properly motivated, and believable white protagonist. Isn't that what I, the producer, am supposed to be looking for in a writer?

CF: I don't get those kinds of offers.

JE: A pity.

CF: Yes, but at the same time, there's not enough material about *black* people in normal, human relationships. I'd like to do those. There aren't enough movies in which we, black people, function as anything besides victims or victimizers. So until that's a reality, I want to write about what I know—push the possible.

JE: There's a phenomenon my wife and I have noted for years. The sweet black guy almost always gets it. The sweeter he is, the more likely he is to be killed.

CF: We always get killed. I made sure in *A Soldier's Story* that the hero lasted until the end of the movie. That was important.

JE: So since we haven't, as a society, reached total color blindness, your goal is to tell more truthful, positive black stories.

CF: Not so much positive as truthful. They're not necessarily the same.

JE: Did you get much criticism from the more militant black groups about *A Soldier's Story* because it was a black, not a white, racist who committed the murder?

CF: Yes, but that's got nothing to do with reality or the truth. What's positive doesn't mean truthful; it just means positive. What's truthful may, in many instances, upset and annoy people. What's true will benefit you.

JE: Let's get back to the genesis and development of *A Soldier's Story*. What's the process for building such a rich and complex set of characters?

CF: I wanted to understand a variety of people in a tight setting, one that's designed for the stage. The play operated within a narrow space. So did *Billy Budd*. They can't get off a ship; they can't get off a stage.

JE: Was *Billy Budd* a book you'd really liked a lot?

CF: It's not my favorite Melville, but it provided a way in which men in close quarters could be examined. They couldn't escape their reality; they couldn't get off the ship. The army's very much the same. You can't just walk away. And they were men who did the same things—they played baseball, very much the way sailors have jobs. The best of the baseball players was the Billy Budd character, C.J.

JE: Was the significance of C.J.'s hanging homage to *Billy Budd*.

CF: Sure.

JE: With C.J., you mined a rich vein in his being a sort of Stepin Fetchit Negro. How did that come about?

CF: It's a constant argument in the black community. It's always going on, this debate about people who are believed to be accommodators and those who won't accommodate.

JE: I've heard that some black kids call black kids who excel in school "white."

CF: That's dumb, but it's part of the same thing, something that's been going on in the black community since we got here in 1619—that is, do you accommodate the situation that you find yourself in, or fight against it? In the early days the argument was, How can you agree to be like the people who enslaved you?

JE: What does it mean "to be like"?

CF: Dress like them, act like them. Be subservient to them.

JE: C.J. was happy. He was spiritually content. Did he not have that right?

CF: In [Sgt.] Waters's eyes, C.J. was somebody who made black people appear subservient.

JE: Waters gave me that impression more than C.J. did. Waters spent most of his time trying to impress his white superiors.

CF: Probably did. But the problem presents itself in a variety of ways. Guys like Waters believe that guys like C.J. are the problem. Others, like Peterson, believe that guys like Waters are the problem. It's a situation that operates among any people who are oppressed.

JE: Do these characters appear to your imagination out of whole cloth? Out of what did you conjure them?

CF: Guys I knew in the army, 1959 to 1963, in Korea and Japan.

JE: You didn't base it on people and situations you ran into during the Civil Rights movement of the 1960s and '70s?

CF: The time of the action in the play and movie was 1944, but human relationships don't change because the time changes. Relationships are what they are because human beings are what they are. It feels contemporary because the kinds of problems they had are similar to problems we have at the moment. Nowadays, obviously, you can't have the same situation connected to war. And the army's not segregated. But even in today's army, you'll find characters like C.J. and Waters. They're still around, and there's still some people who like them and some who don't.

The army's about the only place where black men were fundamentally equal—to their counterparts. You look back at the Buffalo Soldiers. Even when the army was segregated, they were the police force of the West. Blacks couldn't carry guns in those days, but these guys could. That sort of thing didn't happen anywhere else but the military. I think the dilemma for black soldiers has always been: Who do you really represent or fight for—yourself or the United States?

JE: So your job as an artist is to express that dramatically, access-ibly. I have a sense that when your characters clicked into place finally, you had to get out of the way and let them happen. True?

CF: No. Basically, it was a mystery story. Someone had been killed, and you didn't know who did it. And at the end we'd find out that the killers were black. That was it.

JE: You knew from the beginning that the killers weren't going to be white?

CF: I knew that I didn't want it to be about interracial relation-ships alone. No fights between black guys and white guys. It wouldn't have made sense for me, because I didn't want to do something everybody else had done. These guys were trapped with each other; couldn't get away; had to sleep in the same room; trained together.

JE: How much is outlined in advance?

CF: None at all. When I write plays, I write what works for me in the seats; what I like watching when I'm sitting out there. Movies, on the other hand, are written from something in my mind's eye that keeps running. The movie was written with me sitting down in front of a yellow pad, writing down picture by picture what was going to be on the screen. In other words, I start the movie in my head, from the titles on. I watch it, writing down what I see. It runs, then stops, and I keep making sure that I didn't miss anything in all those shots. I clean up—go back and say, "I need something else there; another shot." Then I move the pic-tures forward from where they stopped, write them down, fix them, on and on. It runs like a movie in my head. I see all the shots and write what I see.

JE: Was *Soldier's Story* shot the way you saw it in your head?

CF: Essentially.

JE: When did you know you'd finished? How did you know you'd gotten it right?

CF: I leave things. I stop. Two or three weeks later I pick it up again and see something else that needs to be done that I didn't see before.

JE: Can you overdo it?

CF: It's possible to overdo and underdo it. Underdo is worse, because if you overdo you can cut. It's hard to add at the last moment. A writer usually knows when he has to stop. There comes a point when the writer and the project have to disengage, to separate. I can't tell you in terms of days or weeks, but there's definitely a point to leave it alone. Not think about it.

When you come back to some projects after time away, you suddenly realize they stink.

JE: Is there any correlation between how fast you're writing and how good it seems to be?

CF: I don't think so. I just did a piece for Showtime. They're doing three short movies about the Vietnam War. The first version of the piece took a while. Before writing the second version, I saw that I'd overwritten; I'd created in thirty minutes a history that ran from the 1940s to the 1970s. It was too much. I realized that I couldn't tell all of it in thirty minutes. So the second draft told a shorter story. It dealt only with the Vietnam War. I wrote it in three days; it came out of nowhere, playing in my head. But the whole writing process for the second thirty minutes took about a month.

JE: Is there anything you can do to facilitate that reel running in your head?

CF: No tricks. In this case, it was simply the realization that I needed to be writing only about Vietnam, not all these other wars. How long does a realization take? As long as it takes.

JE: What's the story?

CF: It's a soldier with two Vietcong chasing him; a whole series of events that connected his humanness to the humanness of the Vietnamese.

JE: Is the soldier black?

CF: Yes.

JE: Did he have to be black? Is there anything specifically black about him?

CF: He's a black sergeant. And he had to be black because there are not enough stories out there where the story of Vietnam is told through the prism of the African-American fighting man. So, yes, he's black.

JE: Black families have traditionally been proud of their sons' service to this country.

CF: A great source of pride. When I left college, there were only two choices: get a job or join the Army. I decided I didn't want to go to the university anymore, and chose the army.

JE: Why did you leave school early?

CF: I was one of fourteen blacks in the '50s at Villanova University. I wanted to be a writer, and every attempt I made at writing was thwarted by the English department in those days. They ended up giving me an honorary doctorate after I won the Pulitzer Prize. The only person who helped me there was a librarian, who gave me a copy of James Joyce's *Ulysses*. It was a first edition. She'd only read thirty pages and told me she couldn't get through it. "You're always reading all the time," she said. "Here. Finish this for me." She'd let me go through the stacks, and I'd read poetry and anything else in the stacks that you weren't supposed to be able to get your hands on. In those days, you couldn't get in the stacks at Villanova. You were supposed to write out a slip for the book you wanted and have someone fetch it for you. But she let me go through the stacks.

JE: Is the screenplay you're writing about Miles Davis finished?

CF: Not completely.

JE: Where did you begin?

CF: From 1975 until about 1980 or '81, Miles quit playing. He just put down his trumpet. I picked up the story then. He was living in New York, on the West Side.

JE: Why did you choose that as a starting point?

CF: Because he's not doing anything then. Miles went into seclusion. He was sick a lot. His hip was bothering him; other things. He'd been playing then as a lead-in for his sidemen, like Herbie Hancock. That had to be an insult to Miles. He'd open for, say, Santana. People weren't listening much to jazz anymore. They liked rock. He'd opened for the Grateful Dead. After a while that has to kick your ass. So Miles just backed off.

JE: Did he have money?

CF: Oh yeah. Miles always had money. He was born well-off. His father was a doctor in East St. Louis. When Miles came to New York in 1944 and played with Charlie Parker, Miles could afford the room; Charlie Parker couldn't. Charlie roomed with Miles in Miles's place. He was an aristocrat. He led a far different life than ninety-nine percent of the musicians out there.

JE: As a storyteller, do you think it's a better story because he's an aristocrat?

CF: Yes, because your inclination is to see musicians in a particular kind of way that doesn't apply to Miles. When was the last time you saw a story about an aspiring black musician growing up on an estate?

JE: What's the movie based on?

CF: Miles's autobiography that he wrote with Quincey Troupe, conversations with people in his family, musicians he played with, people who knew him.

JE: What's the most important thing to keep in mind as a writer, a dramatist?

CF: To tell the truth.

JE: How do you know whether you have enough talent to tell the truth?

CF: I don't know how to answer that. I just never believed there would ever be an obstacle in the way to stop me. I always assumed I'd be able to overcome whatever looked like it was blocking me. If you want to get anything done, you have to have that attitude. You have to believe that you can do it.

JE: Years ago, before you had the exterior validation of success, how did you know that what you'd written was good? Didn't you ever think you were just bullshitting yourself?

CF: I always knew that if I cracked up at what I was writing, then it was funny. Same thing with serious, dramatic writing. When I'm feeling something that makes me cry, makes me feel bad, I know it's right. If it affects me, it's good.

JE: You couldn't have known that in the beginning, though.

CF: No, but I knew that if it moved me, it would move someone else. It's all about discovery. The discovery is in the writing. Even if you know what the outcome is going to be, there's still discovery in the writing. It's all discovery. As you work, there's a process that happens. In certain kinds of situations, a dramatic moment will arrive. You'll know it's true by the way you feel; how it affects you.

As you write, you're thinking about language, about dramatic tension, about characters, about where it's heading. They're all going on at the same time. You can't do it the first time you sit down to write. You have to read a great deal. Read a lot, an awful lot, to get a sense of how writing is done. It takes a while to develop your own voice.

JE: Does writing get easier the more you do it?

CF: No, it gets harder. It's harder now than it ever was.

JE: How so?

CF: I'm older. There are more things that I don't believe in anymore. The older I get, the more jaded I get. You have to come back to what was beautiful and what is possible. You have to stay away from cynicism. It's hard to overcome experience and age and all the things that you see happening, to say, "Well, maybe there's potential for something extraordinary happening right here." But a writer has to overcome, has to rediscover the extraordinary.

ROBERT TOWNE

Robert Towne has the deserved reputation of being one of Hollywood's best screenwriters. If his entire career had consisted of writing only China-town (Oscar winner for 1974's best original screenplay), he'd still have earned his place in the screenwriters' pantheon. Not far behind (if it's behind at all) comes The Last Detail, a film that is often overlooked. Though I was familiar with his long list of credits, I was surprised to find how many excellent films his uncredited scriptwriting hand had influenced, including Bonnie and Clyde, The Godfather, and Marathon Man.

He responds to questions thoughtfully, with care and precision, in a voice whose tone and cadence sound exactly like Warren Beatty.

We met early one evening in his Santa Monica office.

JOEL ENGEL: Did you write for television before writing films?

ROBERT TOWNE: About '62 to '64 I wrote for television—*Man From Uncle, The Lloyd Bridges Show.*

JE: That was one of the last anthology shows.

RT: It was. I also wrote for *The Richard Boone Show.*

JE: Interesting idea: same cast, different stories each week.

RT: That was the last thing that Clifford Odets worked on. He was story editor. In fact, he gave me a bit of dialogue. I wrote a show about Francis Gary Powers, the U-2 pilot who'd been shot down over the Soviet Union [May 1, 1960]. The story was about Powers having been moved to a camp in southern Russia. The Russians would send not only political prisoners there, but, in an effort to clean up Moscow, they'd also send amputees and people who'd been maimed in the war. That way Moscow didn't look so ugly to tourists. It was a camp of real losers.

My story was about two men whose presence embarrassed their respective countries: Powers and a lieutenant in the camp. The Powers character decided to escape, not for escape's sake, but to climb a mountain that he'd been staring at all these months. Unbeknownst to Powers, the lieutenant has begun negotiations to get Powers exchanged as the equivalent of [Soviet spy] Rudolf Abel, which is in fact what happened [February 10, 1962]. The Russians wanted Abel back very badly, and though his capture had badly embarrassed the U.S., we wanted Powers back. In the middle of negotiations, the Russians discover that their prisoner—who was much less valuable than Abel was—had escaped. They were trying to hold the American negotiators at the table while this lieutenant at the camp went to recapture Powers so the exchange can be made. He has to pull him off this mountain. It becomes a race.

Clifford liked the story. He suggested a piece of dialogue between the negotiators. Because the Russians were playing games, not wanting to admit that they'd lost their prisoner, the American negotiator believed that the Russians didn't want to go through with the exchange. The American was a chain-smoker. He nervously picks up a cigarette—filtered. Until now the negotiations had been conducted in Russian. But at this critical juncture, the Russian says to him, in perfect English, "You're lighting that at the wrong end."

JE: How long had you been writing before you sold something?

RT: I think I sold something the minute I tried to, but that's a little misleading. It was Roger Corman, who'll give anyone a chance because he doesn't pay more than two bucks.

JE: What was your first Writers Guild sale?

RT: Probably something for TV.

JE: How long had you been writing at that point? A year? Two years?

RT: Probably about two years.

JE: How long would you have continued to write had you not sold?

RT: There's no way to know that. The thought never entered my mind that I wouldn't sell. That may sound arrogant or foolish, but it was simply my state of mind.

JE: Why did you want to write for the screen and not prose?

RT: Movies were not chic when I started; they were fun. Movies were not that thing that talented writers did; they were that thing that Scotty Fitzgerald or William Faulkner or people like that did to make money between writing serious novels; between Clifford writing the great American play. They would come out to pick up some quick cash and then get back to the business at hand.

JE: It was still considered slumming.

RT: It was aesthetically slumming; pandering for big bucks. Screenwriting was that thing that Nathanael West and Dorothy Parker and Fitzgerald and those people did between their serious work to make some money, and tried not to do it too long in order not to become hopelessly compromised.

There was a play by Budd Schulberg called *The Disenchanted* about Fitzgerald that came out about the time [1959] I started writing. It perfectly embodies the ideas of those people who wrote for the screen but never considered it a serious occupation for a serious writer. In fact, in a 1984 article that was partially about me, [*New York Times* critic] Vincent Canby wrote that he didn't know why anyone who took writing seriously could be a screenwriter for five minutes.

JE: What's the answer?

RT: The answer is in the doing. You can't answer someone who says something like that.

JE: Wasn't Canby's remark made in the context that the writer's vision is inherently compromised by the producer and director and actor and editor and studio?

RT: Perhaps. I think it was partly that. I think it was partly that a screenwriter, almost by definition, has no vision.

JE: Don't you have a vision? Don't you see the movie in your mind's eye while you're creating it?

RT: Of course I do. When I write a screenplay I describe a movie that's already been shot. That's what I do.

JE: Did you turn to directing because the movies you'd written did not match your vision of the finished product?

RT: It started really with *Greystoke* [*The Legend of Tarzan, Lord of the Apes*], in which there was no dialogue. At that point I knew that I had to start doing it myself, because you can't turn over a bunch of camera angles to somebody and say, "Shoot this," and then, if it's not done adequately, say, "You screwed this up." It's more than you can expect the page to convey. That was as good a screenplay as I've written, but you simply cannot expect to describe at twenty-four frames per second those pictures, have somebody shoot them, and expect them to be even remotely what you had in mind; it's just not reasonable to expect that.

JE: Did *Chinatown* turn out the way you'd envisioned?

RT: Yes and no. That's a complicated issue. It's not altogether bad that it didn't turn out exactly the way I wanted. That movie is truly an amalgam of me and [director] Roman [Polanski]. I don't think it's altogether fair or correct to say simply that it didn't turn out the way I'd imagined when writing. Roman made too much of a contribution. At the time the movie was being made and came out, I was angry about the end of the movie, which was not what I wanted. We had a disagreement that was well publicized at the time. In hindsight, I've come to feel that Roman was probably right about the ending, that I don't think that what I had in mind could have been done; that an end with the ambiguity and ambivalence that I had in mind simply could not satisfactorily be done as the tag to a movie with that much complexity; the end had to have a level of stark simplicity that at the time I thought was excessively melodramatic. Roman rightly believed that the complexities had to conclude with a simple severing of the knot.

JE: What was your ending?

RT: My ending originally had her kill her father, and be unable to tell why, which was to protect her daughter; so she had to go to jail. Gittes couldn't help, because she just didn't want to harm her daughter by discussing the incest as the motive. Everything else would have been the same except for the ending.

JE: Interesting, ambiguous ending.

RT: Yes. It even had a nice line of dialogue in it. There was a lawyer in it who early in the film declines an offer to have his cigar lit. He says, "No, thanks. It's one of two things I always do myself." Later, when it's clear that the lawyer can't help her and that she's going to go to jail for the rest of her life, Gittes asks him what the other thing is that he always does himself. "Put on my own hat," he says. And with that Gittes puts his hat on and walks out of the office—accept responsibility for your actions. It was good, but it's more of a literary ending, and very difficult given the complexities of the cinema story to do that adequately. What I wrote was good, but Roman, I now think, was right in recognizing that it was excessively complex.

JE: It also gave us the immortal line, "It's Chinatown."

RT: Yes. Let me get back to the question of why screenwriting. In a collection of James Agee's screenplays and criticism that was published posthumously, he made a remark that is the perfect summation of what my own feelings were at the time. He said, "I concluded that I have often been bored by a bad play, but I can rarely remember being bored by bad movies." I thought to myself that that was right; that's what I felt. I love movies, and I'm not bored by them; I'm just going to write them the best I can. I felt that there need not necessarily be anything aesthetically inferior about them.

Since that time, I've often been bored by the movies; at the time I had not. Nor had Agee. There's a reason for that. In those days, no movies were boring, because they weren't pretentious. They were either damned good, or cheesy, sleazy B movies that certainly didn't bore you; lively and full of entertainment. So if you went to see some cheesy film with James Craig or Bonita Granville or Rod Cameron or Yvonne de Carlo, they were never boring, no matter what. They may not have been very good; may not have aspired to much. They did, actually, aspire to one thing: never to bore you.

JE: Does the process of being able to visualize the film in your mind's eye happen only after the story is worked out, or does it happen concurrently?

RT: It's concurrent. What I generally do, whether it's an original or an adaptation, of which I've done very few until this last year, is I write a treatment, or I write a story, or I tell a story. I tell myself the story; I tell my wife the story; I write it down; I tell it over and over again, until I have strung together those sequences that I think will make the movie. When I proceed to write the script, I find that I'm as likely to go 180 degrees in the opposite direction of my own treatment as I am to go with it; sometimes it's useful when I use it, and sometimes it provides the vehicle for me to argue with when I don't. What dictates that is, as you start the process of writing a screenplay—or probably anything— you're dreaming a dream. The job is to make a dream come true. It starts as a daydream, which is to say that you're the one who's actively pushing the fantasy. If you get lucky, at a certain point the conscious part of you goes to sleep and it becomes a night dream. It takes over. You lose conscious control over it. The characters have a life of their own, and you just have to follow the logic of them and say, "Oh, that's what they do."

JE: Does getting to that point require an already fully imagined character?

RT: No. You imagine it, and you're pushing it. But when you really start the process of writing, which means the moment-to-moment life of these people—those things that no one can foresee until the moment they're doing it—that's when the characters assume a life of their own.

JE: Have you ever completed a successful screenplay that was the product of a constant daydream, as opposed to the characters acting in your subconscious?

RT: I used the terms metaphorically.

JE: I'm asking in metaphoric terms. Did you ever have to push a story that wasn't realizing itself?

RT: I've had to push stories more than I wanted to. There are hybrids—*The Firm*. It has a lot of good stuff in it, and has stuff that is wonky. It's a combination of trying to work with material that you can only go so far with, or, given the constraints of the time, one could dream some part of it as a night dream and some, being unable to wait, as a daydream. I think that's the process, generally speaking, for me.

JE: Is it a pleasurable process? Do you look forward to it, to writing?

RT: Sometimes, yes, I do. It's a funny thing. I didn't when I was younger. I didn't like it. Didn't like the act of writing, in part, I suspect, because I didn't think I could do it. I mean, I felt I was good, in a way. But in another way, I felt I was the one who always had to do it. As I've gotten older, I've been able to be more accepting of the fact that there's some little gnome at work inside of me; sort of like I'm the maiden who's been ordered to spin flax into gold in "Rumpelstiltskin." I can't do that. But contained somewhere inside of me, I've concluded, is this little dwarf, this vicious little prick, who, if I go to sleep and let him go to work, he'll do it; and it's fun to watch him work.

JE: Do you know when he's going to come out?

RT: You go to work, and go through the process of the work, and there's a certain point where you realize you're just following the story. And you say, "Oh, yeah, that's what the guy was doing." You just know that the characters have assumed their own life, and all you have to do is watch them carefully. That's what's fun; that's when they surprise you.

JE: Do you have to be at the desk, or can you be driving, walking, shopping, showering for that to happen?

RT: Oh yeah. I don't suddenly feel that I'm zoned out, or anything. I am describing after the fact what happens. During the time I'm just sitting there talking like I am with you right now. It's not mysterious. It's like describing a battle after it happens. At the time, no one really knows the sequence or the order. Wellington once said that a battle was like a ball: You attended it and were aware of some of the dances, but very rarely did anyone dance all the dances or be everywhere in the ballroom to know everything that was happening. Any description of that ball afterwards is to some extent superficial. It had its own life, like a battle has its own life, like writing a screenplay has its own life. I can describe it afterwards, and say it's like I've got a dwarf in there. But at the time I'm just writing. I feel good because, *Oh, that's it.* Like I discovered something. The best that I feel is when I feel I have nothing to do with it. Not surprisingly. As if, *Oh, what a great thing somebody gave me.* It allows you to feel that it's good, because nobody feels that what they write, personally, is going to be good. It allows you to enjoy it, to be surprised by it.

JE: When you were writing *Chinatown,* did you have a sense that something extraordinary had happened or was happening?

RT: No. I remember vividly that I had a sense, at about page eighty, that it had kicked in, and I just started watching it happen. I mean, I didn't know that I said that to myself at the time, only in retrospect. To extend the dance metaphor, you start off leading, and you like to end up following.

JE: What is it that you gave to the story that jump-started its self-activation?

RT: I don't know that I can point to any one thing, per se. Passion, mainly; really caring about it.

JE: Is speed any indicator at all of how well or how poorly a particular script is going?

RT: Sometimes yes and sometimes no. I have had a reputation for being very slow, and yet people who know me well know that I can also be very quick. Otherwise I couldn't have gotten involved in *The Firm,* going from start to finish in a relatively short time.

JE: What did the other two writers, David Rabe and David Rayfiel, have to do with it?

RT: In the case of Rabe, nothing; I never saw his screenplay. The first writer on an adaptation is assumed to have written the work. It's not a good rule. David Rayfiel is another matter. He had done an early version of it that he and Sydney [Pollack, the director] felt was structurally not working, and both he and Sydney, who are friends of mine, called me. We all worked out an outline, or a new treatment, frantically. And then I was pretty much left to myself to write all night, with the two them revising during the day.

JE: The novel was changed substantially.

RT: Yes, but we tried to do it so that it didn't look that way.

JE: Your movie had a much better ending than the book.

RT: I thought so, too. That was the thing that I had the hardest time convincing them of. They thought that that was going to let the Mafia off the hook. My arguments were manifold. You can't just let a guy take the money and run; it's disgusting. He should learn to care about something. Yeah, they said, that's true, but it'll look as if he's just afraid of being killed. I said that it wouldn't. Then Sydney said, "Well, I don't know. If you could just have a scene where these Mafia guys were talking about trying to kill the lawyer, and one of them says, 'If I could get my hands on that—' And then the lawyer walks in at that moment." I said, "Sydney, that's what I'm talking about." "That might work," he said. So I wrote the scene. Now if this scene didn't work, there was no ending for the movie. Then I read it to him and David Rayfiel and [producer] Lindsay Doran, and they laughed. That was it. We had six or seven or eight weeks to write the whole thing.

I think if we'd had a little more time we could have taken about fifteen minutes out of it. Sydney said, "I didn't have time to make a short film." To make the release date, the entire editing process was done in four weeks.

JE: What's your favorite screenplay among the ones you've written?

RT: I don't know that I have a favorite. I think the least interesting part of the work is the end product. It's there to be used, to be enjoyed; it's very pretty. But the very process of creating it is to discard it. Once you get it from inside to outside, it's gone. All those concerns reside in you. Once you objectify them, in a sense you've exorcised them. They're gone. They don't belong to you anymore. You've purged them. When the sand gets in the oyster's craw, the oyster's response, to protect himself, is to spin this thing around the sand that becomes this beautiful pearl. The object is not to admire it, but to get rid of something that hurts.

JE: The process of writing.

RT: Yes. I think it's the process that's all important.

JE: Do you pass the need or the desire to get the script made? Is the script itself reward enough?

RT: No. I don't think you ever pass the need to get it made. I'm just talking about the process of writing, which is terribly important. You can look at the process of getting it to film as an extension of writing. You never stop writing the script until it's practically released.

JE: How do you know when it's done?

RT: When it's in the theaters.

JE: There's never a moment when you say, "Eureka! That's it"?

RT: It's what Yogi Berra said about a ball game, "It ain't over till it's over." You're rewriting it while it's being shot. You have to. Too many things change. Actors you never anticipated. Actors you lose. Locations you lose. Other things you can't tell during rehearsal.

JE: So even before you were a director, you were welcomed on the set as a writer?

RT: Always.

JE: That puts you in a small minority, doesn't it?

RT: It does. That's partly because of my success, but also because of the kind of success. Starting off as a script doctor means rewriting things when they're being shot. Right from *Bonnie and Clyde* on.

JE: I didn't know you worked on that.

RT: The last draft. Also, *The Godfather*. The longest scene in it was something I wrote. The scene between Marlon Brando and Al Pacino in the garden.

JE: "I drink more wine than I used to."

RT: Right, that scene. That wasn't in the book. Francis [Coppola, the director] didn't have a scene between Michael and don Corleone, and he needed it. So I came back and did that scene as well. The point I'm getting at here is, by definition, you have to be on the set: "This is the footage that I've shot, Robert, and this is where the scene should go, and I don't have the damned scene. What should I do?" "Well, I think you ought to have a scene between father and son saying 'I love you,' but you can't just have them saying that." You're intimately bound up with the process when the movie's being made. It's been rare that I've had that excluded feeling most writers experience.

The larger point that you're asking about is, When is the screenplay completed? The answer is, When you have gone completely through postproduction. When Sydney was shooting *The Firm,* he ran into problems right in the middle of shooting that had to be solved with a new scene. I had written a sequence where Tom [Cruise] was to hold a fire hose and jump down the stairwell to get away from the villains there. Well, Sydney couldn't find an open stairwell. They did have a building that had a boiler room. Faxing back and forth, we finally came up with Tom taking the briefcase and pummeling poor Wilford [Brimley]. Sydney would describe the room in a fax, I'd send some notes, he'd send some back, and that's how the scene developed.

JE: I'm reluctant to ask such an immensely dense or naive or even stupid question, but it's begging to be asked. What do you have in your brain that, say, Sydney Pollack doesn't have, so that he has to ask you to solve this problem?

RT: I don't want to be altogether glib, but I would say that I probably have more time. This poor guy has been thrown into the midst of a movie on which he's working eighteen hours a day; he can't think about this. Presumably, he hires me to have another good mind. So I would answer: time and talent, one of which he has, the other he doesn't while in the middle of shooting.

JE: That leads me to another, equally naive question. Doesn't that say that a director and a producer who want to make a good film should go for the top talent, rather than the new kid on the block?

RT: You should always go for the best talent available. That may or may not be the new kid.

JE: How do you judge the new kid based on one film, or even two films?

RT: You don't. I think it was Kazan who said that ninety percent of directing is casting. That's true of casting actors, screenwriters, cameramen; it's true of casting everything. Get everyone who's good, and you've done an awful lot of your job.

JE: Are you a good oral storyteller?

RT: Pretty good, yeah. I've become good at it. I wouldn't say that I was a natural-born raconteur. Over the years I've gotten better. It's necessary. One of the things that is not done enough is to have people tell their stories so that their audience says, "Then what happens?" Once you can do that, once you can face somebody and tell the story without being embarrassed or falling down, then you realize that you've got a real basis for something there. After all, that's how stories really started. A storyteller's art was primarily verbal. I think that you really should try to do that. I try to do it because it's a way of testing it. It's going to be dramatized, and telling it out loud is a form of dramatization. If you're sensitive at all, when you're telling a story you can see almost immediately how the audience is reacting to it; your audience helps you shape your story a bit.

JE: Can you tell it out loud to yourself? Does there have to be someone to make eye contact with?

RT: You need to sense and feel someone's reaction, much like an actor. Let's say you're trying out a show on the road, you do it in front of an audience before you get to Broadway. Same with a story. Just the reaction is enough to give you clues. I don't mean just laughing or crying. There's that sense where you see someone get imperceptibly bored. You see you've lost them, or you see they're confused, or if they're leaning forward they're excited. You can tell how it's working a little bit better; it shapes your story. Your listening audience shapes your story for you just by the way they listen.

JE: Is there anything that's unique to screenwriting—something that it requires not required by any other form of dramatic writing?

RT: One thing is that the process is incomplete unless and until the movie is made. A screenplay is no more complete than an architect's rendering of a building is complete until the building is erected. It's not a finished product; neither a play nor a screenplay is. A novel, a poem, a short story—those are finished products; they don't need anything additional. What distinguishes, I think, a screenplay from a play is that the screenplay is less complete than the play. It's more incomplete because the variables involved are so much greater. A play is meant to be done on a stage, and a proscenium stage is a little bit like a laboratory; it doesn't vary that much. You rehearse and rehearse and rehearse. By the time you're done with that part of the process, it's kind of complete. You don't have to guess. Movies, on the other hand, are made with these cumbersome French knights, which are movie stars.

You get them dressed in armor, hoist them up on their horses, and send them off into the field of battle. A cumbersome process. Disentangle them from another war. Some of them don't do certain things. So with these people costing from five million to fifteen million dollars, and you have a short window of time before they go off to the next war, there's not a lot of time to rehearse. There's not much time to test the text, except when you shoot it. So shooting a screenplay is rather like a combination of rehearsal and performance, whereas a play is a performance of the rehearsal process. A movie has more variables, like the weather, for instance, which is one of them. It is a much more uncontrollable process. You cannot control it the way you can a play. Audiences may vary a performance from night to night in a play. Indeed in a movie theater, audiences react differently from night to night; they change the movie kind of figuratively, not literally, the way playgoers can change it. What you learn as a director is that the director has complete authority and no control.

What I'm getting at is this: What's unique about screenwriting is that it's an act of prophecy. The screenwriter is a bit of the gypsy with a crystal ball. You say, "I'm writing this on a page and it's going to be blown up on a screen so damned big that you can't believe it, with actors I don't know if anybody's going to get, in settings I don't know where and how can be done; and it's going to turn out this way. . . ." You're guessing. There's a bit of gypsy in you. An act of prophecy.

JE: What I don't understand, I guess, is, if the scene is played just as you've described it on the page—in orthodox fashion— what happens from here to there that sometimes goes wrong?

RT: Here's one example, and I certainly don't mean it in any way as a pejorative to the actor; I'm just using him as an example.

I write *Chinatown*. I have a certain actor in mind, which I did. He's unavailable, and Walter Matthau plays the part. What's different about that movie?

JE: Everything.

RT: Right. What I'm saying is, it takes almost nothing to make it completely different. That's a lot, changing Jack Nicholson to Walter Matthau, but it's only one thing.

JE: Matthau could say the exact same lines, and still everything has changed. It's like a spread sheet—changing one entry changes everything else.

RT: The most difficult thing to capture, and what finally makes a movie, is its tone. Tone is a very delicate matter. It requires a keen understanding from everyone involved, the director, producer, stars, writer; it's called the Lubitsch touch. If you have Ross Hunter, for example, as the arbiter of an Ernst Lubitsch film, it's going to turn out differently.

JE: So it's not exactly an accident that good films get made, but there's a lot more going against a good movie than a good play. Is that what you're saying?

RT: There's a lot of serendipity in a good movie being made. If *those* people happen to be available, and the confluence of talent comes together at that particular point, then . . . But it's not an accident. Luck, maybe.

JE: Do you remember where the idea for *Chinatown* came from?

RT: It was a combination of things. There was an old magazine called *West* that the *Los Angeles Times* published with the paper every Sunday. Looking through it one day, I came upon a bunch of photographs, one of a green Plymouth convertible under a streetlight in front of J. W. Robinson's [department store]; one of a Packard convertible in front of a Pasadena mansion; one taken near the train station. They were accompanied by prose from Raymond Chandler's novels, describing Los Angeles. I'd never read much Chandler, though I did after that. In reading these words and looking at these pictures, I realized that I had in common with Chandler that I loved L.A. and missed the L.A. that I loved. It was gone, basically, but so much of it was left; the ruins of it, the residue, were left. They were so pervasive that you could still shoot them and create the L.A. that had been lost. That touched me.

Later, one day I was walking up in the hills in the Pacific Palisades. I got up on a bluff and I suddenly felt like I was ten years old. It happened to be one of those days like the days had been when I was growing up in San Pedro. I could smell the ocean coming in, even though I couldn't see it. And the saltwater sort of mingled with the weeds and the chaparral and the mustard plant and the eucalyptus trees on the hill, and I remembered that when I was growing up you'd go driving and smell the orange blossoms and tar in the road. And the city was so beautiful.

Anyway, at the same time some asshole was trying to build a development in a canyon called Deep Canyon around Benedict Canyon. Quincy Jones and I tried to fight it together. Poor Quincy. For the next year and a half after we lost he had about fifty huge tractors in his front yard hauling millions of cubic yards of dirt out of there. The developer destroyed the canyon. It just so happened that I was trying to beat City Hall while I was reading a book titled *Southern California Country* by Carey McWilliams. There's a chapter in it called "Water, Water, Water," which was about how we in 1905 had destroyed the Owens Valley so that we could bring the water here, so that speculators could use it for the San Fernando Valley.

My dealing with City Hall and seeing how crooked and corrupt things were; reading the book; seeing the photos and text in *West* magazine; my memory that afternoon of my childhood Los Angeles; Columbia Pictures refusing to do *The Last Detail* for reasons having to do with censorship and the MPAA ratings board and the film's language; being unable to get *Shampoo* made—all of these things contributed. In 1972 I went to Jack [Nicholson], who'd backed me on *The Last Detail;* neither of us wanted to do it unless it was done right. I said, "What if I write a detective movie. Would you be interested in doing it?" He said yes. All the disparate elements came together, and that's how the story came out.

JE: Did you find the voice of the movie, the private detective, through the Chandler influence?

RT: No. It was Jack's voice. I had been in acting class with Jack for five or six or seven years. I created the detective J. J. Gittes around his personality. In fact, I used Chandler in the way that I explained how I write a treatment and argue it. Chandler's detective is the rusty knight, a sort of hard-boiled Don Quixote. He has ideals: "I won't do divorce work," won't do this, etc., etc. Well, my detective won't do anything else *but* divorce work because that's what most private detectives did. I played upon the disparity that Chandler had created and the reality that I knew to be the case. The only ones who made any money were the guys sneaking around and peeping into bedrooms or the ones who dealt with movie stars to protect them. These guys did the sleaziest work of all.

JE: You can do that for one or two movies with your character, but not a series of novels. You'd lose the romance that carries the reader.

RT: Of course not, but that's the difference between a movie and a novel. Or the difference between a movie and a television series. A movie is a one-shot deal. Drama is something in which a character changes. You cannot have a running character in a novel and change him too much. What do you do for the next novel? That's one of the limitations, actually, of a novel that features a running character. A movie character can change; it's self-enclosed. You can start him off as an uppity little pimp and then have him get religion. Drama is change. A running character, in a sense, is the opposite of that; he's a character without change.

JE: Do all your film ideas have such poetic births as *Chinatown* did?

RT: *Shampoo* also got started in a confluence of influences. I was going with a beautiful girl, a dancer—in fact, Fred Astaire's last dancing partner. She was also an actress, but mainly a dancer. Anyway, she had been married, which I didn't find out right away. I was twenty-three, and it was very unusual at the time for your girlfriend to have been married and divorced. She told me his name. Gene Shacove. I asked what he did. She said he was a hairdresser. It shocked the shit out of me, that such a beautiful girl would marry a hairdresser. Or that a hairdresser would marry a girl. Both were shocking. I asked what happened. She said, "Well, we'd been married about six weeks. He woke up one morning and said, 'I don't feel like being married anymore.'" I said, "What?!" then asked what happened to him. She said he had a real successful shop. I asked if she ever saw him. "Yeah," she said. "Every week. He does my hair." They were still very good friends. It turned out that he asked her who she was seeing. She told him about "this young guy who wants to be a writer." He said, "Don't waste your time with him. He's not going to amount to anything. This fringe asshole." She couldn't resist repeating this to me. So I said, "Wait a minute, where is this asshole?"

This went on week after week, and I got sick of hearing it. I was curious to see who this guy was, so I went down there to pick her up one day. I walked in, and there he was with his hair dryer, going like a bee from one flower to the next. The most beautiful girls, one right after another. I could not believe my eyes. The only rooster in the hen house. It was a revelation to me. I was absolutely staggered. Then I found other guys, like Dusty Fleming, who did the same. A whole subculture of wildly heterosexual guys with a great sense of design, who worked on human heads instead of pieces of paper. I was fascinated by it; thought it was a terrific subject.

Then one day Warren Beatty, whom I'd never met, came by. He'd liked a script I'd written for Roger Corman, *The Long Ride Home,* but was worried about working with Roger. He asked about any originals I had. I asked what he had in mind. He wanted to do a movie about a compulsive Don Juan. He believed he'd had *What's New, Pussycat?* stolen. I said I'd been interested in doing that since doing a television show for *Breaking Point;* Cliff Robertson played that kind of role, which peaked my interest. He asked how I would do it. I said that I'd do it somewhat like [Wycherley's] *The Country Wife.* It's a restoration comedy about a man who convinces people that he's been rendered a eunuch by his doctor, so all the men trust him with their wives. Warren said he thought that that was interesting, and asked how it would be done. "Would you use an actor who everybody thought was gay?" I told him I'd use a hairdresser.

He looked at me. It took him about thirty seconds. He said, "You're right."

JE: It coalesced at that moment?

RT: That was it. I had been thinking about *The Country Wife* and I'd been thinking about what to do with the hairdresser. When he asked the question, it just—wham!—came together.

Of all the movies I've done and have not directed, *Shampoo* probably came closest in tone to the way I would have done it had I directed it. On the other hand, I was never off the set. There were the three of us there [Towne, director Hal Ashby, and producer-star Warren Beatty], and when I felt a scene wasn't working and had to be rewritten, I said so and rewrote it; it was reshot.

JE: You saw this as it was being filmed or in dailies?

RT: In the case of a particular scene, I saw the dailies and felt it didn't work. It was a scene in which Goldie [Hawn] confronts Warren and says, "There were other women, weren't there?" Originally he said, "Everybody fucks everybody, you know." I saw it, and it wasn't any good. He looked like he was bullying this little girl. It didn't have the context of what I wanted. I hated it.

JE: Were you the only one to notice this?

RT: At the time I was, yes. I realized, for a start, that one of the things that was wrong with the scene was that Warren was standing up. I had written him sitting down. Now that may seem like a strange thing, but this tall, large, well-built man who looks, at the very least, like a running back, is towering, with a head of hair that looks like a dragoon's helmet, over this poor little blond girl, saying, "Grow up, everybody fucks everybody." It was awful; it was didactic. I told Warren he shouldn't have been standing up. He said, "Well, you were watching when we were shooting. Why didn't you say something?" I had no answer; nobody does.

Everybody's so mesmerized. That's one of the good things that happens. It's why you have to constantly be in touch with yourself, to be aware of what you're feeling: *Why am I feeling the way I am?* Most people's instinct when they're watching a movie being shot is to try to make allowances for something, not to attack it. Most people say, "I guess that's all right." Part of being a social animal is to be accommodating. You've got to overcome that when you're working on a movie, whether as director or writer or producer or actor.

After going for a walk and thinking about the scene, I realized it should be very personal. I decided that, one, he should be sitting down. Two, he shouldn't want to tell her and she should drag it out of him; that way it's not didactic. Three, it should be intensely personal: "This is what I did, this is who I am. Sorry. That's the truth." I wrote it that way and it was shot that way. I think it's instructive.

JE: There's a sense of romance that pervades your work.

RT: I guess so. Truth is, I'm kind of a romantic.

JE: *Tequila Sunrise.*

RT: I'll tell you something, I was forced to change a lot in the film because of the studio's [Warner Bros.] discomfort with his being a drug addict. My original ending had him die. It had great tone, because the tone that was lost came from this guy who wanted out of the dealing game, but at the same time, like an old race horse tied to a milk wagon, the bell rings and he wants to run. There was excitement, and the action was fun; he couldn't help himself. That meant that, in the end, either he or the girl was going to get killed. There's no other way out. It would have been a great movie.

JE: Warners wouldn't go for your vision, so you had to compromise.

RT: Yes. That's the long and short of it. They will always feel that they made more money because of it, and I will always feel that they would have made more if they hadn't. He would have been a more romantic figure had he died. After his death, the character played by Michelle Pfeiffer takes care of his kid.

JE: I like it.

RT: I did too.

JE: Isn't romance the juice of a story?

RT: I think people go to the movies to be transported, to have an experience different from their humdrum life. I think romance is powerful, whether you mean it in the classical sense of the word or the traditional Hollywood sense, which are not the same things. The classical sense means Promethean, Byronic; Hollywood sense means *Pretty Woman*.

JE: Is it still as much fun for you now? Do you get the same thrill seeing your work on the screen?

RT: Yeah.

JE: Is the process as much fun?

RT: The process is as much fun. What's more annoying about it now is the attendant difficulty of getting to the starting gate, the attenuated process of deal-making. The corporations taking over studios. Conglomerates. Personal ownership is gone. Now they bring in fleets of in-house lawyers who attentuate the process. What used to be quick can now take months. It can vitiate your momentum, bleed your enthusiasm or interest. By the time you finish the dealmaking, you sometimes feel that you've already made the movie. That, and because the cost of making films nowadays is so expensive that the executives are less venturesome, tends to take some of the joy out. Executives' only criterion these days is, Will the audience go, or won't they go? Sure, that was always first among equals, but there was a time when other things were important to a Goldwyn, a Warner, even Harry Cohn; it was important to have a Frank Capra there. John Huston's films did not make money, but it was considered an honor to have him work for you.

JE: So when you're writing, do you always have to wonder whether this scene is going to be an audience pleaser?

RT: I don't feel that I'm that different from my audience. I just tend to keep in mind what I would like, and generally feel that the audience will like it as well.

JE: What do you read for pleasure?

RT: Here's what I've read in the past year: *War and Peace, Anna Karenina,* John Keating's history of the second world war, [William] Manchester's biography of Churchill, [David] McCullough's biography of Truman. I tend not to read novels.

JE: One last question. What was the thinking behind the slitting of Gittes's nose in *Chinatown*?

RT: I was trying to think of something that would scare me. I remember thinking of slitting the mouth or ears, but that seemed gruesome and witless. There was just something about slitting a nostril that is both painful and terrifying, and also oddly appropriate for a nosy guy. He's a detective who puts his nose in other people's business. There was just something slightly humorous about it, and at the same time it's really terrifying. I think that combination, for a guy who's a peep, a snooper, seemed just right. I didn't want it to be something that was potentially fatal, just scary and funny. It's a curious thing about that scene. Many people have called the movie violent. But it actually has very little violence in it.

JE: There's a dominant subtext of violence and menace and danger.

RT: The use of the nose-slitting is something that suggests violence rather than is violent. It's humorous and appalling. It suggests worse things to come. As Roman's character [the man doing the slitting] says, "Next time I'm going to get serious." That admonition to the hero is also in a sense an admonition to the audience: *The next time something happens, it can be serious.* I think the threat of violence is there precisely because the act is both appalling and funny.

RICHARD
LAGRAVENESE

I thought that Richard LaGravenese's script for The Fisher King *was superior to the movie made from it. It had a sense of inventiveness and originality. Its characters were fleshy and had heart. After meeting their author, it's easy to see why. Suffice it to say that I would be shocked to hear that he had been signed on to write producer Joel Silver's next bang-a-minute extravaganza.*

At the time we met, in his apartment overlooking Central Park, La-Gravenese had just completed a long string of assignments earned after the success of The Fisher King. *(I had not yet seen* The Ref, *which came out a few months later.) The phone rang often with questions from directors either preparing, shooting, or editing scripts he'd written.*

RICHARD LAGRAVENESE: When I was a boy, my passion was for the movies. I didn't know how I would end up in that world, only that I wanted to be in it. I never thought I would be writing. In fact, up until my twenties, I figured I'd end up as an actor. But I was writing all along the way. I just never really paid attention to it.

I remember when I was nine, in the fourth grade, we had a reading period. If you finished your work you got to read a book on your own. We were sort of Dr. Seuss fanatics. We'd always run to the back of the room and grab a Seuss book. One time I got sick of reading the same things over and over, and instead of reading I wrote a short story. The teacher made me read it in front of the class.

I guess it just flowed naturally. Later, when I was part of a comedy team, I wrote our bits, which just came rather easily to me. When I was a struggling actor, I used to write monologues for myself and for other actors as a way of earning money. That, too, came easily. My acting teacher gave my name to [writer and director] Joan Micklin Silver, who was putting together a revue called *A . . . My Name Is Alice*. After I sold her some material, it hit me that I should ride the horse in the direction it was going. Acting was wonderful and very creative, but I hated auditioning. I hated being at the mercy of looks and things I couldn't control, and it was not as fulfilling as writing. So I stopped with great ease and just focused on writing.

JOEL ENGEL: What was the first screenplay you wrote?

RL: Neil, the husband of an old college friend, had worked for the original *Saturday Night Live*. He had pitched a movie idea to producer Aaron Russo and made a deal, then hired me to write it with him. But because it was his story, he had complete control. It was such a nightmare experience, I rarely talk about it. It came out as *Rude Awakening;* originally it was called "The Guatemalan Papers." My partner had conceived of this very sophisticated satire about ex–1960s people living in Guatemala, who live in this idyllic, Eden-like society but are completely bored. They have nothing to fight against. They long for a cause. This was during the era of Reagan and the Contras and the Sandinistas in Nicaragua. They come upon these papers that prove the United States was about to invade, sort of like Vietnam, and create a skirmish as a reason. So these people plan to come back to the States to expose the plan.

We wanted to do it like *Dr. Strangelove*. Well, Aaron saw it as the 1960s meets the 1980s. He ruined it; it looks nothing like what it started out as. What's on the screen now is an embarrassment. We worked on it for about three years for no money. He kept insisting that it would be made. In three years, I think, I made about five thousand dollars. The good thing was that it was my professional entrée. And during that period, I wrote *The Fisher King* on the side, because this was so frustrating.

JE: What was the genesis of the idea?

RL: The moment of genesis was in 1986, when one day I saw two men crossing the street together. One was handsome and young, the other looked to be slightly retarded. The relationship just struck me as interesting. They seemed so bonded to each other, so affectionate, and yet they weren't touching at all—connected in an invisible way. Something about that interested me. So I began writing about these two characters, making notes. At the same time, I also wanted to write about narcissism. Over the next year and a half I wrote, I think, three different drafts. I'd finish a draft and then put it away for about six months, then pick it up again. You see, except for working with Neil, I had no real encouragement that this was the thing I should be doing. So, when I was working on the screenplay, every time I lost faith I'd put it aside and try to do something else. That's why it took three years. But each of the three drafts is completely different from the others.

In the first one, the character that Jeff Bridges ultimately played was originally a cab driver. The part played by Robin Williams was homeless as well, but more of an idiot savant. It was very dark. They wind up going to a casino at the end. I should also mention that this was before *Rain Man* came out. I remember reading in the *New York Times* that this film was about to come out about an idiot savant and his brother, a nice-looking young man, and I freaked. How could two people come up with the exactly the same idea at the same time? So I threw it away.

JE: Just like that, you threw it away? That must have been painful.

RL: No, because I just wanted to be original. It turned out to be a good thing. I ended up really exploring. I kept the two characters and tried a completely different vein. The second draft was more like a sitcom—very superficial, at least in terms of plot. It was about how Jack was a ne'er-do-well son of a rich man who'd just died. He can't come into his inheritance unless he marries off this cousin, who was Lydia, and he finds this street bum and tries to marry them off. There was also this mean, matriarchal character. Then I threw that whole draft away, except for Lydia, whom I kept for the third draft. Out of each draft I kept something. I liked the character of Lydia. She moved me. She was a sweet, fumbling, weird character I liked.

JE: Based on anyone you know?

RL: No. Well, based a little on *A New Leaf,* the Elaine May film; that draft in particular. Before she evolved into her own, she was more innocent and clumsy. In the third draft I gave her the voice of a kind of bitchy girl. When you hear Lydia she's kind of smart-assy, as opposed to being sweet and gentle. That came in the last draft. After I finished I put it down for a few months. It was really my wife who said that I should finish, that there was something there. At that point I thought it might be just a writing sample, or some quirky independent film. I never thought it would get made the way it did. So I went back to it and decided that the Jack character would become a shock jock along the lines of Howard

Stern. Originally, he was more like Stern. When the script got through Disney, he became more David Letterman. He began more angry than political.

JE: What inspired you to change him to a shock jock?

RL: On weekends, my wife's father would lend us his car. I'd have to drive the car back from Scarsdale to the city, and because I had to do it before the parking changed, we'd have to leave at about six in the morning. So I would turn on the radio and listen to Howard Stern. Ordinarily, I don't listen to the radio. It was on those drives that I realized what an interesting character this was. I have a very negative reaction to the kind of humor that evolved out of the '80s. There's a meanness, a cruelty, a cynicism, an irresponsibility, to it that I really don't like. The meaner you can be. Nothing is sacred. I like satire, which is what *Saturday Night Live* started out to be. What it evolved into, where you couldn't believe anything anybody was saying, just got annoying to me. I couldn't stand it. And the sloppiness. As a talk show host, you could go out there, do your stand-up routine, and if it wasn't funny, then that was the joke. If you didn't get it, then you were stupid.

JE: Andy Kaufman.

RL: I think he was satirizing just that.

JE: Maybe. But they took him seriously.

RL: Letterman, in the early days, he'd go up there with a bad monologue, and that was the joke. I thought, *Why can't they just get good writers to write good jokes?* That annoyed me, that they wanted us to think something was funny because it wasn't funny.

Not funny is not funny. That was just bad writing. Why are we applauding this?

This was Howard Stern five or six years ago; he was just shocking people. Though he did do some funny stuff. I remember when Lorne Greene was dying. Stern used to call up the hospital to find out how Lorne was doing, and the nurse would talk to him.

Anyway, I thought there was an irresponsibility and a narcissism that I wanted to touch on, so that's where that idea came. It took a little while until I connected the Robin Williams character with the tragedy. Once that happened, the script kind of wrote itself.

JE: Once the elements come together, what do you do to get out of the way of the story, so that it can write itself?

RL: For *Fisher King,* it wasn't hard. I'd never been schooled in screenwriting. I came to this as a lover of movies, and the reason I love them is because I love performances. If and when I direct, it won't be because I admire camera angles or anything like that. I watched movies as a kid because I loved actors. I loved watching Bette Davis, I loved watching Spencer Tracy, I just loved their performances. That came from my parents. They were older. When they talked about performances and actors, they sort of glowed. I inherited that.

JE: Did they have any connection to show business?

RL: My dad was a cabdriver. My mom was a mom. They had me late in life, at least for the 1950s. My mom was in her late thirties, my dad in his midforties. Their movies were from the '30s and '40s. My mom used to wake me up, make me stay up till three o'clock in the morning to watch *The Good Earth* with her. They never showed it when I should have seen it, but Louise Rainer gave this incredible performance, so I'd have to watch it. Mom turned me on to movies like *Dodsworth* and *Summertime* and *All About Eve*—movies that I'd rank in the top ten scriptwise.

JE: I don't know if you can be an excellent screenwriter without really loving movies. That may be true of all artistic endeavors to some degree, but movies seem to really need a kind of reverence for the form if the movie is going to be engaging.

RL: Then there are those who love movies so much that everything they write is derivative. All it is is homage to different styles, which I find empty. All this fascination with B movies, which I don't understand. I never really got into that. Reviving these B movies as A movies is weird.

JE: Maybe that reflects the business of filmmaking as opposed to the passion of making films.

RL: Passion gets looked down upon. That's the thing about Oliver Stone. You may like him or not as a filmmaker; he often tends to be a little on the nose; he tells you what to feel and think every second. But I really believe that this guy is filled with this, you know, anger. There's something there. Like him or not, I respect what he does. It's rare to see such passion nowadays.

JE: As a writer?

RL: It's become very hard to put your heart out there. It was easier when I didn't know anything about the business. One of the reasons I don't live in Hollywood is not to be too close to the business. Being in the film industry and living in Hollywood is like being in the car industry and living in Detroit; you hear too much. I don't want to hear what the marketplace is looking for or what's going or who's got what deal. All that stuff. I think it's because I'm too weak. I get too affected by it. I don't read the trades anymore. I don't read *Premiere* magazine anymore. Knowing too much about trends and fads can kill your creativity. With *Fisher King,* I innocently did what I thought. Since then, I've done nothing but assignments, no spec scripts. I'd never earned a real living before, and my wife and I wanted to have a child, wanted to have a home. There was a point where I could have stopped, and I kept on committing, because I was frightened to be out of work. This was before *Fisher King* came out. I doubted that *Fisher King* was real. I didn't have the confidence to think that it was going to last; maybe it was a fluke. So I took jobs. And why not? They were asking. That, coupled with the fact that there was a co-dependency there. When you grow up as kind of an outcast, and all of a sudden these people you admire from afar are asking to work with you, it's like being a kid in a candy store; it's very hard to say no. So I said yes, and got to work with wonderful people. I kind of look at it like I went to grad school. I crammed in three or four years. I don't know how many scripts I've written. I learned a lot. Look, I got to work with Steven Spielberg.

JE: On what?

RL: It's an adaptation of a book called *The Talisman.* Stephen King and Peter Straub. I also wrote an animated version of *Cats* for Spielberg.

JE: You've been busy.

RL: I've been working nonstop for well over a year, and got burnt out creatively. I told myself that I'm going to finish the commitments I have, then I'm going to take two months off and really not work, just read, and rejuvenate, and absorb. Number one, I don't like the writing that's coming out of me now; I think it's mechanical.

JE: Do the people you're writing these scripts for think that?

RL: Well, things are getting made. But for me, I'm doing it out of my last thread. My fear now is that, unless I put everything aside for a while, whatever gift I have will disappear because I've abused it so badly.

JE: I think you share that with most other talented people, especially writers.

RL: That's good to know. I always imagine that other people are really confident.

JE: It's been my experience, talking to talented people for a living, that, often the people who don't question their own talent are the untalented.

RL: Like your soul, you can mistreat your gift. That energy, if it's not channeled in the proper respectful manner, will come out in destructive ways. Do I do a particular script because it's a high-profile project? No. I've worked with people because I wanted to work with them, not always because the material was something I wanted to deal with. I've made it something I wanted to do, but the initial reasons weren't always pure. It wasn't just because I was so turned on by the story. I'd think, *Well, I like the story, I think I can make it work, and it would be nice to have this job because I'll feel more secure.* Or, *Wow, look who's asking me.* Those reasons have to go away. I have to check whether I lean toward doing something as a temptation or a gift. I'm constantly doing that. Sometimes, when I don't know whether to take an assignment, I'll just arbitrarily say one day, "Yeah, I'm doing it." Then I check what happens, what happens to my body, what happens to my feelings. The next day, I'll say, "No, I'm not doing it." Then I check what happens. Am I relaxed, relieved, nervous?

JE: So the point is to be true to whatever drives you.

RL: If my creative energy needs a rest, that's what I have to respect.

JE: How do you know when the work is good? Where does the objectivity come from, if there is any? A writer is not necessarily the best judge of his own work.

RL: I know when it's not good, though I do tend to be overcritical. When I think it's not good is when it reads unoriginal to me, like something I've seen before.

JE: How would you know?

RL: Because I know movies really well. And I know dramatic structure well, and character well. When it's not authentic.

JE: But you're always questioning yourself and your talent. So aren't there times when you look at your work and your stomach turns and you think—

RL: It's shit. Yeah. Those are the days I walk away from it. I don't work that day, because obviously my head isn't in a good place. Before I start work I try to clear that energy up. I meditate. I sit in the chair and focus and clean out my mind and try to get in touch with what I'm feeling; talk to myself a bit. Because I wake up frightened every day, so I have to overcome fear every day.

JE: Do you think there are other writers who don't wake up frightened?

RL: Yeah, I do.

JE: Maybe you're right, but just the process of filling up blank pages or screens with words all the time is atrociously difficult. What could be harder?

RL: Wherever ideas come from, you can't be arrogant enough to believe that they're just coming from you. And what if that day they're not coming?

JE: I'm intrigued by the idea of putting the work aside for the day when you don't think it's right. Isn't there a day when you feel that panic, that fear; then sit down to work, still feeling it, and get past it?

RL: Sure. There are days when I can transform it.

JE: Then why not just work through it all the time?

RL: Because there are days when it needs to be, I think, transformed in a different way. Just because I'm not sitting in front of my computer typing doesn't necessarily mean that my creativity's not working. Sometimes, taking a day off, going to a movie, visiting a bookstore, walking the streets, you relax and suddenly get filled with insights and ideas. You're still working, even though you're not paying attention to it. Then you come back fresh, and you actually have an idea. Sometimes that's part of it.

JE: You're actually able to relax when you walk away?

RL: I can, depending on the situation. If I really give myself permission to go—"You're not in shape to write physically today; go and take a walk, go and just sit"—it actually works real well.

Let me get back to what we were talking about—distinguishing between when the writing is good or not good. I've gotten better at being able to tell, without being the neurotic critic, but being more of the constructive writer. What I've learned, or am beginning to learn, is that when the writing is authentic, as opposed to being clever, I know I'm on the right track.

JE: You can tell the difference between authentic and clever?

RL: I'm starting to. When you write a lot, you can start to tell when you're opting just for a clever idea or a clever line of dialogue, as opposed to telling the truth about what has to be going on in that moment for a character or a story. It's taken a long time, because when you have to write fast and have a lot going on, you tend to be clever. Clever, you get quicker residuals from. But in the long run it doesn't pay off. You can impress people with cleverness, but in the long run it doesn't last.

JE: The people who make decisions about which movies get made seem to prefer clever.

RL: That's what I mean. But the movies that are worth seeing go deeper.

JE: Any examples you can point to of either clever or authentic?

RL: In my own stuff, I hope that by the time the drafts are finished they're not going to be clever but authentic. I can write dialogue that'll flow, on and on and on. It'll make sense, but it's not telling the truth about what a character may feel or not. Sometimes I'll put in a good joke or a funny line, but it doesn't tell the truth; it hides it.

JE: Tell me some of your favorite screenplays over the last ten years.

RL: *Tootsie.*

JE: That's an interesting choice, because it was written by a dozen different writers. It wasn't one person's coherent vision.

RL: It's a great screwball comedy. *Witness. Bull Durham. Do the Right Thing.* I think *Risky Business* was the best coming-of-age screenplay in many years.

JE: How do you get your characters to spark?

RL: With the spec scripts, and to some extent with the assignment scripts as well—because I'm actually more drawn to the characters than the stories—I start with character; I'm not a strong story writer. It takes a great deal of work for me to work on a story. Characters come to me because I'm interested in who people are and why they do what they do. I tend to explore what I think are different aspects of myself ultimately. In *Fisher King,* for example, I felt that I was each of those six characters; different aspects of my self.

I think I begin with myself. The idea I have for a new spec script is about an agoraphobic. What it started from was my own fear, wanting to deal with it, with cowardice.

JE: Of what?

RL: Life. I want to take those fears and put them into a character. A lot of us, I think, believe we're cowards. We all have fears. It would be interesting to define what cowardice and courage are through a character in a film. I want to explore a character who feels so overwhelmed by his fear that he labels himself a coward. How he overcomes that would make an interesting movie. I don't know how, as yet. At this point it's just thematic, but that's the starting place. I have the character.

It was either David Rabe or David Mamet who said that a writer writes what he wants to learn. That applies to me. Themes that I like to explore have to do with questions and problems I have about myself. Characters who sacrifice really intrigue me. I have another spec idea about two sisters—one who's good, one who's bad. Why I read Jungian literature is because archetypes and archetypal energies fascinate me; and the whole thing about myth—what these characters represent. I'm reading a book now called *The Gregory Myth,* about symbolic incest, which is another fascinating relationship to explore. It's incest in a positive way, meaning the marriage of the masculine and the feminine spirit within. If that is not done, what happens is you get the physical incest. That's what we were talking about before: If the energies aren't respected in the right way, they manifest in a distorted way. The story of Gregory begins with him chained to a rock on an island. It's all about how he got there.

With *Fisher King,* I found the grail myth in a Jungian book. It was an analysis of the grail myth with male psychology. The characters of the *Fisher King* story—the Fisher King and Parsifal the knight—parallel different psyches of the male personality in male psychology. So to answer the question of how I make characters real, I begin with these archetypal energies that I believe are present and real in all of us, and find characterizations for them in order to tell stories with them. Then people can learn from them what they need.

JE: Obviously, you would prefer to inhabit a screenplay with flesh and blood in every role. But does every character have to have an absolute air of authenticity? Can you get away with having the most minor characters simply be there to advance the plot?

RL: I'm learning. Initially, I did both. I had throwaways and not. What I'm striving for is to write where every part is alive. For me, it's what Preston Sturges and Billy Wilder did, and Charles Brackett and I. A. L. Diamond. Sturges would have a scene with a bartender. You'd never see him again after that scene. But, it was a great character moment. He was real and three-dimensional. That's what I strive for. I should tell you, you don't get a lot of understanding from studios on that kind of thing. "Why does he need to say this?"

JE: It costs more.

RL: Well, you want to make every moment real, a jewel. It's hard to get that done. If and when I direct, I'd like to be able to do that.

JE: You do want to direct?

RL: I've been offered several things, but I haven't had the time to write what I'm going to direct. I don't want to do other people's stuff, because I'm not a director, I'm a writer.

JE: How about working with a producer who has a strong sense of what he wants, like Scott Rudin?

RL: I have worked with Scott. Terry Gilliam and I wrote a screenplay this past year that Scott produced. It's called "The Defective Detective." It was a story of Terry's that he asked me to write with him. What he said was, *Fisher King* [which Gilliam directed] was him entering my world. Now he wanted to see if what I do can work in his world. It's a fantastical idea. My job was to bring character to it.

JE: You seem to have a particular moral vision. As a writer working in Hollywood, do you ever feel like a square peg.

RL: Something that just drives me nuts about this industry, these executives in Hollywood are the ones who determine what we see in film. But they don't lead real lives, they don't have real relationships, and they're telling us, "Well, no, people don't really act like that." How do they know? They live in ivory towers. They don't know what people are really feeling and thinking. That's why so many of the films coming out these days are so shallow and thin. And of course one thing feeds the other. So the standards are being systematically lowered, as Woody Allen noted. The audience says, "Yeah, okay, yeah, that's okay; it's good." The last few years I feel like I'm on another planet. What critics call masterpieces, I can't stand. *The Bad Lieutenant,* for example, was supposed to be brilliant, dark and brilliant. What are they, nuts?

JE: That goes back to the subject of cynicism. Hip is cynical.

RL: It's getting tiresome. Though it is, I think, swinging back a little. Films like *In the Name of the Father, Schindler's List, Philadelphia,* those are very positive as part of a movement. I haven't been able to understand why critics have been so quick to praise a film simply because of its violence. Like *Reservoir Dogs.* I think they read meaning into it I don't think it had. Quentin [Tarantino, the writer-director] was just doing it for fun. He loves violence. He thought it was entertainment.

JE: A very cynical type of entertainment.

RL: Quentin loves B movies. He's the king of 1970s B movies. Loves them. That's what he sees them as—"Hey, it has no responsibility other than being a movie."

JE: You don't believe that.

RL: No. Art reflects and puts out certain ideas into the atmosphere that are real.

JE: That's the classical idea of art, that it ennobles.

RL: And elevates.

JE: Why does it seem, with the exception of the films you just mentioned and maybe a few others, that there are so few movies representing that? Aren't they being written?

RL: I think they are. More than likely what happens is, executives see a script full of humanity. And they know they should make it. And they're going to make it, but it's the changes that happen between the decision to make it and the time the film is released that is the dangerous period. Their instincts sometimes drive them to do the right thing, to make those kinds of films. But along the way they get suckered into the fears of what people are going to want and what's going to sell, and the idea gets whittled away. That, to me, is worse than saying no at the outset.

JE: If character is your forte, where do you go for help with story, with plot?

RL: I have a friend who's a producer whom I trust, and also my wife; I talk out the idea a bit with them. With *Fisher King* I literally wrote each page as it came; literally let the story unfold by itself. I had the time to do that. On the adaptations, obviously I've had something to work off of. On original work, I tend to want to let the story find its next scene. I'm not a good outliner. I'm actually trying to discipline myself to do that. But I only get so far in outline; I don't do the index card thing that a lot of writers do—one scene per card on a bulletin board. To me, the most original work happens when you let it flow, when you're not constrained by something predetermined from an outline. Outlines, to me, are very rational.

JE: That takes courage—to be willing to go out there with your story, not knowing where you're headed.

RL: Well, I know for a lot of screenwriters, particularly the veterans, the edict is to know where you're headed, to know what your ending is. With *Fisher King,* I had an ending. It just wasn't a story ending. I wanted the Jack character to commit a completely selfless act, to go from narcissism to selflessness. That was my ending. I had no story. I just knew what the idea was; what I wanted to communicate. That's what I have. So as I'm writing, I do have a direction. I just let the story tell me how to get there.

ANDREW
BERGMAN

Before we began our conversation, one week before It Could Happen to
You *opened, Andrew Bergman told me that he wasn't very talkative, but
rather laconic. He wasn't lying. Bergman has written films that have often
doubled me over with laughter, but his answers to questions about the
comedic process indeed proved the adage that comedy is serious business.
Next up for Bergman, he said, was an adaptation of the book* Striptease
and an original political comedy, The Ottoman Empire.

The interview took place over the phone from his home in New York.

JOEL ENGEL: Let's start with *The Freshman,* a film I particularly
enjoyed because it was so fresh and inventive.

ANDREW BERGMAN: The germ came from a *New York Times*
clipping I'd been carrying around for maybe three years, about a
former Mafia informer who had apparently turned straight but
was arrested again in Seattle running an endangered species racket.
He was importing cockatoos and komodo dragons into the country. I just thought, *Well, there's something here.* He wasn't eating
them, that was mine—eating the last of something.

JE: It's such a funny conceit, the idea of making a meal out of
the end of a species. I'm sure it'd be a thrill to a particular psyche.

AB: Of course. What a high.

JE: So from that original idea, how did you bring in all of the other pieces—like the kid with the father who's an animal protectionist and the love story?

AB: It took a long time. That was the hardest script I ever wrote. It took forever. I kept painting myself into one corner after another. I couldn't figure out what the hell to do with it. The innocent kid. In a way, it's not all that different from *So Fine*. It's just a younger version of the naif brought into this world of idiocy.

JE: You had the innocent from the beginning?

AB: I started with him and the father. That I knew. That relationship became progressively less important as the script developed, but it was the starting point.

JE: So you had to have the innocent kid thrown into this world because you needed something to play off of, the conflict.

AB: The usual—being in over one's head.

JE: After that, it's just imagination, putting your feet up and staring out the window?

AB: A lot of that. And a lot of rewriting. I'm a compulsive rewriter, which the computer has made even worse, because it's so much easier to rewrite than in the old days, when I was cranking them out on a typewriter.

JE: Is there either a quantitative or qualitative difference between using a typewriter or pencil and a computer?

AB: Revisions are much easier. There's no physical barrier between you and changing what you want to change. A friend of mine maintains that books are getting longer and longer and longer, because physically it's easier to write a six-hundred-page book now. When you have to sit down at a typewriter to revise, you can much more easily say, "Oh fuck it. Who needs that chapter?" There's something to it. Everything seems to be getting longer—movies, books. Not better, just longer.

JE: Do you rewrite as you go along or wait until you've completed each draft?

AB: As I go along; it's so easy to do on a computer.

JE: Do you ever rewrite out your best work because it's so easy?

AB: I hope not. My producing partner [Mike Lobell] will sometimes say, "What happened to that scene?" I'll say, "I don't find it funny anymore." He'll say, "You may not find it funny anymore, but nobody's actually even seen the joke." I just rewrite things out of boredom.

JE: When did you know you were funny?

AB: I was always pretty funny. I was the youngest child. Younger children try to be funny as a way of getting attention. I was small as a kid—all of those things, always one of the funny kids in class.

JE: Well, yours is dry humor, not slapstick, not attention-getting kind of humor. It's situational, not dependent on punch lines.

AB: Never jokes. The biggest laughs are never jokes. That's my strength: situation and character. Sometimes the characters are the situations, as in *The In-Laws*.

JE: Another wonderful film.

AB: It was fun. I stand behind it.

JE: How did it originate?

AB: Warner Brothers came to me and said, "We'd like you to write the sequel to *Freebie and the Bean.*" I said, "Who the hell wants to write *Freebie and the Bean?*" They said, "Well, it's not really that; it's that Alan Arkin and Peter Falk want to make a picture together." They seemed like such a natural combination to be together; they're such opposites. One is such a snail, the other a hysteric. What a wonderful opportunity, I thought, to create situations in which Peter is constantly eating into Alan. That's really all the movie was.

JE: What's the next creative step toward the realization of that movie after you've had that initial thought about these two characters, one eating into the other?

AB: When you think of situation, you think of juxtaposition. The rule I always have is: either ordinary people doing extraordinary things, or extraordinary people doing ordinary things. You or I hailing a cab isn't interesting; Queen Elizabeth hailing a cab is interesting. It's as simple as that. Or, a schlemiel involved in South American politics is better than a nonschlemiel. That's one rule.

Then it's about taking disparate things. I'm not a big reader of critics, but there's a guy named [Michael] Sragow who's always been a big fan of mine. He always seemed to have a handle on stuff I did. In his review of *Honeymoon in Vegas* for *The New Yorker,* he described it as "pastiche." I thought that was interesting. It's sort of like collage, taking things people know already, then rearranging them. They know Bert Parks and they know

Brando, but they never saw Bert Parks and Brando in the same shot. Or, they know Bert Parks and they know Dylan, but how about Bert Parks singing "Maggie's Farm"?

So I think there is something in pastiche that rings true. Less so, actually, in *It Can Happen to You*. It's different from anything I've done before.

JE: More linear?

AB: That, and it's a straightahead romance. It's different.

JE: You didn't get screen credit on *It Could Happen to You,* but I noticed in the Writers Guild guide that you wrote a script titled "Cop Gives Waitress Two Million Tip," which is the same story.

AB: It wasn't my original script. I was sent a script originally with the names Jane Anderson and Stephen Metcalfe on it, which I proceeded to rewrite. Those were the credits that were going to be on the film. TriStar then submitted the script for arbitration after Jane Anderson went to the Guild. She wound up with sole credit.

JE: The film definitely has Bergman rhythms and sensibility to it.

AB: I only wrote seven drafts of it.

JE: You get more out of Nicholas Cage than anyone else. You used him to great advantage in *Honeymoon in Vegas*. I can't think of another actor who could have done that role so appealingly.

AB: I love him to death. I never thought of him for the part. He came in to read for it. On the page, the James Caan part was the better part, but Nick changed all that.

JE: When you write—

AB: Very rarely do I have someone in mind for the part. Obviously, there were instances when I wrote scripts specifically for someone, like *The In-Laws,* like *Fletch,* which was adapted from a [Gregory McDonald] novel with Chevy Chase in mind as the star. When I heard that Brando was definitely going to do *The Freshman,* I obviously rewrote it just for him. Usually, I may have someone in mind just to make it more specific, but that's not to say that the part is written *for* that person. It's more a job of tailoring after the fact to a specific talent.

JE: How often do you base characters on people you know?

AB: I base them on combinations of different people, their characteristics. Every writer's tape is always rolling, observing people. I eavesdrop in restaurants; I eavesdrop everywhere. I live a life that's not insulated from the world. I live in New York. I go on buses and subways. I see what people are doing, what they're wearing. I'm not imagining what people are thinking; I'm still a part of the world.

Recently, I was walking on Eighth Avenue and saw a woman in a bathrobe and slippers hailing a taxi. A cab pulled over and she got in. Nobody noticed her, nobody pointed, nobody cared. That's what's so wonderful. Only in New York would you see something like that; there's nothing extraordinary about it here.

JE: When you worked with Mel Brooks on *Blazing Saddles,* were you there to provide gag lines or situations or both?

AB: We were just there to be funny. I'd written the original screenplay. But since I was twenty-six years old at the time, I automatically assumed that I was going to be bounced off the script. But Mel Brooks thought I should stay on, that it was my baby.

JE: I didn't realize that that was your original idea, your script.

AB: The original idea was a black sheriff in the old West. Doing a send-up of all Westerns was Mel's take on it. At that point in my life, twenty-six years old, I said, "Hey, whatever." I was just amazed to be in the room. It was the first thing I'd ever done. I didn't know what my strengths and weaknesses were.

JE: You'd never written anything before?

AB: The first screenplay.

JE: How wonderful.

AB: It was pretty great. The thing I learned was, *You never know.* None of us thought anybody was going to see the movie. We wrote it as a big private joke. Mel was a cult figure at that time. That was more gag-oriented, I would say. More brainstorming, *Show of Shows* style—three are at the table, five people are at the table. It was the last time I worked that way.

JE: How much different was the original draft from the movie we see?

AB: Hugely different. The sheriff was more a Paul Bunyan figure, more folkloric in nature; it was more a black-white story—not of toll booths and farting.

JE: I'm betting that the cowboys farting around the campfire was a Mel Brooks idea.

AB: Yes. The toll booth was mine; farting was his.

JE: Did you like that film?

AB: I thought it was very, very funny, though I think for pure Mel, *The Producers* is funnier—his essence. My younger son, who's eleven, has just gotten into *The Producers,* which means he watches it every day. It's very funny. Some of the stuff is paralyzing.

JE: Who else making comedy do you like?

AB: Very few people are making comedy nowadays. Woody still makes me laugh. *Manhattan Murder Mystery* definitely made me laugh. Who else is there? *Four Weddings and a Funeral* was hilarious.

JE: I thought so too. But I don't think it's the same kind of humor yours is.

AB: I do. It's very much character and situation.

JE: But it seemed to have more gag lines than your films.

AB: Yes, but the humor came from situations. I can't remember a joke in it.

JE: Your films have a sort of cumulative effect. I get hooked at the beginning on this situation you're setting up, which continues to get odder, more absurd.

AB: They run the risk, always, of being slow at the beginning. It's a calculated risk that I have to take in order let the viewer know who the characters are. That's really been my method, taking that risk. People can wonder if it's ever going to get going. Of them all, *It Could Happen to You* is probably the only one not to follow that.

JE: Your films work idiosyncratically, like an acquired taste. The longer you watch, the more sucked in you get. The characters become involved in increasingly interesting situations.

AB: Well, they have their own reality. In and of themselves, the lines the characters say may be funny, but they're certainly funnier in context.

JE: My impression is that each successive draft adds another layer or two on.

AB: As a rule, that's true. You put down the story then laminate these other things over it, until you reach a point where it's too thick and you start scaling things back.

JE: Do you enjoy the writing, or would you rather take a finished script and direct it?

AB: Finished script? Everyone dreams of being handed a finished script they can shoot; it almost never happens. I liked starting with someone else's script, as I did with *It Could Happen to You*. Writing is awfully hard. Directing is, too, but in a different way. With directing, it's social, and there's coffee and bagels and people and jokes. Writing is just you, feeling like a moron eighty percent of the time. In my old age I like directing more and more and writing less and less.

JE: You feel like a moron much of the time because . . .

AB: Because I can't figure it out. I can't get it. Can't get to the next part of the movie, and I feel like a dumbbell.

JE: What do you do when that happens?

AB: I work through it. Norman Mailer said that professional writers are people who write on a bad day. That's what I do. Very rarely do I say, "That's it, I'm outta here."

JE: Do you have to be in a good mood to write comedy?

AB: No. You should be in a bad mood to write comedy. Comedy comes out of anger so often. There's nobody more pissed off than comedians. They're a very angry group of people. There's not a song in my heart, no.

JE: But *Honeymoon in Vegas* has a song in its heart.

AB: I really wanted to write a boy-girl story.

JE: There's something wonderfully twisted about that particular boy-girl story. Can you remember the story's birth?

AB: The first draft stunk, then it slowly started getting better, draft by draft.

JE: You know the story's going to have a lot of complications when the main character has to tell his fiancée that he's lost her in a poker game. Did that come from your playing poker?

AB: I used to be in a poker game. I miss it. Being in Vegas for a month, shooting the picture, was a nightmare. Living in a Vegas hotel is sensory deprivation. It was a relief to finally go outside and shoot the night stuff. Vegas at night is great. It's eighty-five degrees, everybody's out there. The best night shooting in the world.

JE: Was *Soapdish* an original?

AB: That was a rewrite. Robert Harling [who wrote *Steel Magnolias*] had written a script that was lying around at Paramount. I had finished *The Freshman* and was looking to make a quick buck because I'd spent a lot of time on *The Freshman* for a low directing fee. So I called my agent and said, "You know, I've never done this, but I'd like to do a rewrite. Get me something to do for three weeks." I'd never, until that time, done a rewrite, and I haven't done one since.

JE: Aren't you asked all the time to tend to comedies as a script doctor?

AB: Yes, but I don't do them. I'd rather do my own work. You can get caught up in it, making all this money working on other people's stories. You're like a garage mechanic, which is not how I see my role in the world. I'd rather not put in new carburetors.

Anyway, he sent me two scripts, one of which was *Doc Hollywood*. I thought it was sweet but didn't know what the hell to do with it. The other was *Soapdish,* which I thought I could work with.

JE: Was your intention to become a comedy writer?

AB: I still don't think of myself as a comedy writer. I think of myself as a writer. I never thought I would do it professionally, but I began writing as a kid and always liked it. I thought I would be a history professor and write novels on the side, late at night.

JE: Are you saying a "history" professor as a metaphorical example?

AB: Not at all. I have a Ph.D. in American history.

JE: I didn't know that. That's why you didn't begin writing professionally until you were twenty-six. You were in grad school.

AB: Right. I wrote a doctoral dissertation on American movies in the 1930s, which became a book called *We're in the Money*. I came out of that thinking that I'd rather be involved in the movie business than the history business.

JE: Do you still have an academic inclination?

AB: I'm still sort of an academic. I have that side of me. I think that's why *So Fine* was about academia; it was a metaphor for me in the movie business. Ryan O'Neal going into the dress business was really me going into the movie business.

JE: Ryan O'Neal seems to me to have been interesting casting.

AB: He's a great physical comedian. First of all, Warner Brothers wasn't going to let me do the picture unless we had a major star in it. Ryan was it. I mean, he's not the logical person to play an English professor who's Jewish. But I really wanted to make the picture, so I said, "Screw it." Ryan is a great physical comedian—I think one of the great wasted talents. He's extraordinarily funny.

The movie was a bomb, but I must say that, to this day, some of the funniest things I've ever done were in that movie. Jack Warden's performance was hysterical. The opera sequence. The whole ongoing thing between Warden and the buyers. For sheer, piss-in-the-pants funny, the movie has some of the best dialogue I've ever written.

JE: Do you know something is truly funny when you write it, or do you need external validation?

AB: If I laugh, it's funny. Now, it may not be funny to an audience. For instance, the preview audiences at *Honeymoon in Vegas* didn't respond at all to Chief Orman, the Peter Boyle character [a singing shaman of sorts]. They didn't get it at all, but I thought it was funny.

JE: Are you saying that it's unimportant whether the audience laughs?

AB: Not at all; it's very important. But I'll go to my grave insisting that some things are funny that the audience didn't think were funny, like the Boyle character. Critics thought that was funny, by the way. Most audiences thought the funniest thing in *The Freshman* was the lizard running through the shopping mall. I didn't think it was the funniest. I thought it was the worst.

JE: It was pretty funny.

AB: Nah, it was dumb—and I wrote it.

JE: Matthew Broderick was terrific in that.

AB: Yes, he was. He's an excellent re-actor. He was adorable.

JE: Do you laugh while you're writing?

AB: Sometimes—if it's funny.

JE: Is there one film you'd gladly put on your epitaph?

AB: To me, it's the body of work. It's like saying "Which of your children do you like the best?" Well, you like them all for different reasons. I like each of my movies for different reasons as well.

JE: Before you directed, was it difficult to hand over scripts to the director, and thereby lose control?

AB: It really wasn't. First of all, *Blazing Saddles* turned out so well. *The In-Laws* also turned out well. I didn't turn to directing because I felt that directors were butchering my scripts. I did it because I just wanted to direct. *So Fine* was in 1981; I'd only been in the business for eight years. It wasn't as though my search through the desert had finally come to an end.

JE: Are you constantly writing down ideas?

AB: No. Maybe some writers do that, but not me.

JE: You don't take notes in order to add layer after layer—a sudden thought in the shower ultimately becoming the center-piece of act three?

AB: No. None of the above.

JE: So you sit down each day at the computer, tabula rasa, and that's it?

AB: Yep. It's a hard way to do it, let me tell you.

JE: So you stop working when you're not working?

AB: I'm done for the day. My mind is always working, though. It's like Con Edison: Somewhere a light bulb is on. Things are happening in my brain, so maybe the next day a connection is made that wasn't made the previous day. But basically, the way I write is by jumping out of a plane without knowing if the parachute will open. It's dangerous.

JE: What's the most fun you've ever had writing?

AB: There have been different kinds of fun. *Blazing Saddles* because of the group experience. I never laughed so hard in my life, between Mel and Richard Pryor, that was a hilarious room. Rewriting *The Freshman* for Brando was great, because it was such fun to know that I was going to have this unbelievable weapon: He was going to be doing that wonderful send-up [of his *Godfather* character]; that was particularly delicious. Knowing he was going to be saying those lines was heaven.

JE: Did you think of Brando for the part?

AB: I had a contact with him because he was a big *In-Laws* fan. He had called me out of the blue in 1987 just to talk about the film. So when we started casting *The Freshman,* my partner said, "Why don't we send it to Brando?" I said, "Come on." He said, "No, I have a feeling he's going to go for this." He did.

JE: How was the part originally written?

AB: It was for a much younger guy.

JE: He was wonderful, imitating himself imitating the Godfather.

AB: Well, he did a new guy. He started with the don and then made him another guy. He kept saying, "Oh, he'd never say that." I would say, "Pretend it's your own little joke. Put quotes around it." Once he got that, he was off. He went even further. It's like a Falstaff version of don Corleone.

JE: Convivial, yes. That's right. The avuncular presumed killer. When you were working with Mel Brooks and Richard Pryor, did you feel you were their equal?

AB: Yes, I did. Richie was sort of on the outs at that moment; a sort of washed-up comedian at that point. We're talking about 1972. He was kind of nowhere. And Mel was coming off two flop pictures. So it wasn't like I was terrified to walk in their presence. Anyway, I've never been a person who's intimidated. That's how I was able to work with Marlon Brando. I'm not intimidatable.

JE: Are you confident about your work?

AB: Depends which day you're asking. Today, I'm confident.

JE: Would you ever attempt a collaboration? Can you see yourself working with another writer?

AB: I don't think so. It depends on the person or the project. That's not my inclination, but if there's a wonderful idea and a wonderful writer, why the hell not.

JE: Is there anyone you can call for help when you're stuck?

AB: No. No one does what I do. I'm not saying that out of ego, it's just that I do a specific thing that other people don't do.

JE: Your wife?

AB: She can help me out in a generalized way, because she's a shrink; she can't help me out writing. But my kids, my partner, they're good sounding boards. Mike's been my partner for fifteen years, so I know he's not going to blow smoke up my ass. The danger is that people will say "great" when it isn't. That's the worst thing that can happen. I know that if it isn't great that Mike will be honest with me.

JE: Let's go back to something you mentioned before. What is it about comedy that lends itself to rechanneled anger?

AB: Humor is a defense. It's something you do instead of getting angry. It's more socially acceptable.

JE: Quips more than situational humor like yours.

AB: Quips, yes, that's an example. Instead of punching someone, you quip. But generalized as well. Humor is still a way of dealing with frustrations of various sorts. *Honeymoon* is about a guy who's continually blowing up; that's where the humor is.

JE: There's a lot of humor that's based in anger. I'm not sure that I'd classify yours that way. Sure, this was about an angry guy, but that's not necessarily the same as angry humor.

AB: It's not that the humor itself is angry, it's that humor is a way of dealing with anger.

JE: The synthesis you create of situations and realities is driven by a worldview that's not bemused.

AB: I wouldn't describe myself as bemused. I may act in a way that's bemused, but my nature is not bemused.

JE: Your comic take is different than, say, Richard Pryor's, which was about anger; or Mel Brooks, who sees himself as a Jew stuck in a Gentile world. Neither of them feels at home in the world. I don't get that from you.

AB: I don't know that I feel out of place. I'm a first-generation American, so my relationship to this country is different from someone whose family has been here several generations. In some ways, I have more of a European sensibility. My humor is not traditional stand-up Jewish humor. It's not Mel's; it's not even Woody's. It is not ethnic. That's a store that other people have run successfully. I didn't want to open up the same store.

SCOTT FRANK

I first met Scott Frank in 1992, when Dead Again *came out, to write a piece on him for the* New York Times. *Since we'd spent so much of that two or three hours together talking about screenwriting and imagination, Scott was the first person I thought to include in this book. "Writers are the weak link in filmmaking right now," he told me then. "The scripts that sell for the most money usually have titles like* Hell-bent *and* Back, Texas Lead *and* Gold, The Rest of Daniel. *They're high-concept and half-baked. I don't hear writers say anymore, 'I love this idea; I'm on fire with this idea.' Instead you hear, 'I'm gonna write this script in two weeks and sell it for a million-five. It's a concept: Arnold Schwarzenegger as a woman—and she's a cop.' "*

I was then, and remain, impressed by how much consideration Frank has given to the creative process and to what makes movies enjoyable. A genuinely warm man, he speaks with enthusiasm and passion.

The interview was conducted in his second-story office behind his Los Angeles hillside home.

JOEL ENGEL: Until recently, you were an extremely slow writer—sometimes half a page a day. Now you say that you've learned to write faster. How'd you do that?

SCOTT FRANK: In some ways I am writing faster. In other ways I'm still up to my old tricks. I wrote a lot in the last year—a lot of things that were not my own ideas. I adapted a novel, and I co-created a television series [*Birdland*], but even the original core idea came from someone else; and then I adapted the "Fallen Angels" short story. I had gotten to a point in my writing, when I was writing my originals, where I would agonize. The ratio of what I threw away to what I kept was fifty to one, and I really wanted to find out why that was and why I was so afraid to move forward and why it took so long. So I decided to take on assignments for which I was forced to write quickly. One adaptation I did, they wanted a first draft in twelve weeks. For the "Fallen Angels" episode there was a very hard start date that I had to have the show by. And for the television series, you know, you're always running in front of a train, because they're shooting one right after the other. You're always rewriting other people, and you're always rewriting yourself. We wrote one episode in four days that shot two days after we finished pulling it out of our typewriters.

JE: A sixty-minute episode in four days?

SF: Yes. One day I wrote twenty pages.

JE: So what did you learn?

SF: Well, I learned that sometimes there is no right or wrong. The problem was, I was trying to land on what's right. "This is the right way to go." With my own work, I was always looking for the solitary "right" way. What you realize is that, in storytelling, there's only what works. There could be a wide variety of things that work, not just one thing. The lesson learned is that when you fly by instinct, you kind of know what works. It might not be the best choice, but it can still work. There are different levels of how well something can work. That was the lesson I learned, and I still believe that you must take your time and that most writers write too fast and don't do enough rewriting today— screenwriters in particular. They write too fast and they don't rewrite. Look at the films. You'll see a film that will be a great idea that's not fully realized—a lot of characters that were left undone. A lot of it will be good, but *this* part won't be good. Even *The Fugitive,* which everyone loved, the last third of that movie is stupid. He was getting in a fight with this doctor. He should have been fighting with the one-armed man in some interesting way. It was the exact reverse of what should have been happening. Suddenly this doctor is this very physical guy who we're suddenly supposed to be afraid of?

One of the differences between screenwriting and writing a novel is that in the novel, you can get into a character's brain. If you so love the character whose head you're in, you don't care if the plot isn't working right. You can be the writer. But I do believe that the main reason you go to movies is to see a story being told. You want the experience of living through this story. What happens in most screenplays is there's always one thing that I call "The Problem." It could be your third act, it could be your ending, it could be your opening, it could be one character, but it's The Problem. And every draft has it. They may even bring in new writers to try and solve The Problem, but it's always there. And what happens is, because getting a green light is such a precious commodity, once the movie gets going, people say, "We'll solve The Problem on the run." And then it'll be, "We'll solve The Problem in casting." Or, "We'll solve The Problem while we're shooting." "We'll solve The Problem directorially." Then it will be, "We'll solve The Problem in editing." But it's always there, and what happens is The Problem ends up on a screen fifty feet tall.

It's there because no one ever dealt with it, and because movies are about getting made. Sometimes getting it made is more important than getting it made well.

JE: It takes on a life of its own. Like with *Godfather III.* "We don't have time for another draft."

SF: "We just need *Godfather III.*" There are certain sequels where, if they're in focus, people are going to go for the first week, and they're going to make a certain amount of money. Which is a shame, because I'd love to see, for example, a great *Dirty Harry* sequel. I'd love to see one of those movies be great. Why can't they be well written? I'd love to see a well-written *Die Hard* sequel. The weak link in all filmmaking right now—and I truly believe this—is the writing.

JE: That has to be the weak link because, technically, everything else has gotten better.

SF: Even acting. The acting is almost always good. The technical aspect—movies are made beautifully. The one skill that we've lost is storytelling. So what movies are supposed to be, they're not. The problem is screenwriters don't focus enough on storytelling. For a while, their movies became conceptual: The story didn't matter. It was Eddie Murphy in Beverly Hills. Who cared? You just wanted situations. It could be episodic. It really didn't matter. You wanted to see him in an expensive store. You wanted to see him in a restaurant. Tom Cruise in an airplane. Tom Cruise in anything. There are certain kinds of movies that were so high-concept that the plot really was unimportant.

But what's happening with all the different mediums now coming into play, with all the different markets and avenues, the audience is sort of changing. You see movies like a *Driving Miss Daisy* or a *Fried Green Tomatoes* and you go, "How the hell did that ever make $100 million?" It shouldn't by rights have made $100 million.

JE: By those rules.

SF: Yes, by "those" rules. But what you realize is that people are hungry for character and story.

There really is an audience that really wants real storytelling. And so for me, I only know how to write what I know how to write. There are other people who can write great action concept movies and do them well, but I think in terms of plot. By doing all these assignments, I wanted to reduce my writing to its simplest form so I could look at it, and so I could see just how I worked: If I were forced to write quickly I wouldn't have time to kind of censor myself the way I had in the past.

JE: I don't know what that means, "reduce my writing to the simplest form."

SF: Just telling the story. Just having to tell the story. Sometimes with my own work I'll take huge amounts of time off, trying to get reinspired. I'll be stuck on this one section. I'll literally want to inspire myself just for that one section of the story. I'll try and figure out a way to kind of catch it again, just for that part of the movie. *This middle part, I don't know what the problem is. It's sinking in the second act here.* To solve the problems, I read and take notes and take a lot of time off. And I began thinking that instead of doing that, what if I just work on a lot of things? Would I be able to solve the problems just by having to solve them?

JE: While you're working on that script or working on another script?

SF: Working on others.

JE: You were unable, when you got to a problem part, just to skip over it?

SF: I start with character, and from character create my plot. The more complex the characters, the more complex the plot. At first, I load it up full of character and plot, so there's too much—jammed, almost like a novel. I do everything: I digress. I tell every story about every person. Laying it out that way, I end up with a very long draft. Then I begin cutting.

But what happens is the characters and the ideas remain, almost like a phantom limb. You're know it's still there even though it's been cut out of the story. You're still aware of these things that have been in the story, and I don't think that you can have that kind of richness unless you start off with a lot of character and a lot of plot. If you try to build from nothing, it feels that way. You can't mine something from nothing. If you start from an interesting character, and build on why he is who he is, and what he wants, you can build a fascinating plot, whether it's simple or complex. I personally happen to be more attracted to complex. One of the keys to being a good storyteller is the element of surprise. People can't know where you're going; they have to be surprised. That doesn't necessarily mean twists, just that the viewer can't be ahead of the movie. That's crucial.

JE: When you say you start from character, do you mean that you start with an idea for a character, then flesh it out with observation and imagination?

SF: My process is very messy. I begin by writing about all the characters. I take months. Along the way I begin to picture them in certain scenes, and those would illuminate the character. I get ideas, and ideas beget other ideas, and I just keep going. I just write anything about my character—little stories about situations in his past or her past. I write situations that they're going to encounter in the story that I know have to be in. For every character, I write all the scenes that I know have to be in there. I end up with fifty pages of notes.

I just keep writing and writing and writing. Every character's whole story—where they're going to end up; why they're with this person or that person; what their kind of flaw is; who's haunted by what, which is my favorite theme—people being haunted by something from before. I love that whole notion, whether it's past lives or five years ago or five minutes ago, because I believe there's one moment in every person's life that defines him for the rest of his life, whether he's aware of it or not. There's this moment that you keep going back to and you keep trying to redo in some way or another.

JE: Regardless of whether you've overcome it?

SF: It's still a defining moment. And it's there for you either subconsciously or consciously. There's this thing that you keep, and you kind of design your life to play that moment out again and again and again. For me, every character is like that.

JE: Do you know the defining moment of every major character?

SF: Have to.

JE: And it doesn't usually even end up on the page?

SF: No, though sometimes it does because it's very dramatic and interesting, and I want it to be on the page. The most dramatic thing for me is to have someone encounter his worst nightmare.

JE: So having these defining moments for your characters gives them a direction that they're pointed in, and that creates the plot?

SF: And that creates the plot.

JE: Do you often start with the character and have no sense of plot?

SF: Sometimes I get them both at the same time. In the case of *Dead Again,* it all came to me whole cloth. I got a major chunk of the plot and a major chunk of the characters literally in a five-minute period of time.

JE: What were you doing when that happened?

SF: I was supposed to be writing another script at the time [which became *Plain Clothes,* directed by Martha Coolidge], but I was stuck. I'd had this title, *Dead Again,* in my head forever. I just thought it was a funny idea for the name of a movie. I love film noir, and thought it had a noir yet wry sound to it. Just sitting there daydreaming, thinking about that title, I thought, "What if it told two stories?" Obviously the title suggests some kind of reincarnation.

Then I started thinking about this man who has no identity whatsoever and is forced to protect this young girl. Initially she was a fourteen-year-old girl who has some mental problem: She doesn't know who she is. He's supposed to protect her and yet find out who she is. In so doing, he finds out she's this woman from forty years ago who perhaps killed him in a past life. So he's protecting the person who killed him. That was it. Originally it was going to be like *Lolita*—Raymond Chandler does *Lolita*. He falls in love with this fourteen-year-old girl, and in the end she kills him again. Obviously, the movie changed greatly after that, once I started writing.

JE: When an idea comes to you, do you write it down or let it germinate inside?

SF: At a certain point I write it down, but if it's really strong I keep it in my head. There will be an idea that's been in my head for a year or two, and at a certain point when I'm really kind of ready for it, I think that I'm so love with this this idea—when I haven't stopped thinking about it for a year or two—that I want to write it next. "Widowmaker," the script I'm doing now, is an idea I've had in my head for a long time.

I began with this character in my head, and just started writing about him. From the character came the whole sense of plot, and I also had the title—I had the title and drew the character.

JE: What was the original inspiration?

SF: Wouldn't it be interesting if you had a guy who as a young boy was absolutely terrified of everything, especially of his father, and the way his father treated him and his mother. This guy grows up to be a hired killer. He loves to kill people. How did that happen? What was the turn in his life that made that happen?

The joke was, wouldn't it be interesting if it never happened but someone just *told* him it happened? His mother is responsible for his father's death. But the boy, at fourteen, has gone to jail for the killing because the mother says, "If you go to jail, you'll only be in for two years. If I go, I'll be in there forever—and there's your baby brother. Who's going to be a mother to your baby brother? So be good. We all wanted him dead anyway, because we were all afraid of him. This was a good thing."

JE: You seem to like, or at least to write about, the theme of identity—either finding one or denying one.

SF: You get into trouble when you try to be someone else. The joke is, for this man, he isn't this man, but he's become this man, therefore he has to live with himself. The irony in this story is that he really isn't trying to deny who he is.

JE: It's one thing to start building a character; it's another to create incidents that illuminate the character. Is that purely imagination?

SF: Yes.

JE: Is there a trick to unleashing that imagination?

SF: Relaxing, and not trying to unleash it. There is a very small percentage of the time at your typewriter when you're operating on pure inspiration. Imagination is a part of that. Imagination sometimes involves more work than inspiration. Inspiration is that thing that happens when you're not even thinking; you don't know where you are, don't even know what's happening. Your fingers are just clicking as fast as they possibly can. You make the most typos. You're operating purely on inspiration. Maybe two percent of the time are you operating that way. Everything else is designed to get you there. Everything else is to relax you, or focus the juices, or make yourself ready. It's all busy work until getting to that point, then you have that small burst of energy. Then you work from that, writing, rewriting; it gives you other ideas for fixing other things that may have gone before, so you go back and do that. Then you get another little piece of inspiration. You keep adding on, little by little.

JE: That's why you can't skip ahead.

SF: I begin each day rewriting what I did the day before. The last part of the day, I may write something new—if I get to there. And I may not.

JE: Do these moments of satori come every day?

SF: Sometimes. But sometimes they come once a week. And sometimes, for weeks on end, it's like busy work. I'll sit there, day after day, proofreading. I feel myself doing damage to the script. I then have to admit that, okay, I'm in a spot; a victim of creative inertia. Whether it's the planets or something in my personal life or fatigue, whatever it is I have to get myself out of that groove. For me, it's some sort of sleight of hand or distraction creatively, maybe reading. It's not, for me, working on something else, as it is for other people. The juices are too precious, so I don't want to do that.

JE: When you read, are you able to shut it out of your mind so that you can actually concentrate on what you're reading? Or is it like a split-screen image?

SF: I don't turn it off. I move it to the back of my mind. I read something that may be kind of like what I'm working on.

JE: Are they interacting, the two of them?

SF: Absolutely. I'm thinking, *Oh, so that's how he solved that problem*. Or, *This is interesting*. You're looking for a new way of seeing.

Sometimes you just can't force it. For me, when I try to force it, holding a gun to the back of my head, I can't write. That's when I'm stuck. Because there are also times when I'm just lazy and just don't want to confront it. On television shows, you do have a deadline all the time, and you do have to write through it. Sometimes it's not as inspired. A lot of the writing I've done in the past year gets the job done, but I don't think about it all the time the way I do "Widowmaker." I don't think about [my adaptation of the Elmore Leonard novel] *Get Shorty* the way I do about "Widowmaker." I don't think about *Birdland* or "The Fallen Angels" all the time the way I do about "Widowmaker." I'm writing good stories, and I know they're well done, but they're not inspired the way my own stuff is. That's why I take so long on my own stuff. I build on every moment; there's not just a moment to get me to the next moment.

JE: In television, there's such a thing as "good enough."

SF: Yes. Which you're forced to do, because there's not enough time. At least for me. There are very inspired television writers, which I don't think I am. I do believe that the bulk of good writing in Hollywood right now is on television, not in movies. The consistently best storytelling is happening on television. For whatever reason, my process doesn't accommodate that. I'm left feeling unfinished.

JE: "Widowmaker" is a spec script?

SF: Yes.

JE: So you can afford to take your time with it.

SF: I work with people who know that I have a rather long process. And I involve people, too; I keep it for a while, then give it to them; then keep it for a while, then give it to them. A lot of scripts that turned out to be bad movies are really first drafts. That happens a lot when the director is the screenwriter. He feels as a screenwriter that he doesn't have to take notes from a director anymore, and the director thinks that the screenwriter got it right the first time out.

JE: When the two are the same, the director can be the writer's worst enemy—like a lawyer representing himself.

SF: Movies are a more exact science than books. Movies are ninety minutes to two hours, and you really have to hit those beats. In a book, you can go off and lose him and get him back and lose him. People pick up a book, put it down, pick it up, put it down. Movies don't have that luxury. The audience is sitting there saying, "Okay, excite me." You have to be specific. And by its very nature, film is collaborative. It's a question of finding people who can protect you from you, and who know how to let you go and aren't going to inhibit you to follow your own voice. That's why writers who find that with a particular team tend to work with them over and over.

JE: You're also supposed to get help from studio executives. I remember talking some time ago to a writer who was pitching a story to some executives. Giving background and color, she told them that it had elements of *Tobacco Road* in it. One of the executives wagged a finger at her and said, "No smoking." The question is, How literate does an executive have to be in order to help you?

SF: The more literate a producer or studio executive is, the more resourceful he or she is. When you have a problem you can say, "Remember that great moment in *Tess* when she put the letter under the door and it went under the rug?" Or something like that. You can call upon allusions that might be appropriate to the script, maybe give some insight or inspiration. To be unaware of those things as even just cultural touchstones means that you're limited. You may also not know good from bad. It helps.

JE: What do you think of Joel and Ethan Coen's movies?

SF: I love watching their movies. I'm always very entertained. But I don't know if I ever really care about what's happening. I find that I'm interested and intrigued and having a great of time. And I keep thinking, "That's so smart. That's so clever. That's so smart. That's so clever." But for me it goes back to this character thing. What interests me is watching a movie and wanting what the character wants. When you're thinking about a character, that's the base issue. Even more important than the defining moment is, How did that defining moment define what the character wants now? That's the most basic question you can ask about any character, and you should be able to answer it: "What does he want?" Watching a movie, the audience should either want what the character wants or not want what he wants, and at the end the character should either get what he wants or not get it in a very dramatic way.

The other thing a movie script has to have is conflict. Not just the overall plot, but even within a scene. Let me give me you a dumb example: If a character wants a cookie, he shouldn't just be able to get his cookie out of the jar. The jar should be hard or impossible to get at. He has to climb on a ladder and the ladder breaks, and he's in a hurry.

Every scene has to have inherent conflict. Nothing happens easy. If a guy goes in to get information from someone and they just give him information, that's boring. But if he goes in to find out what color hair the other guy has and ends up finding out he lives right down the block—whatever the conflict is—that's interesting. As a writer you always want to be thinking, "How can I turn this scene? What's in the way? What's the conflict here?"

JE: When the lights go down, you say, "All right. I'm suspending disbelief right now. Okay, filmmaker, you've got X number of minutes to keep me suspending it."

SF: Right.

JE: "And if you do something that violates the reality you've spent X number of minutes setting up, I'm gone." What often happens to me, I start watching myself watching the movie, rather than watching the movie.

SF: I can only comment on what I know how to do and what I respond to as an audience member. I try to write movies that turn me on while I'm writing. Sometimes they don't work. Sometimes, I still feel very immature as a writer—like I'm still at the beginning. I used to have this big, big bug up my ass about directing; now I have this bug up my ass about figuring out how to become a better writer because I can't believe I've gotten away with it to a certain degree. I want to get better because I know I have good ideas. What's in my mind's eye is infinitely better than what I do on the page.

JE: Doesn't every writer feel that way?

SF: Probably. In my own case, I want to just narrow the gap a little bit. The more tools I have, the better I'll be able to mine what's in my head.

JE: What are the tools and how do you get them?

SF: I'm not sure. I think it's just writing a lot. It's a question of experience. The way to become a better writer, like the way to become a better anything, is to do it more—to just write a lot, and to think about it, and to become aware of it, and to stretch. A lot of writers get in this place where they know what they're doing and they know how to write a certain kind of thing, so they keep on doing it. The way you get better at anything is to stretch a little bit. That doesn't mean writing outside your voice. But it does mean taking on a little more.

JE: Do you see a lot of movies?

SF: I see a lot of movies, but I probably read more books than I see movies.

JE: They're really not related at all.

SF: No. Prose writing is a great way to learn about character because I think the best character work is done in fiction. The plots are aren't always that satisfying to me, but I always love the character work. It always makes me continue to think harder about my own work: *Is this guy just too simplistic? Is this just too simplistic?*

JE: Are there any films that you look to when you're stuck? Something that has such a brilliant screenplay that you just have to study it again? Are there scenes that so move you, that you have to see the scene for a kick in the pants?

SF: Not really. There are films that inspired me when I was younger, that made me want to write moves. But I don't go back to them to see how they did it. It was more the feeling I got watching them. Like *Dog Day Afternoon*.

JE: Can you point to a scene that made you say, "Wow"?

SF: When Al Pacino walked out and started chanting, "Attica."
I was fourteen years old. I looked around the audience. Everyone
was so into it. It was the first time I'd ever been in a movie where
the audience was so caught up in that guy and what he wanted,
and wrapped up in what went on in that little bank. When he
came out and started chanting, "Attica," I've never felt more exhilarated in a movie theater.

Then there's *Harold and Maude,* which was a very bizarre experience for me. Again, I saw it when I was very young. It had a
huge effect on me—how I wrote, how I saw the world. What I
loved about it was the blending of tones. On the one hand, it was
very black and very funny, and on the other hand, incredibly sad.
And I liked the movie because it delivered on more than one
front. It wasn't just a comedy. It wasn't just a love story. That's
what was so interesting about it. And I loved the transitions, the
way the movie flowed. Actually, a lot of Hal Ashby's movies are
my favorites. He's probably my favorite director of all time. He
started as an editor. Editing and writing are very similar.

Buster Keaton was another person who had a huge effect on
me. The way he saw the world was so pronounced and so different from anything I'd seen before. His stories were so constructive. You saw the foundation underneath it all. They were so
cleverly constructed.

Billy Wilder is my other favorite director. *Sunset Boulevard* is
one of my all-time favorites. *Laura* [directed by Otto Preminger]
is another one. That's probably the movie I've seen more than any
other.

JE: Let's go back to something you said about *Dog Day Afternoon,* that it has inspired the way you write. Be more specific
about that.

SF: "Attica" was a moment. Movies for me are moments. A synthesis between plot and character in which the audience is going, "Yeah!" And they're with you. It's a manipulation because, on some level, you go to the movies to be manipulated. You go to laugh or to feel sad or to feel scared or to be exhilarated. What *Dog Day Afternoon* had was moments. It would be wildly funny one minute, wildly sad the next—all because we knew those people. You knew the characters. You cared about all those people in the bank. You cared about Charles Durning [policeman in charge]. That was the kind of feeling I wanted to try to capture with my own work.

Also, it was a straight-ahead plot. But it did make a left turn out of nowhere, when it was revealed why he's robbing the bank. It completely threw me. It went where I never expected it to go. That's another rule, I think, that every movie has to have. These days, you see a trailer for a movie, and a lot of the time you know what's going to happen.

And then there are other movies that have turned me on by their plot: *Chinatown. The Parallax View.* I loved *Parallax.* It was funny and it was very scary and it had this great plot, and the suspense was amazing.

Even *Dirty Harry.* I remember seeing *Dirty Harry* when I was twelve years old. That's a great movie. It's been ripped off, so you forget how good it is. But it really worked. I mean, it was as fascist as fascist could be, but it was a great movie. It made that point, and it was entertaining and scary. I remember thinking, *I love Harry, I love the bad guy, I love what's happening.*

I am mostly a B movie person. I love B movies because they usually have the best and most interesting plots. They're mostly about situations; you know, they're usually not as conceptual, especially older B movies. *Dirty Harry* is a great B movie.

JE: Do you think you would have liked working in the old studio system?

SF: I would have liked writing movies in the '40s. I would have loved it. Those movies were, again, all about great plot. *Lady from Shanghai. Citizen Kane. Citizen Kane* had a huge effect on me because I thought, *Yes, I like this structure. This is how I think.* I think in terms of this structure, kind of backwards and forwards. I'm never bored watching that movie, because it's just that wonderful structure. The structure is almost as big a star of the movie as Orson Welles.

JE: How long can you sustain a burst at one time, a creative burst?

SF: It depends. I've had bursts that have lasted for days, where I'd write and write, and I'd get up and I'd keep writing and writing. Usually it's when I'm rewriting, when I've broken the back of the story and have gotten notes on the story, and I'm rewriting. It's when I know what to do and how to fix it.

JE: When you're not working, are you able to leave the work behind and be in the here and now with your family?

SF: No, I'm never in the here and now, ever. I'm working on it, but I have a big problem. That's why I'm very dangerous to be in a car with, because I'm always kind of thinking. Everything sets me off.

JE: You're just a born storyteller.

SF: My biggest problem is I come up with lots of ideas, and I flood my stuff with lots of subplots. I love investing every character, no matter how little screen time they have. But my problem is sometimes I get lazy. Sometimes I get to the point where I don't want to solve the problem.

JE: Give me an example.

SF: *Dead Again.* There's a twist where you realize that he's she and she's he, and the big thing that needs to be solved is, why? What's the payoff to that twist?

JE: For me there is only one inconsistency. In one scene you had he, who was of course she in the past, recounting something that he as she couldn't have known about.

SF: Actually, there are a couple like that. Outright cheats. The opening, the whole opening is a cheat. What is the opening? It's a dream. Is it real?

JE: But you can do that because you're setting up the parameters of what this universe is.

SF: Well, that's the thing. Maybe someone said this to me, but I firmly believe that you can have your cheats and your coincidences in the first thirty minutes. After that, you can't.

JE: The problems in the script are always going to show up.

SF: Unless you fix them, they become huge. They're on screen now. With titles and music.

JE: Let's go back to the differences between novels and screenplays, but from a practical viewpoint.

SF: Good screenwriters just write what you see. That's all. And whenever you can tell something visually, that's what you do. Novels are the exact opposite. Some of my favorite novels are told mostly through the dialogue. Screenplays are also told a lot through the dialogue, but key things that can be done visually are done. In a book, two people just saying things, and saying them in an interesting way, and thinking about interesting things can be good reading. You can't do that in a movie.

JE: Movies run on characters' actions, not their thoughts. It's usually hokey having a voiceover telling a character's thoughts.

SF: Right. The first thing people do when they adapt a novel is try to have a voiceover, as a way of preserving the writer's voice. When people see a book turned into a movie and they're disappointed, I feel like saying, "Well, it's a different thing."

Sometimes they're just bad choices. *Bonfire of the Vanities* and things like that—horrible choices made right down the line. But also there are times when the experience is going to have to be different. I mean, I agree with Sydney Pollack's choices in *The Firm*. I understand that watching someone xeroxing for twenty minutes in a montage is going to be kind of dull; so you begin reinventing that, and you have to reinvent everything that sets it up, and so on and so forth.

Also, movies as opposed to books are much more about setups and payoffs, because it's in such a short amount of time. The setup-and-payoff factor is much more satisfying in movies. Especially in mysteries, you want those solutions to be payoffs. Whereas in a book, say, a James Ellroy novel, sometimes the character who did it is someone who's introduced only here and there. It wouldn't necessarily have been "legal" for him to be the killer in the movie.

Movies and books use very different muscles. One is much

more constructive than the other. You can certainly still feel a structure to a novel, but you have much more leeway to go off and digress.

JE: Are you conscious of having to have a certain number of crashes and booms by, say, page twenty-five?

SF: I don't think it's so much a conscious, *Okay, by this page I have to do that*. It's more a feeling—*It feels like we're taking too long to get to this point. This character is being introduced, and they're going to have a major relationship, and it's page one hundred. I have a problem. I've made a wrong turn somewhere.* As far as crashes and booms and big moments, it's more just instinctive. Stories have peaks and valleys.

JE: They naturally synthesize during the creative process?

SF: Yes; it just comes out. Early on, I just go by my gut. Then when I go back and rewrite, I may reorder. I have a very pragmatic side. I look at the story and I say, "This information would work better here and would have more resonance. This scene would be more powerful here because we don't want to wait to see it."

JE: Do you trust anybody to read your stuff while you're writing it?

SF: Very few people. [Producer] Lindsay Doran. Bill Horburg.

JE: How about your wife?

SF: No. Not that I don't trust her. It's that I would rather she read it when I'm done with it. What I'll do is, I'll tell her the story when I have the story. Because I still feel like I'm trying to woo her, I like to put my best foot forward on paper—only show her the finished script. I'm still trying to impress her, so that's pretty much why.

I feel very vulnerable when I show people my stuff because it's really like, "Tell me what I look like." There are very few people who can read a rough draft and understand where you're going and not go, "Whoa. Needs to be proofread." For some reason, people can look at rough cuts of movies and know what's going on without saying, "There's no music. You need music." But a lot of people can't read something rough and understand it. The thing about Lindsay Doran in particular, more than any other person I've met in the business, is she knows how to speak to writers. She speaks that language very well and understands the process very well, backwards and forwards.

Whereas in studios, you deliver a second draft that has suffered from the give and take. In my experience, the second draft is always worse than the first draft—only you don't know it. You get notes from people, and no matter how good they are, you begin to call everything into question. You rewrite the movie—glomming onto this and that—and it's like the Frankenstein monster. It's a useless step. Then executives at the studio flip out. "Fire this guy. Bring on someone else, because he's burned out. He's written out." And that happens periodically.

Then maybe a fifth draft will have the same problem as the second draft, because it's in the process. You're going to take a step back and ten steps forward. You have to know that there is a time when you can become exhausted. But there are very good people who know how to reenergize you. They'll say, "Let's figure out why we've gotten to this wall. Let's get reexcited. Let's figure out a solution that will reexcite us." Sometimes doing serious work on the script means throwing out something or changing something massive. I liken it to playing chess. Sometimes when you're really stumped, you do something drastic, and sometimes that helps; it opens things up. It can really help.

The other mistake writers make is not being true to their own voice or to the material. They suddenly start fighting someone else's fight, making it like something else. They see a movie and say, "Oh, my God. Mine can't be like that movie." Then they begin changing all these things. They panic. I sometimes make panic decisions: "Okay. I have to cut everything." And that's when I know I have to have someone read it.

JE: You start doubting yourself completely?

SF: Yeah. Almost every day that I sit down at the typewriter I doubt myself completely. There's a moment where I say, "Fuck it." Then I just have to tell myself, "You're really great. You are the best."

JE: You literally say that to yourself?

SF: I don't know that I actually say the words, but I kind of get myself in that position. I've got to trick myself into getting into it because there's always a point in the script when I say, "I'm writing a fucking movie about reincarnation. I don't believe in reincarnation. This is stupid. This is dumb. This has people using expressions like 'past lives.' This is laughable. This is not the kind of movie I ever thought I would be writing. I'm stuck, but now I've got to finish it." And what happens is, I come up with some scene or some line of dialogue or some moment that suddenly reinspires me, and I'm rocketed back into it. Which is why I take so long to think about them, because if you're not passionate you won't ever get over that point.

William Goldman once said to me, "I think I'm a fraud every time I sit down at my typewriter. So I tell myself every time I sit down that I'm the best there is, and then I start going." In his case, he's right. But whenever I sit down I feel the same way, that at a certain point no one is going to like what I'm writing. And when I turn in my scripts, during those few days when I'm waiting to hear from someone, I'm a mess.

JE: You can't call in sick.

SF: On everything I ever work on, I sit there and think, "You know what? I've stolen all this. I know I've heard this before. I know I've seen this stuff before. I've stolen all this." There are other times when I say, "This just isn't working at all. No one will believe this." And then there are those times where I have these weird panic attacks—suddenly everything looks bad, even though it isn't. Intellectually, I know it couldn't be, because yesterday it looked great and I was walking in the house an hour early and jumping around and playing with the kids and throwing them in the air and thinking great thoughts because I'd just written a scene that made me feel incredible. Then, the next day, I sit down and say, "Who am I fooling?"

JE: Which voice do you trust? What's the answer?

SF: The answer is to keep going, either to keep writing and calm down, or to somehow give yourself some sort of perspective, either by going away from it for a while or by letting someone read it.

JE: Even midstream?

SF: Even midstream. At that point I usually begin taking notes. I write about it—write anything I know about it, whatever it is, whether it's "How can these two people meet?" or describing a scene I know is really good.

Sometimes I'll move ahead and write a scene I know that I want to write that I've been saving, but very rarely. Usually, if I begin to have a panic attack I feel like the whole thing is wrong, that it's on the wrong track.

JE: How long will the panic attacks last?

SF: Sometimes a day, sometimes a month.

JE: A panic attack can last a month?

SF: Yes. At a certain point I wake up. Usually my wife, bless her heart, says, "Finish your script. It's a great idea." She wakes me up.

JE: What's the relationship between the work and your emotional well-being?

SF: If the work comes from a more personal place, the stakes are higher. Because you care about the idea. If it doesn't work you'll be devastated: *You must not be any good because the idea didn't work.* Not only would you be devastated, but you're going to be out of a job and washed up.

JE: "This is my whole life."

SF: You've heard the way people talk about other writers when they write a bad script, so now they're going to be talking about you when you write this bad script. You know you shouldn't think about these things, but you can't help it.

JE: So no matter how much success you've had in the past, it doesn't mitigate that sense of panic?

SF: Yeah. I always feel like I'm a fraud and I'm going to get found out tomorrow. I always feel like this is all going to be taken away from me tomorrow. Somehow I'm going to shoot myself in the foot.

JE: Are you a good verbal storyteller?

SF: Yes.

JE: Do you get pleasure out of sitting at the computer?

SF: I love it. Which brings up the one essential thing that all screenwriters have to know: The greatest joy that you get from screenwriting is screenwriting. It's not the movies that are made out of your work. The single greatest joy you'll ever have is when you're sitting there writing. You truly are a writer. I mean, that's where the joy comes in, because the movie will never be what you thought it would be. It's impossible. Given the collaborative nature of movies, how could it be? There are so many people interpreting your work. It's going to be impossible for it to turn out the way in which you conceived of it.

JE: *Dead Again* was shot just like the script.

SF: Actually, he [director Kenneth Branagh] shot the script word for word, but the tone of the movie was a lot different than what I envisioned. I wrote what I thought was *Rosemary's Baby*. I thought it would be sexy and that the scary stuff would be scarier—for instance, when she stabbed him at the beginning. It's very theatrical in the movie, but not very scary. He did a much more theatrical version, which I completely respect. And I think that's the key. As a screenwriter, your expectations have to be brought into line. The best you'll feel for one of your films is respect. Very rarely will you say, "That's better than what I thought it would be." The real joy comes from the writing.

JE: Do the characters live in your head?

SF: All the time.

JE: Any reluctance to kill off the ones who need to be killed off?

SF: I always have reluctance, but I seem to do it without any problem. I do the most damage toward myself by cutting. I'm the most vicious cutter of my own work.

JE: Do you have any reluctance to finish a script and say, "It's done now"?

SF: I'm never done. Even when they're shooting, I'm never done. There are twenty-five other things I wish I'd solved.

JE: How do you know when you've done enough?

SF: When someone tells me, and they start shooting that first day.

Screenwriter Credits

The following is a complete listing of the screenwriting credits of the writers interviewed in this book. "AAN" indicates the script was nominated for an Academy Award, while "AA" indicates the screenplay won the Oscar for that year.

ANDREW BERGMAN

The Scout (1994), with Albert Brooks and Monica Johnson
Honeymoon in Vegas (1992)
Soapdish (1991), with Robert Harling
The Freshman (1988)
Fletch (1984)
Oh God, You Devil! (1984)
So Fine (1981)
The In-Laws (1979)
Blazing Saddles (1973), with Mel Brooks, Norman Steinberg, Richard Pryor, and Alan Uger. AAN

HORTON FOOTE

Of Mice and Men (1992)
Convicts (1990)
On Valentine's Day (1985)
1918 (1985)
The Trip to Bountiful (1985). AAN

Tender Mercies (1984). AA
Hurry Sundown (1967), with Thomas C. Ryan
Baby, the Rain Must Fall (1964)
To Kill a Mockingbird (1962). AA
Storm Fear (1956)

SCOTT FRANK
Malice (1993), with Walter F. Parkes
Little Man Tate (1991)
Dead Again (1991)
Plain Clothes (1987)

CHARLES FULLER
A Soldier's Story (1983). AAN

AMY HOLDEN JONES
Beethoven's 2nd (1993), with Len Blum
The Getaway (1993), with Walter Hill
Indecent Proposal (1993)
Beethoven (1991), with Edmond Dantes
Mystic Pizza (1988)
Maid to Order (1987), with Perry Howze and Randy Howze
Love Letters (1983)

RICHARD LAGRAVENESE
The Ref (1993), with Marie Weiss
The Fisher King (1990). AAN
Rude Awakening (1989), with Neil Levy

ERNEST LEHMAN
Black Sunday (1976), with Kenneth Ross and Ivan Moffat
Family Plot (1975)
Portnoy's Complaint (1971)
Hello, Dolly! (1968)

Who's Afraid of Virginia Woolf? (1965). AAN
The Sound of Music (1964)
The Prize (1963)
West Side Story (1961). AAN
From the Terrace (1960)
North by Northwest (1959). AAN
The Sweet Smell of Success (1957), with Clifford Odets
Somebody Up There Likes Me (1956)
The King and I (1955)
Sabrina (1953), with Billy Wilder and Samuel Taylor. AAN
Executive Suite (1953)
The Inside Story (1948), with Mary Loos and Richard Sale

MICHAEL MANN

The Last of the Mohicans (1992), with Christopher Crowe
Manhunter (1986)
The Keep (1983)
Thief (1980)

NICHOLAS MEYER

Sommersby (1993), with Sarah Kernochan
Star Trek VI: The Undiscovered Country (1991), with Denny Martin
    Flinn
Company Business (1990)
Star Trek IV: The Voyage Home (1986), with Steve Meerson, Peter
    Krikes, and Harve Bennett
Time After Time (1978), with S. Karl Alexander and Steve Hayes
The Seven Percent Solution (1976)
The Bee Girls (1973)

BRUCE JOEL RUBIN

My Life (1993)
Ghost (1990). AAN

Jacob's Ladder (1989)
Deadly Friend (1986)
Brainstorm (1983), with Philip Frank Messina and Robert Stitzel

CAROLINE THOMPSON

Black Beauty (1993)
The Secret Garden (1993)
Homeward Bound: The Incredible Journey (1991), with Linda
   Woolverton
The Addams Family (1991), with Larry Wilson
Edward Scissorhands (1990)

TED TALLY

The Silence of the Lambs (1990). AA
White Palace (1990), with Alvin Sargent

ROBERT TOWNE

Love Affair (1994), with Warren Beatty
The Firm (1993), with David Rabe and David Rayfiel
Days of Thunder (1990)
The Two Jakes (1989)
Tequila Sunrise (1988)
Personal Best (1982)
Shampoo (1974). AA
The Yakuza (1974), with Paul Schrader
Chinatown (1974). AA
The Last Detail (1973). AAN
Villa Rides (1968), with Sam Peckinpah
Tomb of Legeia (1965)
The Last Woman on Earth (1960)

Index